D1440993

INTERNATIONAL DICTIONARY OF
PROVERBS

INTERNATIONAL DICTIONARY OF PROVERBS

Gerd de Ley

Translated by Peter Darbo and David Potter

HIPPOCRENE BOOKS
New York

Copyright © 1998 Gerd de Lay
Translation Copyright © 1997 Peter Darbo and David Potter

Originally published as *International spreekwoordenboek*
by Standard Utigeverij © 1996, Antwerp.

Hippocrene edition, 1998.

All rights reserved.

For information, address:
HIPPOCRENE BOOKS, INC.
171 Madison Avenue
New York, NY 10016

Library of Congress Cataloging-in-Publication Data

Ley, Gerd de, 1994-
  [International spreekwoordenboek. English]
  International dictionary of proverbs / Gerd de Ley ; translated by
 Peter Darbo and David Potter. — Hippocrene ed.
   p. cm.
  Includes Index.
  ISBN 0-7818-0531-7 paperback ISBN 0-7818-0620-8 hardback
  1. Proverbs. I. Title.
PN6409.D8L4913 1997
398.9/21—dc 21   97-28158
                          CIP

To my good friends
Pol Goossen and Annemarie Picard

CONTENTS

Preface

A book without a preface is like a body without a soul.
Hebrew Proverb

Proverbs know no boundaries—they are truly universal. Over the course
of history common human experiences have been gradually and subtly ver-
balized by way of international commercial and social traffic into many different languages. Therefore, it is hardly surprising that some proverbs appear
in more than one language or country. However nationality scarcely changes
the intrinsic philosophy of a proverb—only the way it is communicated.

For more than twenty years I have been collecting proverbs from around
the world. They reveal much about the wisdom, humor, and character of
other countries and peoples. I have also discovered, as you will, that proverbs are also cosmopolites, and that every exception proves the rule.

I wish you an interesting world-tour.

Gerd de Ley

ABOUT PROVERBS

A proverb is always wise.

Russia

Proverbs are not merely decorations on life. they have life itself in them. they are the bedrock substance of living, built up by many people and many years. they are the beginnings of all literature, the first metaphors and similes, the first comedies and tragedies. they are the first poetry we have.

Robert Peter Tristram Coffin

Proverbs are jewels that on the stretched forefinger of all time sparkle forever.

Alfred Tennyson

Proverbs are the literature of reason.

R.W. Emerson

Behold the proverbs of a people.

Carl Sandburg

Proverbs are maxims on their deathbed.

Maxim Drabon

A proverb without wisdom is like a body without a foot.

Abraham ibn Ezra

A proverb has three characteristics: few words, good sense, and a fine image.

Moses ibn Ezra

Solomon made a book of proverbs, but a book of proverbs never made a Solomon.

England

Proverbs are little gospels.

Spain

A proverb is the horse of conversation: when the conversation lags, a proverb will revive it.

Yoruba

When the occasion arises, there is a proverb to suit it.

Oji

Proverbs are the daughters of experience.

Rwanda

A proverb says what man thinks.

Sweden

Old proverbs are the children of truth.

Wales

Proverbs cannot be contradicted.

Ireland

When the fool is told a proverb, its meaning has to be explained to him.

Ghana

He who uses proverbs, gets what he wants.

Zimbabwe

Proverbs are the people's wisdom.

Russia

Proverbs cannot be bettered.

Ireland

A proverb seldom comes alone.

Maxim Drabon

All proverbs contradict each other.

Georges Simenon

Proverbs contradict each other. That is precisely the wisdom of a people.

Stanislaw Jerzy Lec

A proverb is the lamp of speech.

Arabia

You can't make a proverb out of a feathered frog .

Toon Verhoeven

When a poor man makes a proverb it does not spread abroad.

Ghana

Proverbs are always platitudes until you have personally
experienced the truth of them.

Aldous Huxley

Don't quote your proverb until you have brought your ship
into port.

Gaelic

A wise man who knows proverbs reconciles difficulties.

Yoruba

A good proverb does not strike one in the brow, but full in
the eye.

Russia

Proverbs are abridgements of wisdom.

Joseph Joubert

A proverb can't be judged.

Russia

Proverbs are short sentences drawn from long experiences.

Miguel Cervantes

A proverb is to speech what salt is to food.

Ethiopia

A proverb is shorter than a bird's beak.

Switzerland

Like country, like proverb.

Germany

The wisdom of the street lies in the proverb.

Germany

If everyone says it... it must be true.

Hebrew

A hundred proverbs—a hundred truths.

Spain

Never argue with a fool, a proverb, or the truth.

Russia

Hold on to the words of your ancestors.

Maori

A short saying oft contains much wisdom.

Sophocles

An old woman is always uneasy when dry bones are
mentioned in a proverb.

Africa

Wise men make proverbs, but fools repeat them.

Samuel Palmer

All maxims have their antagonist maxims; proverbs should be
sold in pairs, a single one being but a half truth.

William Matthews

There's always an old proverb that says just about whatever
you want it to.

Maxim Drabon

A country can be judged by the quality of its proverbs.

Germany

The proverbs of a nation furnish the index to its spirit, and
the results of its civilization.

Josiah Gilbert Holland

A proverb is the wisdom of many and the wit of one.

John Russell

There's always an old proverb that says just about whatever
you want it to.

Peter Darbo

A true proverb remains true forever.

Gui Ericx

There is no proverb without a grain of truth.

Russia

THE PROVERBS

Afghanistan

Even the largest army is nothing without a good general.

In bad things be slow; in good things be quick.

He who goes to the blacksmith's shop comes home with scorched clothes.

The deaf laugh twice.

A donkey has two friends: his two hind legs.

On earth it's hard and heaven is far away.

An old friend is like a saddled horse.

Give graciously—even an onion.

Though God is almighty, he doesn't send rain from a clear sky.

You can't flee your lot nor share it with another.

First food, then religion.

Where the heart would go, there follows the foot.

Heaven is dark and yet out of it streams clear water.

Every man thinks his own thoughts are best.

Some men wonder over God's values, others over the cut of a garment.

To speak ill of anyone is to speak ill of yourself.

Man sins... then blames it on the devil.

A palm tree growing in the shade will not bear ripe fruit.

Be patient with your enemies and forgiving of your friends.

The rose is a friend of the thorn.

Try out your shoes on your feet—gauge people against their misfortune.

The ungrateful son is like a wart on his father's face; to leave it there is unsightly, to cut it off is painful.

As the sun's shadow shifts, so there is no permanence on earth.

I'm talking to the door, but I want the walls to hear me.

Don't use your teeth when you can untie the knot with your fingers.

When the tiger kills, the jackal profits.

Every tree feels the force of the wind.

It is easier to wage war with wise enemies than be at peace with foolish friends.

Wealth belongs to the person who enjoys it and not to the one who keeps it.

The best weapon is the one that's to hand.

When the wine is free even the judge drinks it.

The world is the traveler's inn.

Africa

(Angola, Baguirmi, Bambara, Bantu proverbs, Basutoland, Berber Proverbs, Burkina Faso, Cameroon, Congo, Ghana, Ivory Coast, Kenya, Liberia, Madagascar, Namibia, Nigeria, Uganda, Sierra Leone, South Africa, Sudan, Swahili proverbs, Tanzania, Somalia, Togo, Zambia, Zanzibar, Zimbabwe)

If they are offered winged ants, people will eat them.

Anxiety will not let you die of hunger.

Ashes will always blow back into the face of the thrower.

Don't ask me where I am going but where I have come from.

He who rides upon an ass cannot help but smell its gas!

A beggar won't mind being insulted.

The best morsels are never given to a beggar.

If you know the beginning well, the end will not trouble you.

He who betrays you is not one from far away.

A blacksmith has no need of an axe.

Human blood is heavy; he who has shed it cannot run away.

The sight of books removes sorrows from the heart.

Not the place where I was born but where I hang my hat is home.

A bowl should not laugh when a calabash breaks.

Brothers love each other when they are equally rich.

The calf is not afraid of the mother's horns.

The camel and his driver—each has his own plan.

Where the cattle are, there the wolf shall die.

Where the cattle stand together, the lion lies down hungry.

A chicken with beautiful plumage does not sit in a corner.

A chick that will grow into a cock can be spotted the very day it hatches.

No chicken will fall into the fire a second time.

The child hates the one who gives him all he wants.

If a child washes his hands he could eat with kings.

A child's fingers are not scalded by a piece of hot yam which his mother puts into his palm.

Clouds do not always mean rain, but smoke is a sure sign of fire.

You can tell a ripe corn by its look.

"What's all the fuss?" said the crane after the eel had slipped away. "I never liked fish anyway."

Death is always news.

"Come and I'll tell you something," tickles the ear.

We have never seen the earth show her teeth.

When there is no enemy within, the enemies outside cannot hurt you.

The eye envies, not the ear.

In a court of fowls, the cockroach never wins his case.

One who does what he says is not a coward.

If you have escaped the jaws of the crocodile while bathing in the river, you will surely meet a leopard on the way.

A man who cries all the time is not heard.

You can't dance on one leg.

The dead are not seen in the company of the living.

That which is deadly may have a sweet scent.

Too many calls confuse the dog.

A dog never forgets his master.

As the dog said, "If I fall down for you and you fall down for me, it is playing."

A dog does not mind being called a dog.

A dog returns to where he has been fed.

Beat one dog and the others will run away.

The hollow of the ear is never full.

Ears are usually uninvited guests.

Only what you have eaten is yours; other things may not be.

If there were no elephants in the jungle, the buffalo would be big.

An elephant does not die from one broken rib.

Even if the elephant is thin he is still the lord of the jungle.

Do not laugh at the fallen; you may find slippery roads ahead.

If you know his father and grandfather, don't worry about his son.

Fire does not make fire, only ashes.

You can only know the fleas in the bed you have slept in.

Food you will not eat you do not boil.

Even the best cooking pot will not produce food.

Who forgives wins.

If it's not here and now, who cares about what and when?

Heaven and earth shall never meet.

A small house will hold a hundred friends.

There are three friends in this world: courage, sense, and insight.

A wound inflicted by a friend does not heal.

The more intimate the friendship the deadlier the enmity.

The fuel in the lamp consumes itself but lights others.

Whoever has only one garment does not wash it when it rains.

Goats cannot live in a herd of leopards.

He who does not know is forgiven by God.

The plant God favors will grow even without rain.

That which is exceptionally good is a forerunner of something bad.

Good things sell themselves; those that are bad have to be advertised.

Greatness is not achieved with violence.

A guest who breaks the dishes of his host is not soon forgotten.

Treat your guest as a guest for two days—then on the third day give him a hoe.

Haste bequeaths disappointment.

He on whose head we would break a coconut never stands still.

The house of the heart is never full.

A proud heart can survive a general failure because such a failure does not prick its pride.

When the heart acts the body is its slave.

In hell there are no fans.

The horse never refuses a homeward gallop.

Noise and hunting don't go together.

Hunt in every jungle, for there is wisdom and good hunting in all of them.

If it's a big man that is hurting you, smile at him.

Don't show a hyena how well you can bite.

Indecision is like a stepchild: if he does not wash his hands, he is called dirty, if he does, he is wasting water.

The key that opens is also the key that locks.

Looking at a king's mouth one would never think he sucked his mother's breast.

The knife that has been lent, never comes back alone.

Africa

No one is without knowledge except he who asks no questions.

Practice with the left hand while the right is still there.

A lie has many variations, the truth none.

The smaller the lizard the greater the hope of becoming a crocodile.

The lizard that jumped from the high iroko tree to the ground said he would praise himself if no one else did.

Don't try to get blood from a locust; God didn't put it in there.

A stern look is not a slap in the face.

The very fact that we are looking for something usually stands in the way of our finding it.

There is no physician who can cure the disease of love.

What lowers itself is ready to fall.

When a man says he does not mind, then he really does.

When a man says yes, his chi [personal god] says yes also.

A man who pays respect to the great paves the way for his own greatness.

You must judge a man by the work of his hands.

If you are threatened by a man, sleep at night, if it is by a woman then stay awake.

Marriage is a snake to slip into your handbag.

He ought to be feared who sends you with a message, not the one to whom you are sent.

If it hurts to spend your money, you will go hungry.

I don't sow ground nuts when the monkey is watching.

If the moon is with you, you need not care about the stars.

When the moon is shining the cripple becomes hungry for a walk.

He who waits for the moon waits for darkness.

He whose mother is naked is not likely to clothe his aunt.

The mouth which eats does not talk.

He who has the necessities has no shame.

A needle cannot hold two threads or a mind two thoughts.

It is the path of the needle that the thread is accustomed to follow.

News does not sleep on the way.

Say no from the start; you will have rest.

Let a wrong-doing repeat itself at least three times: the first may be an accident, the second a mistake, but the third is likely to be intentional.

Through others I am somebody.

Those whose palm-kernels were cracked for them by a benevolent spirit should not forget to be humble.

Without human companions, paradise itself would be an undesirable place.

The last partridge will take the most arrows.

Live patiently in the world; know that those who hate you are more numerous than those who love you.

Those who wear pearls do not know how often the shark bites the leg of the diver.

People think that the poor are not as wise as the rich, for if a man be wise, why is he poor?

The potter eats from broken plates.

Poverty without debt is real wealth.

Where there is no wealth there is no poverty.

It rained on the mountaintop, but it was the valley below that got flooded.

A razor may be sharper than an axe, but it cannot cut wood.

A reflection does not see itself.

Repetition is the mother of knowledge.

If you get rich, be in a dark corner when you jump for joy.

For the sake of the rose the thorn is watered too.

Scandal is like an egg; when it is hatched it has wings.

Smooth seas do not make skillful sailors.

Where there is no shame, there is no honor.

The quarrel of the sheep doesn't concern the goats.

Before you buy shoes, measure your feet.

He who is too sure of himself and acts without thinking is heading for his downfall.

Silence gives rise to peace and with peace comes security.

Small matters breed important ones.

Smile... heaven is watching!

The snail leaves its trail wherever it goes.

He who takes a light to find a snake should start at his own feet.

The sparrow says: "I have not eaten... so the parrot will not eat either."

The spring makes the stream flow.

If you don't stand for something, you will fall for something.

What is in the stomach carries what is in the head.

People should not talk while they are eating or pepper may go down the wrong way.

The thrower of stones throws away the strength of his own arm.

If you want to know how the true story goes, wait till the arguments start.

The success of a man is through the soles of his feet, that of a woman is from her legs.

The sun will shine on those who stand before it shines on those who kneel under them.

There are three things that a man must know to survive in this world: what is too much for him, what is too little, and what is just right.

If sweetness be excessive, it is no longer sweetness.

If a man makes soup of his tears, ask him not for broth.

Nothing wipes your tears away but your own hand.

A man does not run among thorns for no reason; either he is chasing a snake or a snake is chasing him.

Thorns themselves will not harm you—you hurt yourself on the thorns.

Travel and you will see them, sit and they will come to you.

The wise traveler leaves his heart at home.

The tree that is not taller than you cannot shade you.

The tree breaks that takes all the force of the wind.

To trouble me is better than to forget me.

Two is good, one alone cannot wash his back.

He who loves the vase loves also what is inside.

The viper assumes the colors of his surroundings.

Nobody wages war with ghosts.

Where water is the boss, there must the land obey.

The water can only flow thanks to the well.

Return to old watering holes for more than water; friends and dreams are there to meet you.

They who dig the wells never drink from them.

As long as the white man stutters, the interpreters have a lot of work.

If you have five wives, then you have five tongues.

Differences between husband and wife should not be aired in the marketplace.

He who is drunk from wine can sober up, he who is drunk from wealth cannot.

The wise man is father of the fool.

A woman is like a banana; one alone can turn the whole bunch rotten.

A woman wearing trousers? What has she got hanging in there?

A woman listens only to the advice of a fool.

A woman's strength is a multitude of words.

The world has not made a promise to anybody.

The wrongdoer forgets, but not the wronged.

The word "yes" brings trouble; the word "no" leads to no evil.

Albania

Patience is the key to paradise.

Don't put golden buttons on a torn coat.

Where a horse of a Turk passes the grass will not grow again.

When you have no companion, look to your walking stick.

A tailless dog cannot express his joy.

Fire is a good slave, but a bad master.

If you fear God, you won't fear humans.

Hard heads suffer much.

Even the hen looks toward heaven when she drinks.

He who hesitates, regrets.

More lambs than sheep are slaughtered.

In times of need a pig is called uncle.

If your neighbor is an early riser, you too will become one.

The stomach has no windows.

The sun at home warms better than the sun away.

There was anguish before there was man.

You cannot turn blood into water.

He who leans against a big tree will always find shade.

He who is not drunk on a Sunday is not worth a greeting on Monday.

He who can read and write has four eyes.

In the eyes of the mouse the cat is a lion.

If you have figs in your knapsack, everyone will want to be your
   friend.

Fire, water and government know nothing of mercy.

When a Greek shakes your hand, count your fingers after.

Stroke the dog and he will mark you with his dirty paws.

A dry bone is never licked.

Love is sometimes difficult but death even more so.

Brotherly love for brotherly love, but cheese for money.

The monk gets married to please his friend.
The man who has eaten enough will never believe a hungry one.
One eats figs whilst the other pays.
The fox will catch you with cunning, and the wolf with courage.
If you are in the house of a friend, bad times are soon forgotten.
Work like a slave and eat like a gentleman.
When a hundred men call a wise man a fool, then he becomes a fool.
The wolf loves the fog.

Andes Mountains

No one knows as much about the pot as does the spoon.

Angola

The crocodile is only strong in the water.
Don't despise the nut, one day it will be a palm tree.

Antilles

The monkey will never wash with the same water twice.
In the hangman's house you will always find a rope.
You cannot fly with wings made of butter.
An old hen makes strong soup.
There are no virgins in a brothel.
The more hair a dog has, the more fleas he will have.
The dog says: "Master, my life is far too good, hurt me in the tail."
You eat an egg, but you don't understand how painful it was for the chicken.
Don't give a child a name until after it is born.
Never throw the cat at the dog.

A cat will teach her young ones all the tricks, except how to jump
backwards.

The rainbow would be even more beautiful if the show was not for
free.

The rope will break where it is thinnest.

Arabia

Advice given in the midst of a crowd is loathsome.

Ask advice of an ignorant man and he will think you are his enemy.

Follow the advice of the one who makes you cry, not from the one
who makes you laugh.

Every age has its book.

Trust in Allah, but tie up your camel.

There are four things Allah cannot do: lie, deny himself, die or look
favorably on sin.

Those who argue with each other on the highway will often make up
in the lane.

The barber learns to shave on the orphan's face.

Make your bargain before beginning to plow.

Do not ridicule the thin-bearded when you yourself have no beard.

Beauty is power.

Beauty doesn't exist, men only dream it.

Beauty never travels in a group.

If begging should unfortunately be your lot, knock at the large gates
only.

He who only thinks about what is in his belly is worth less than what
comes out of it.

The benefits you get become the debts you owe to others.

Blind eyes see better than blind hearts.

The eyes are of little use if the mind be blind.

A book is like a garden carried in the pocket.

To threaten the brave with death is like promising water to a duck.

Bravery without intelligence is not bravery.

Another man's bread will not fill your belly.

Better to have bread and an onion with peace than stuffed fowl with strife.

Make do with bread and butter until God can bring you jam.

It is not the bullet that kills you, it is fate.

If the camel once gets his nose in the tent, his body will soon follow.

The chameleon does not leave one tree until he is sure of another.

A borrowed cloak does not keep one warm.

Live together like brothers and do business like strangers.

If you are offered a bull, do not ask how much milk he will give.

The mouth of a canon is less dangerous than that of a scandalmonger.

If you are a friend of the captain, you can wipe your hands on the sail.

Great care is no defense against Fate.

The dreams of a cat are full of mice.

If you buy cheap meat, you'll smell what you have saved when it boils.

Children are buttonholes that hold their parents together.

An eloquent cock crows as soon as it comes out of the egg.

Without the companionship even paradise would be boring.

A man who was always complaining was quite rightly sent to hell. "Why are you burning damp wood?" was his first comment.

Be sure to have a controversial opinion, and men will talk about you.

Conversation is like making love; the man is the question, the woman the answer, and the union of both will bear fruit.

The corn will bend but it still ends up in the mill.

A thousand curses never tore a shirt.

Do not stand in a dangerous place trusting in miracles.

When danger approaches, sing to it.

The house of danger is built upon the borders of safety.

Better a handful of dry dates and content therewith than to own the Gate of Peacocks and be kicked in the eye by a broody camel.

Dawn does not come to awaken a man a second time.

Every day of your life is a page of your history.

When you die, your sister's tears will dry as time goes on, your widow's tears will end in another's arms, but your mother will mourn you until the day she dies.

Death rides a fast camel.

Death is a black camel that lies down at every door. Sooner or later you must ride the camel.

Only death itself can end our hope.

My debtor is a worse payer even than I am.

It is better to die in revenge than to live on in shame.

Diligence is a great teacher.

The dogs bark, but the caravan moves on.

Every dog is a great barker at the door of his own house.

Better to be a free dog than a caged lion.

If a dog offers to help you across the river, don't ask if he is suffering from the mange.

A grateful dog has more worth than an ungrateful man.

Doubt is the key to all knowledge.

Nothing but a handful of dust will fill the eyes of man.

He promised me earrings, but then only pierced my ears.

Don't think you are eloquent just because a fool applauds you.

Better a thousand enemies outside the tent than one within.

Kiss the hand of your enemy if you cannot chop it off.

Envy has no rest.

Evil people know one another.

If you have never seen evil, look closely at yourself some time.

The excess of one is the shortage of another.

Excuses are always mixed with lies.

Arabia

Experiences are the spectacles of intellect.

Ask the experienced rather than the learned.

The tongue of experience utters the most truth.

A fable is a bridge that leads to truth.

All kinds of fame belong partly to others.

Both the fast and the slow will meet each other on the ferry boat.

In the presence of Fate, the physician becomes a fool.

Fate loves a rebel.

Fear the person who fears you.

Show no fear to the man who picks up a big stone.

Men fear, but time fears the pyramids.

It may be a fire today—tomorrow it will be ashes.

The fire is winter's fruit.

The first will get the credit, even if the second is better.

The soul of a fool is always dancing on the tip of his tongue.

Never trust a fool with a sword.

If you give in to a fool, he will say, "This is because they are afraid of me."

Rather a slip of the foot than a slip of the pen.

Forgiveness is more satisfying than revenge.

He that counts his friend's mistakes will be abandoned by him.

Your friend will swallow your mistakes, your enemy will present them on a plate.

In the small lanes there are no brothers or friends.

Never tell your friends what your enemy may not hear.

Attend funerals avoid weddings.

Every future is not far away.

He who predicts the future lies, even if he tells the truth.

The best act of generosity is that which is quickly done.

The awakening of a giant shakes the world.

Unwrapping a gift wraps up enmity.

Arabia

The doorstep weeps for forty days whenever a girl is born.

If you have given away much of your wealth, then you have given a little of your heart.

He who lives in a glass house should not throw stones.

If you don't know where you are going, look back to where you've come from.

When God shuts one door, He opens another.

God gave the giraffe a long neck so that He would not have to bend the palm tree.

All earthly goods we have only on loan.

A good man is one who rejoices in the well-being of others.

A good deed dies when it is spoken about.

Good qualities never cancel out the bad, just as sugar is no antidote for poison.

The grave is our mother.

Habit is the sixth sense that dominates the other five.

There has to be a first time for everything—even our most natural habits.

The angry hammer works off his fury on the steel.

When what you want doesn't happen, learn to want what does.

Haste is the invention of the devil.

Every head has its own kind of headache.

If you cannot take things by the head, then take them by the tail.

One day in perfect health is a lot.

A heart free from care is better than a full purse.

He who has health has hope, and he who has hope has every thing.

The strength of the heart comes from the soundness of the faith.

Heaven on earth is to be found on horseback, reading books and between a woman's breasts.

Once you have decided to hit someone, then hit them hard because the retribution will be the same whether you hit hard or not.

He hit me, started to cry, and went straight to the judge to sue me.

Arabia

He who wants to sell his honor will always find a buyer.

A small tumbledown house is better than a communal palace.

The soul of an idiot is always dancing on the end of his tongue.

Act like you are an idiot and everyone will respect you.

An imbecile can manage his own affairs better than a wise man the affairs of other people.

He who uses bad incense must be careful not to burn his sleeves.

An insult is but a short garment: it reveals the one who wears it.

Insults must be written in sand and compliments carved in stone.

Sometimes even the intestine and the stomach disagree.

It makes no sense to try to forge the iron whilst it is still cold.

When the judge's mule dies, everyone goes to the funeral; when the judge himself dies, no one does.

If the king says that it is night in the middle of the day, look up at the stars.

An unjust king is like a river without water.

The word of the king is the king of words.

You won't gain knowledge by drinking ink.

He who starts a lawsuit makes a hole in the dike.

A lazy man will be an astrologer.

He left us and we rejoiced; then an even more unbearable person came.

Never celebrate someone's leaving, until you know who will succeed him.

He that has long legs will go far.

Lending nourishes bad feeling.

The rope of a lie is short.

He who lies for you will lie about you.

Beware: some liars tell the truth.

The liar's mother is a virgin.

Life, like a fire, begins in smoke and ends in ashes.

Arabia

The lion said: I am the best one to take care of my business.

An old lion will be mocked by the dogs.

Whoever lives within himself is burning with love.

He who looks up too much gets a pain in the neck.

He who loves thinks that the others are blind; the others think that he is crazy.

Love lasts as long as does the reproach.

Love makes a man both blind and deaf.

Love sees clearly, hate even more so, but jealousy sees the most clear, because it is equal to love plus hate.

In order to really love someone you must love him as though he was going to die tomorrow.

After lunch, rest; after dinner take a walk.

If man be a river, then woman will be a bridge.

Men laugh with their heart, women only with their mouth.

You know a man by the sweat of his brow and the strength of his word.

A man's worth depends on his two smallest organs: his heart and his tongue.

There are two kinds of men: those who could be happy and are not, and those who search for happiness and find it not.

Mankind is made out of forgetfulness.

Marriage is like a besieged fortress: those who are outside want to come in, and those already in want to be out.

If we are both masters, then who shall lead the mules?

Misfortune is easier to bear if you share it with many others.

There is no greater misfortune than your own.

You can always find good elements in the misfortune that strikes you.

Mistrust before you trust.

He that has no money has no friends.

Money can build roads in the sea.

The monkey looks into the mirror and sees a gazelle.

Arabia

The mother of someone who is killed can sleep; the mother of the murderer cannot.

If you want to hit your mother-in-law, be sure to split her head.

Moustaches hide the imperfections of the mouth.

If a man's mouth were silent, then another part would speak.

A mule can go to Mecca, but it will not come back as a pilgrim.

A mule who goes in search of a fine set of antlers, will come back with his ears cut off.

The nail supports the hoof, the hoof the horse, the horse the man, the man the world.

God has spared the naked man from washing his clothes with soap.

Choose your neighbor before your house and your companion before the road.

If your neighbor visits Mecca once, watch out for him. If he makes a second visit, you had better avoid him. After the third visit you had better move to another street.

God grant us no neighbor with two eyes.

Even the one-eyed man winks to women.

He who walks through a field of onions, will smell like an onion.

A good orator makes us see with our ears.

You only own that which you have earned.

He gets his passage for nothing and then winks at the captain's wife.

The man with no patience waits for daylight, and when it comes he'll be blind.

The cure for bad times is patience.

Peace is only possible after war.

Whoever knows how to use a pen never adds his own name to the "guilty" list.

A man cannot be a good physician if he has never been sick himself.

Put things into their places, and they will put you into your place.

Play alone and you're bound to win.

The poor always smell.

A poor man would like to have some fun, but he cannot find the right place.

So long as the pot is boiling, friendship will stay warm.

Beware the man who lavishes too much praise on you, he will later run you down.

It is better to cut off the head that has no pride.

Better make profit out of manure than losses with musk.

A promise is a cloud; fulfillment is the rain.

He fled from the rain and sat down under the waterspout.

The dry reed does not seek the company of fire.

The best part of repentance is a little sinning.

Reproaches are the soap of the heart.

If you want to take revenge on a man, send him a really beautiful woman.

Once you have found your rhythm, you will then know your God.

When a rich man wants children, he gets dollars, when a poor man wants dollars, he gets children.

Righteousness is half of religion.

Throw him into the river and he will come up with a fish in his mouth.

Examine what is said, not him who speaks.

A scholar's ink is worth as much as the blood of the martyr.

Two scorpions living in the same hole will get along better than two sisters in the same house.

Do not tell secrets in front of servants.

So long as I can keep a secret it is my prisoner. If I let it slip then I am its prisoner.

An army of sheep led by a lion would defeat an army of lions led by a sheep.

The tree of silence bears the fruits of peace.

Silence is the interpreter of happiness.

Silence is a cure for grief.

Look and keep silent, and if you are eating meat, tell the world it's fish.

It is easier not to commit a sin than to repent it.

The slave must be content with the joys of his master.

Seven days king, seven days minister, slave for the rest of your life.

Whoever knew you when you were small will not respect you when you're big.

He who has been bitten by a snake is scared of a rope on the ground.

If you want to kill a snake, chop off its head.

The soul will only be at rest when it stops hoping.

Spirit is the sword and experience the sharpening stone.

A sponge to wipe away the past; a rose to sweeten the present; a kiss to greet the future.

Spurs that are too sharp make even the mule rear.

He who steals an egg will steal a camel.

If a man believes in a stone, that stone will serve him well.

Men learn little from success, but much from failure.

Sunshine without rain makes a desert.

Let the sword decide only after the plan has failed.

Talent without skill is like a desert without an oasis.

Men must sew up tears with gentleness.

If there were no tears, our ribs would burn.

Time is the master of him who has no master.

They have sowed the seed of the word "tomorrow" and it has not germinated.

The greatest tranquility is when we desire nothing.

Not to use trickery is also trickery.

Everything is small at the beginning and then grows; except trouble, which is big at the beginning and still grows.

When you shoot an arrow of truth, dip its point in honey.

He who is a slave of truth is a free man.

Arabia

It is good to know the truth and to speak the truth. It is even better to know the truth and speak about palm trees.

Rather the cruelty of the Turks than the justice of the Bedouins.

Only he who understands is really sad.

Unfortunate is the man who has no fingernails to scratch his head with.

He who would visit a vice, never has far to travel.

Ask me what are my virtues, not about the color of my skin.

God bless him who pays visits—short visits.

Visit infrequently, and you will get closer.

He who walks alone shall surely arrive first.

Walls are the notebooks of fools.

War is a disaster for winner and loser alike.

The most useful holy war is the one fought against your own passions.

More than one war has been caused by a single word.

Don't pour away your water on the strength of a mirage.

Any water in the desert will do.

You cannot carry two watermelons in one hand.

Two weaklings conquered the fort.

It is a sign of weakness just to let things happen.

Dwell not upon thy weariness, thy strength shall be according to the measure of thy desire.

If someone says "There is a wedding ceremony in the clouds," then the women would soon arrive with their ladders.

The whisper of a pretty girl can be heard further off than the roar of a lion.

Ask for your wife's advice and then do the opposite.

If a wife is unfaithful then the husband is partly to blame.

Where there is a will there is a way. Where there is no will there is an excuse.

Wisdom consists of ten parts—nine parts of silence and one part with few words.

There are five ways in which to become wise: be silent, listen, remember, grow older and study.

What wise men suppose is worth more than the certainties of fools.

What the wolf mourns is food for the fox.

You will get no nourishment from the flesh of a woman.

A woman's belly is a garden with many kinds of fruit.

Obedience to a woman leads to hell.

A woman's mosque is her home.

A fat woman is a blanket for the winter.

Give me wool and tomorrow you will have a sheep.

Words from the heart reach the heart, words from the mouth reach the ear.

There are some words that look like salted jam.

A learned man without work is a cloud without rain.

The world is like carrion; those who love and eat from it are dogs.

The worst things in life are:
    To be in bed and sleep not,
    To want for one who comes not,
    To try to please and please not.

Wrath begins in madness and ends in repentance.

He who has approved of wrongdoing is as guilty as he who has committed it.

Youth is a kind of illness cured only by the passing years.

Argentina

The one who loves you will also make you weep.

Children's love is like water in a basket.

No woman can make a wise man out of a fool, but every woman can change a wise man into a fool.

Three daughters and a mother are four devils for a father.

A dog that barks all the time gets little attention.

A man who develops himself is born twice.

If you have a tail of straw, then keep away from the fire.

Armenia

Advice is a free gift that can become expensive for the one who gets it.

When the cart breaks down, advice abounds.

Better to be an ant's head than a lion's tail.

He that asks knows one shame; he that doesn't knows two.

The bee gets honey from the same flower where the snake sucks her poison.

Birds are caught with seed, men with money. ,

They asked a bullfrog, "Why do you croak all the time?" He replied, "I'm enchanted with my voice."

The butterfly who settles on a branch is afraid that he will break it.

A calf is not found under an ox.

Because the cat was given no meat, he said it was Friday.

Thunder clouds do not always give rain.

At death's door a man will beg for the fever.

Dogs that fight each other will join forces against the wolf.

When they gave the donkey flowers to smell, he ate them.

He's looking for the donkey while sitting on it.

Whoever drinks on credit gets drunk more quickly.

A drowning man will clutch at straws.

Stand away from dwarfs, for it's God who hit them on the head.

The eagle was killed by an arrow made with his own feathers.

All men have three ears, one on the left of his head, one on the right and one in his heart.

How can one start a fast with baklava in one's hand.

Before the fat one slims, the slim one will die.

To ask a favor from a miser is like trying to make a hole in water.

You cannot put a fire out with spit.

When asked, "What news from the sea?" The fish replied "I have a lot to say, but my mouth is full of water."

The tongue of the fool is always long.

A pain in the foot is soon forgotten—a pain in the head is not.

When your fortune improves, the columns of your house appear to be crooked.

He who looks for a friend without a fault will never find one.

Friendship is not born of words alone.

The friend who helps me and the enemy who does me no harm, make a pair of earrings.

Dine with a friend but do not do business with him.

Choose a friend with the eyes of an old man, and a horse with the eyes of a young one.

A girl with a golden cradle doesn't remain long in her father's house.

The gravity of the earth is so strong that the old grey man walks crooked.

Quiet horses kick the hardest.

You don't satisfy your hunger by watching others work.

Love did not grow any garlic.

As mills require two stones, so friendship requires two heads.

A mule laden with gold is welcome at every castle.

A mule can swim seven different strokes but the moment he sees the water he forgets them all.

You cannot hit the point of a needle with a fist.

No one will give a pauper bread, but everybody will give him advice.

To pick up in a clumsy way is stealing, to steal in a skillful way is to pick up.

He who cannot pray at home will celebrate mass somewhere else.

On a rainy day many offer to water the chickens.

If you cannot become rich, be the neighbor of a rich man.

If a rich man dies, all the world is moved; if a poor man dies, nobody knows it.

All riches come from the earth.

He who speaks a lot learns little.

The only sword that never rests is the tongue of a woman.

Tears have meaning but only he who sheds them understands.

When the thief has stolen from a thief, God laughs in heaven.

Where is there a tree not shaken by the wind?

Always tell the truth in the form of a joke.

It is better to carry stones with a wise man than accept the meal of a madman.

Ashamed of what she sees in the daytime the sun sets with a blush.

The stones of my native country are warmer than the ovens of Babylon.

Give a horse to the one who likes the truth so that on it he can escape.

The voice of the people is louder than the boom of a canon.

The water in which one drowns is always an ocean.

Wealth can give legs to the cripple, beauty to the ugly, and sympathy to tears.

A woman is like the moon—some nights it is silver others gold.

If a woman hears that something unusual is going on in heaven, she would find a ladder to go and look.

The dowry that a woman brings is like a bell; every time she passes by she hits you with the clapper.

The woman who loves her husband corrects his faults; the man that loves his wife exaggerates them.

The world is a pot, man but a spoon in it.

Australia

The flounder does not return to the place he left when disturbed.

Austria

A light is still a light—even though the blind man cannot see it.

There are more chains than mad dogs.

If you shoot your arrows at stones, you will damage them.

The earth does not shake when the flea coughs.

The cripple is always the one to open the dancing.

The hunt is like a dance for men, for the women the dance is the hunt.

The situation is hopeless, but not serious.

A marriage is a procession in which the cross goes first.

To be drunk every day is also a regular life.

A blind chicken will often find an ear of corn.

What I do not know will not keep me warm.

Babylonian Proverbs

Friendship lasts but for a day, business connections forever.

The gods do not deduct from man's allotted span the hours spent fishing.

Don't trust the smile of your opponent.

Bahamas

A big blanket makes a person sleep late.

Cunning is better than strength.

The shoe knows if the stocking has a hole in it.

Balearic Isles

The best mirror is an old friend.

Lovers always think that other people are blind.

Bambara Proverbs
(Africa)

God gives nothing to those who keep their arms crossed.

Fear is no obstacle to death.

A long beard and a rosary will not make you a priest.

He who has a boss is not the master of his burden.

Beware of the goat that is in the lion's lair.

Do not walk in God's ways on someone else's behalf.

If the hare is your enemy, admit that he can run fast.

No matter how long a log floats on the river, it will never be a crocodile.

No matter how many chores you finish in your house, there is always yet more to be done.

No matter how much the world changes, cats will never lay eggs.

The kitchen is older than the mosque.

The child who loves freedom is the first victim of it.

Even in the freshest of milk, you will still find hairs.

There is no mother like your own mother.

The motherless child will suckle the grandmother.

The hare and the elephant don't travel well together.

When you chop off a snake's head all you are left with is a piece of rope.

When you get older you keep warm with the wood you gathered as a youth.

The word of a powerful man is the truth.

A pregnant woman is not afraid if you threaten her with what you made her pregnant with.

He who longs too much for a child will marry a pregnant woman.

Bantu Proverbs

The earth is a beehive; we all enter by the same door but live in different cells.

Every beast roars in its own den.

No man can paddle two canoes at the same time.

A good deed will make a good neighbor.

The bitter heart eats its owner.

There are forty kinds of lunacy, but only one kind of common sense.

Work is good provided you do not forget to live.

Earth is like a prison: we all go in through the same door, but we stay in different cells.

Who suffers from diarrhea, is not afraid of the dark.

The egg teaches the chicken how to breed.

The hunter who always comes home with meat is a thief.

The most stupid chicken always challenges the wildcat.

The power of the crocodile is in the water.

The eye never forgets what the heart has seen.

Away from home the girl picks forbidden fruit.

A dead man does not know where his grave is.

Whenever I work hard for other people, I always sleep on an empty stomach.

Patience is the mother of a beautiful child.

Only heaven can see the back of a sparrow.

Stroke your dog and he will steal eggs.

A thief does not like to be robbed.

The horizon will not disappear as you run towards it.

The road doesn't tell the traveler what lies ahead.

A woman's clothes are the price her husband pays for peace.

Basque Proverbs

Old bachelors and old maids are either too good or too bad.

God is a busy worker but loves to be helped.

A silver hammer can open an iron gate.

Time flies when you are among friends.

There is never trust without loss.

The wolf and the dog agree about the goat—which together they eat.

Beware of women with beards and men without beards.

A strong attack is half the battle won.

He who is a Basque, a good Christian and has two mules, needs nothing more.

More people are threatened than are beaten up.

The thread must be longer than the needle.

God is good, but not crazy.

A face that never laughs betrays an evil heart.

My dog slaps you with his tail and bites you with his teeth.

Honey is bitter for a sore mouth.

Empty houses are full of noises.

Waiting is futile for whomever wants to kiss someone's backside.

He who knows how to live, knows enough.

The needle dresses people but stays naked itself.

Elm trees have beautiful branches but hardly ever bear fruit.

Whoever crossed the river at the fordable point, knows how deep the river is.

There is no point in offering a helping hand to someone who wants to drown.

My skin is closer to me than my shirt is.

Flatterers and traders are related.

The hand of the stranger is heavy.

Sleep with a woman and she will make sure you wake up.

Earth belongs to the brave but heaven to those who deserve it.

What the wolf does pleases his mate.

The woman who takes a wolf for a husband is always looking into the wood.

The sickness of the body is the cure of the mind.

Bedouin Proverbs

Truth may walk through the world unarmed.

I against my brother.
  My brother and I against our cousin.
  My brother, my cousin and I against the neighbors.
  All of us against the stranger.

Belgium

Happy nations have no history.

The beautiful is less what one sees than what one dreams.

Children have a hair of their father.

Those who counsel do not pay.

We have quite enough to do weeding our own garden.

God heals, but the doctor gets paid.

Honor is better than honors.

The horse must graze where it is tethered.

He who arrives too late finds the plate turned over.

Money buys cherries.

In the end a needle weighs heavy.

Who sieves too much keeps the rubbish.

What you say when you're drunk should have been thought about beforehand.

While the sheep bleats it loses its mouthful.

One spot stains the whole dress.
He who does not wish for little things does not deserve big things.
Truth seldom finds a home.
Weeds never perish.

Benin

The disobedient fowl obeys in a pot of soup.
Who throws stones at night, kills his own brother.
The misfortune that comes into town does not wear a turban.

Berber Proverbs

Silence is the door of consent.
You are worth as much as your purse.
We let him in, and now he shows us the door.
If you open the eyes of a blind man he wants to go back to the darkness.
When a thief finds nothing to steal he will steal a dagger made of sand.
Is the white camel made of fat?
You should make a new bucket whilst you still have the old one.
"I won't tie up the mule in a horse's place," says the widow.
Your secret is your blood—when you shed it you die.
If God were not forgiving, heaven would be empty.
God pardons the ignorant.
The barking of the dogs will not disturb the clouds.
He who rides a camel should not be afraid of dogs.
Boil the water and the scum will rise to the top.
Whoever wants to hurt never misses his target.

The land where the stones know you is worth more than the land where the people know you.

Who is brave enough to tell the lion that his breath smells?

Except for my father and my mother everybody lies.

When a man dies his feet get bigger.

A well educated man always has a kind word to say about the place where he spends the night.

I only have my nails to scratch with and my feet to walk on.

The prayer of the innocent has no wings.

Exile is the brother of death.

With tender words you have less luck with a woman than with jewels.

Fire purges everything.

Better to be watched by a wild animal than a nosey man.

Biblical Proverbs

A soft answer turns away wrath. *Proverbs 15:1*

The borrower is servant to the lender. *Proverbs 22:7*

Can a man take fire in his bosom, and his clothes not be burned? *Proverbs 6:27*

Many are called but few are chosen. *Mat. 22:14*

It is better to dwell in a corner of the housetop, than with a brawling woman in a wide house. *Proverbs 21:9*

Faith moves mountains. *Cor. XIII:2*

The spirit is willing, but the flesh is weak. *Mat. 26:41*

Even a fool, when he holds his peace, is counted wise. *Proverbs 17:28*

Answer a fool according to his folly, lest he be wise in his own conceit. *Proverbs 26:5*

The prosperity of fools shall destroy them. *Proverbs 1:32*

The heart of fools proclaims foolishness. *Proverbs 12:23*

As a dog returns to his vomit, so a fool returns to his folly. *Proverbs 26:11*

Your own friend, and your father's friend, forsake not. *Proverbs 27:10*

Faithful are the wounds of a friend; but the kisses of an enemy are deceitful. *Proverbs 27:6*

It is more blessed to give than to receive. *Acts 20:35*

He that is of a merry heart has a continual feast. *Proverbs 15:15*

Before honor is humility. *Proverbs 15:33*

He that troubles his own house shall inherit the wind: and the fool shall be servant to the wise of heart. *Proverbs 11:29*

Every wise woman builds her house: but the fool plucks it down with her hands. *Proverbs 14:1*

Iron whets iron. *Proverbs. 27:17*

A just man falls seven times, and rises up again. *Proverbs 24:16*

A good name is rather to be chosen than great riches. *Proverbs 22:1*

A good name is better than precious ointment. *Ecclesiastes 7:1*

There is nothing new under the sun. *Proverbs 1:8-9*

The rebellious dwell in a dry land. *Psalm 68:6*

Open rebuke is better than secret love. *Proverbs 27:5*

He that repeats a matter separates very friends. *Proverbs 17:9*

The righteous are bold as a lion. *Proverbs 28:1*

If a ruler hearken to lies, all his servants are wicked. *Proverbs 29:12*

No man can serve two masters. *Luc. 16:13*

Seek and ye shall find. *Mat. 7:7-8*

Stolen waters are sweet, and bread eaten in secret is pleasant. *Proverbs 9:17*

Wealth makes many friends. *Proverbs 19:4*

A prudent wife is from the Lord. *Proverbs 19:14*

The wise man looks ahead. The fool attempts to fool himself and won't face facts. *Proverbs 14:8*

Do you see a man who is wise in his own eyes? There is more hope for a fool than for him. *Proverbs 26:12*

He that walks with wise men shall be wise, but a companion of fools shall be destroyed. *Proverbs 13:20*

Wisdom is more precious than rubies. *Proverbs 3:15*

Bolivia

Tomorrow is as good as today.

Borneo

He who storms in like a whirlwind returns like an ant.
The plowshare only cuts deep where the ground is soft.

Bosnia

When an ant gets wings, it loses its head.
Don't be misled by the tears of a beggar.
A brave man seldom is hurt in the back.
When the ass was invited to the wedding feast he said, "They need more wood and water."
The eyes of all cheats are full of tears.
Why would you use poison if you can kill with honey.
He who heeds the first word of his wife must listen forever to the second.
During the battle you cannot lend your sword to anyone.
Two things rule the world—reward and punishment.

Brahman Proverb

Frugality is the sure guardian of our virtues.

Brazil

Never promise a poor person, and never owe a rich one.

The earth is not thirsty for the blood of the warriors but for the sweat of man's labor.

The poor eat meat when they bite their tongues.

The joy of a poor man does not last long.

Poverty is not a crime, but it's better not to show it.

Between the beginning and the end there is always a middle.

Where blood has been shed the tree of forgiveness cannot grow.

The trees with most leaves will not necessarily produce juicy fruit.

God is big, but the forest is bigger.

God writes straight even on wavy lines.

Goodwill makes the road shorter.

Haste is the mother of imperfection.

At home saints never perform miracles.

Love is blind, so you have to feel your way.

A timely "no" beats a hasty "yes."

The saint is suspicious of too many sacrifices.

An old man with a torn sleeve never dishonored anyone.

In the house of a blacksmith the ornaments are made of wood.

If it were ever to rain soup, the poor would only have forks.

As long as I am running my father will still have a son.

A wise man learns at the fool's expense.

A sleeping fox finds no meat.

He who knows nothing, doubts nothing.

Words will not pollute the soup.

You can only take out of a bag what was already in it.

For every ailing foot, there is a slipper.

You cannot cover up the sun with a sieve.

Breton Proverbs

God knows what will happen to women who drink wine, girls that speak old languages, and suns that set too early.

God's goal will be achieved when everyone is content with himself.

No saint was ever popular in his own parish.

You cannot ring the bell and walk in the procession.

The affection of a child is like water in a sieve.

You don't throw the casket in the fire just because you have lost the key.

It is better to bear your cross than to drag it.

He who always wants the last word, ends up talking to himself.

No matter how treacherous is the sea, a woman will always be more so.

Bulgaria

If you want apples, you have to shake the trees.

An axe without a shaft is no threat to the forest.

If you go to sleep with the blind, you'll wake up squinting.

A good cock can never have too many hens.

A crow will never be a dove.

The crow pecks at the ox to clean it—not to feed from it.

One does not get crucified, one crucifies oneself.

New day—new destiny.

Dead horses can't kick.

If you want to annoy the devil stay silent.

He who believes in dreams feeds on wind.

The droplet is always at its largest just before it drops.

If you want to drown yourself, don't torture yourself with shallow water.

The earth is man's only friend.

Only other people's eggs are double-yolked.

If you have no enemies think then that your own mother might have produced one.

The eye that sees all things else, sees not itself.

A fortress surrenders from within.

The fox falls into the trap only once.

Every frog has his own pond.

God gives but does not lock the gate.

God is not without sins: He created the world.

God does not pay every Saturday.

If you light one candle for God, then you must light two for the devil.

Grapes do not grow in a willow tree.

Two happy days are seldom brothers.

No hero without a wound.

Life is a ladder—some will climb up it, others down.

A lion lurks in everyone's heart; awake him not.

If you would live long, open your heart.

He who has been at the mill has flour on his hat.

Give me, mother, luck at my birth, then throw me if you will on the rubbish heap.

Mother Nature, time and patience are the three best doctors.

The neighbor's chicken is a duck.

Seize the opportunity by the beard, for it is bald behind.

From the promise to the deed is a day's journey.

Ravens do not peck each other's eyes out.

When the sea turned into honey, the beggar lost his spoon.

If you cannot serve, you cannot rule.

Why should I shave when God doesn't?

You will sell more sheepskins at the market than wolfskins.

A song belongs to no one.

Let the man who has suffered ask it—not the man who has travelled.

Thirsty men make good prophets.

When the Turk becomes richer he takes another wife. When a Bulgar gets rich he builds himself another house.

The village feeds the town.

From walking—something; from sitting—nothing.

Whip the saddle and give the mule something to think about it.

The wife carries the husband on her face; the husband carries the wife on his clothes.

Pretty wife, old wine—many friends.

If you call one wolf, you invite the pack.

The wolf changes only his coat—not his character.

A house without a woman is like a fire without a bucket.

One gentle word opens a gate of iron.

He who breaks his word shall through his word be broken.

A word about to be spoken is like a stone that is ready to be thrown.

Burkina Faso

When a beautiful woman does not steal, she takes you.

If you haven't been to two marketplaces, you don't know which is the best value.

Burundi

Two lightning flashes cannot come from one cloud.

The best trees grow on the steepest hills.

If you are dancing with your rivals, don't close your eyes.

The fetus that is afraid of criticism is never born.

God gives, but he doesn't sell.

When the master of the house tells a lie, then offer him a chair.

Dogs don't love people, they love the place where they are fed.
Where there is love there is no darkness.
He who loves everything dies of it.
The lazy one is pregnant in the sowing season.
If a young woman says no to marriage just wait until her breasts sag.
A mother's wrath does not survive the night.
A mother's behind sins when it sits down.
Morning will still come with or without the crowing of the cock.
An elephant does not get tired carrying his trunk.
The reception has more value than the invitation.
Don't tell any more fairy tales when the child has gone to sleep.
Better to kiss an ugly woman than to lick yourself.
Too many words blacken your ears.

Byzantium

A grape that sees another gets ripe.

Cambodia

Cultivate a heart of love that knows no danger.
Active hands, full bellies.
You don't have to cut a tree down to get at the fruit.
The boat sails by, the shore remains.
A husband should not talk of pretty girls in front of his wife.
People give, but don't be in a hurry to take.
You can't claim heaven as your own if you are just going to sit under it.
If you are doing wrong, make sure you don't get fat from it.
The elephant that is stuck in the mud will tear down the tree with it.
Don't shoot people you hate; don't lend to those you love.

Cameroon

Stealing may bring profit, but hanging costs far more.
The tiger depends on the forest; the forest depends on the tiger.
Don't let women who attract attention walk behind you.
With water make rivers, with rice make armies.

Cameroon

A bird that allows itself to be caught will find a way of escaping.
A building of sand falls as you build it.
There is no doctor on the day you die.
If love is a sickness, patience is the remedy.
Lying will get you a wife, but it won't keep her.
However little you think of the elephant, you can't say it won't fill a pot.
However swift a man, he will not outstrip his shadow.
He who asks questions, cannot avoid the answers.
The cricket cries, the year changes.
If you do not step on the dog's tail, he will not bite you.
An elephant will reach to the roof of the house.
The flood takes him in, and the ebb takes him out.
Knowledge is better than riches.
Better a mistake at the beginning than at the end.
Rain does not fall on one roof alone.
Thought breaks the heart.
By trying often, the monkey learns to jump from the tree.
When the vine entwines your roof, it is time to cut it down.
A man's wealth may be superior to him.
The heart of the wise man lies quiet like limpid water.
She is like a road—pretty, but crooked.
The day did not know that night had fallen.

If everyone is going to dance, who, then, would watch?

The darkness of night cannot stop the light of morning.

What you don't know, you will not recognize.

The folly of a man is not broadcast like that of a woman.

You cannot produce one human being without uniting two bodies.

It is better to be the victim of injustice than to be unjust yourself.

If the panther knew how much he is feared, he would do much more harm.

It is the pot that boils but the dish that gets the credit.

Beauty is an empty calabash.

Every smart man is an ignoramus who abuses his ignorance.

One father can feed seven children, but seven children cannot feed one father.

When the poor man sets a trap only his dog gets caught.

Singing birds don't build nests.

A friend is worth more than a brother.

The fire cannot be put out with your hands.

Water always finds a way out.

Better little than too little.

If the fight is tomorrow, why then clench your fist today?

Canada

The devil places a pillow for a drunken man to fall upon.

All Hallows moon, witches soon.

Once the last tree is cut and the last river poisoned, you will find you cannot eat your money.

Do not put all your eggs in one basket.

You cannot catch skunks with mice.

Canary Islands

Women and glass are always in danger.

A gentle breeze blowing in the right direction is better than a pair of
strong oars.

Cape Verde Islands

A person without a spouse is like a vase without flowers.

Catalonian Proverbs

A peasant between two lawyers is like a fish between two cats.

He who maligns you in your absence is afraid of your presence.

At a wedding a bride eats the least.

Dancing at the carnival, baptizing on All Saints Day.

A whore in spring, a nun in autumn.

In times of famine no bread is stale.

Where the girls are there are no spider's webs.

If all else fails, sleep with your mother.

The musician who is paid in advance does not play so well.

A mother-in-law may be good, but she is better when mother earth
covers her up.

A mother-in-law made of sugar, still tastes bitter.

There is always lots of time to die and to pay.

Talking of an old debt always starts another quarrel.

Show me your wife and I will tell you what kind of a husband she
has.

Women and cats in the house, men and dogs in the street.

The best word is the unspoken word.

Chad

Do not try to cook the goat's young in the goat's milk.
The humble pay for the mistakes of their betters.
Your beauty is in what you have.
A man with too much ambition cannot sleep in peace.

Chile

That which is a sin in others is a virtue in ourselves.
Anguish is our worst adviser.
He who saves up for another day has no trust in God.
He who divides and shares, always takes the best part.
We all have something of a doctor, a poet and a fool.
One devil that you know is better than twenty that you don't.
He who travels over land has to drink enough water.
He who travels to Portugal loses his seat.
He who is warned in time is saved.

China

Behind an able man there are always other able men.
One never accuses without a little bit of lying.
Active people never have louse bites.
The more acquaintances you have, the less you know them.
Once bitten by an adder, you will never walk through the high grass
    again.
Almond nuts come to those who have no teeth.
To feed the ambition in your heart is like carrying a tiger under your
    arm.

China

To forget one's ancestors is to be a brook without a source, a tree without a root.

Anger is always more harmful than the insult that caused it.

When you are very angry, don't go to a lawyer; when you are very hungry, don't be a poet.

An answer that does not resolve a quarrel makes a thousand new ones.

Who arrives in the darkness departs as night falls.

An old bachelor compares life with a shirt button that hangs often by a thread.

A bad man talks about what he has eaten and drunk—a good man about what he has seen and heard.

You can lean on a bamboo stick, but not on a rope.

One bamboo does not make a forest.

No matter how big, one beam cannot support a house.

A good bee never lands on a fallen flower.

Good behavior is a virtue for the man—bad behavior is the virtue of a woman.

You can't fill your belly painting pictures of bread.

A bird does not sing because he has the answer to something, he sings because he has a song.

The prettiest birds are in a cage.

Great blessings come from Heaven; small blessings come from man.

Never boast—you might meet someone who knew you as a child.

He who cannot boast cannot succeed.

You can't load a small boat with heavy cargo.

One foot cannot stand on two boats.

When the boat reaches mid-stream, it is too late to stop the leak.

One body cannot perform two services.

Better to satisfy the body than to tarnish the soul.

He who has a straight body is not worried about his crooked shadow.

If your books are not read, your descendants will be ignorant.

China

It is better to be without a book than to believe it entirely.

Every book must be chewed to get out its juice.

When you have read a book for the first time, you get to know a friend; read it for a second time and you meet an old friend.

A man is happy when he has books, but happier still when he does not need them.

Borrowed money shortens time; working for others lengthens it.

Draw the bow but don't shoot—it is a bigger threat to be intimidated than to be hit.

If you bow at all, bow low.

The brave person regards dying as going home.

A good breakfast cannot take the place of the evening meal.

He who does not know what to do in his spare time is not a businessman.

When you go to buy, don't show your silver.

If there are many buyers in the market, the merchant doesn't wash his turnips.

From Nanking to Beijing, buyers are never as smart as the sellers.

Always keep calm in an emergency.

It is better to light a candle than to curse the darkness.

He that is not eager to be pawed in cash is not a businessman.

A blind cat catches only a dead rat.

It is difficult to catch a black cat in a dark room, especially when it is not there.

Which cat does not gorge a mouse?

The cat got an order and delegated it to her tail.

The doorway to charity is difficult to open and difficult to close.

Two leaps per chasm is fatal.

If you don't want to be cheated, ask the price at three shops.

The first time you cheat me, be ashamed. The second time it is I who must be ashamed.

He who has never been cheated, cannot be a good businessman.

China

A chicken is hatched even from such a well sealed thing as an egg.

Big chickens don't peck at small seeds.

If you are married to a chicken obey the chicken. If you are married to a dog obey the dog.

If you are going to have a roast, a chicken is better than a phoenix.

It is easier to get a chicken back in the egg than to undo a slander.

If you want your children to enjoy a quiet life let them suffer a little hunger and a little cold.

The jewel of the air is the sun; the jewel of the house is the child.

A good client doesn't change shop in three years, a good shop doesn't change clients in three years.

Whoever tears his clothes must mend them himself.

Away from home they look at your clothes. At home they look at what is under them.

Just because men do not like the cold, Heaven will not stop the winter.

Where there's a will to condemn there is also evidence.

The conquerors are kings; the defeated are bandits.

Don't hang your conscience on your back.

The man whose conscience is clear will never fear a knock on the door at midnight.

The contented person can never be ruined.

To make good conversation there are a thousand subjects, but there are still those who cannot meet a cripple without talking about feet.

You cannot cook two meals in the same pot.

If cooks quarrel, the roast burns.

The corn is not choked by the weeds but by the negligence of the farmer.

A small cottage wherein laughter lives is worth more than a castle full of tears.

Going into a country the first time, ask what is forbidden; on entering a village, ask what are the customs; on entering a private house, ask what should not be mentioned.

Courtesy never offended anybody.

Even criminals have their uses; they keep sleepyheads awake.

The crow does not roost with the phoenix.

To be able to curse once a day improves happiness and lengthens life.

Eighteen daughters beautiful as goddesses are not as good as one crippled son.

As a daughter grows up she is like smuggled salt.

No wise man takes responsibility for an eighteen-year-old daughter.

The day did not know that night had fallen.

By day think of your own faults, by night think of the faults of others.

When the deal is done, discuss it no more; it is difficult to collect dispersed water.

To pretend to satisfy one's desires with worldly goods is like using straw to put out a fire.

It is not the destination that is important, but the journey there.

The man who is not destined to die will be cured by medicine.

Better a diamond with a flaw than a pebble without.

A dictionary can only be read when it is printed.

To die is to stop living but to stop living is something entirely different than dying.

People die voluntarily when it becomes impossible to live.

It's better to die two years early than to live one year too long.

All things seem difficult at first.

If you want dinner, don't insult the cook.

He who cannot suffer discomfort, will not be called for important things.

Distance tests a horse's strength; time reveals a man's character.

Do everything at the right time and one day will seem like three.

To know how to do it is simple, the difficulty is in doing it.

The best doctor prevents illness, an average doctor visits when the illness is imminent, and the unskilled doctor treats your present illness.

China

A clever doctor never treats himself.

One dog barks at something specific, and a hundred bark at the sound.

It's not the fleas of the dog that make the cat meow.

A good dog does not bite a chicken and a good man does not hit his wife.

You don't need a dog to catch a lame hare.

He who does not feed the dog feeds the thief.

If the dog leads the man, the man is blind. If the man leads the dog, the man is married.

Give a dog a tasty name and eat him.

A dog in a kennel barks at his fleas—a hunting dog does not feel them.

Before you beat the dog, find out the name of his master.

Better to be a dog in peacetime that a man in wartime.

If no one comes the dog does not bark.

A dog shows affection even to a poor family.

The best kind of closed door is the one you can leave unlocked.

Whoever keeps his door locked all the time longs for it to be broken down.

The dragon teaches you that if you want to climb high you have to do it against the wind.

He who wants to be a dragon must eat many little snakes.

There is no room for two dragons in one pond.

To believe in one's dreams is to spend all of one's life asleep.

To stop drinking, study a drunkard when you are sober.

A good drum does not have to be beaten hard.

Drunkards talk to the gods.

Drunkenness does not itself cause bad qualities but it does show them up clearly.

The roast duck can fly no more.

Not the cry, but the flight of the wild duck, leads the flock to fly and follow.

One throws up the dust the other gets it in his eye.

The path of duty lies in what is nearby, but men look for it in things far off.

When with dwarfs, do not talk about pygmies.

Three times an early rise makes a whole day.

Those who earn a lot are seldom tired, those who get tired seldom earn a lot.

The earth offers you a grave everywhere.

He who cheats the earth will be cheated by the earth.

When going to an eating house, go to one that is filled with customers.

He who always eats the roots of a plant is capable of any thing.

There is no economy in going to bed early to save candles if the result is twins.

Even a big elephant can be caught in one female hair.

Though the emperor be rich, he cannot buy one extra year.

If thine enemy wrong thee, buy each of his children a drum.

The torment of envy is like a grain of sand in the eye.

A one-inch error at the start can be a thousand miles at the end.

One moment's error becomes a lifetime of sadness.

Don't expect from others what you can't promise them yourself.

Faith and dishonesty are other words for uselessness.

Don't let the falcon loose until you see the hare.

To fall is not painful for those who fly low.

When you fall into a pit, you either die or get out.

He who trips and falls should not blame his foot.

Govern a family as you would cook a small fish—very gently.

Going too far is as bad as falling short.

China

The farmer hopes for rain, the walker hopes for sunshine, and the gods hesitate.

You won't get much fat from a dry bone.

The father in praising his son extolls himself.

He who hides his faults plans to make more.

Only through the eyes of others can we really see our own faults.

The first favor is a favor, the second an obligation.

Don't use oiled paper to wrap up fire.

Kindle not a fire you cannot put out.

Fire makes mud hard and gold melt.

Do not dress in clothes made of leaves when going to put out a fire.

Be first in the field, the last to the couch.

If you are not a fish, how can you know if the fish are happy?

Give a man a fish and you feed him for a day. Teach a man to fish and you feed him for a lifetime.

The fish you cannot catch is always a big one.

There are people that fish and those who just disturb the water.

There is a time to fish and a time to prepare the fish.

There is a time to fish and a time to dry the nets.

He who sees heaven in the water sees the fishes in the trees.

All rotten fish taste the same.

He who flatters me is my enemy, who blames me is my teacher.

The flatterer makes you climb up a tree then takes the ladder away.

There are thirty-six ways to flee, but to run away is the best.

The flowers in your garden don't smell as sweet as those in the wild, but they last much longer.

The country where flowers are expensive lacks the foundation of culture.

Enough food and a pipe full of tobacco makes you equal to the immortals.

A fool in a hurry drinks tea with a fork.

A fool admires himself most when he has done foolish things.

He who asks a question may be a fool for five minutes; he who asks no questions stays a fool forever.

The fool does what he can't avoid, the wise man avoids what he can't do.

Forethought is easy, repentance hard.

You forgive everything of someone who doesn't forgive himself.

Those who have free seats at the play are the first to hiss.

A friend—one soul, two bodies.

It is easier to visit your friends than to live with them.

You can accompany a friend for a thousand miles but at some time you must take your leave.

There is no better sale than when you give a true friend what he needs.

Do not remove a fly from your friend's forehead with a hatchet.

If you have money and wine, your friends will be many.

When men are friendly the water is sweet.

With a frog in the well you don't talk about the ocean.

Ripe fruit falls by itself, but it does not fall into your mouth.

All the past died yesterday; the future is born today.

You can be cautious about the future but not the past.

He who can persuade someone not to gamble has earned money for him.

Those who play the game do not see as clearly as those who watch.

All gardeners know better than other gardeners.

One generation builds the street on which the next will walk.

Genius can be recognized by its childish simplicity.

No one is more afraid of ghosts than those who don't believe in them.

The gift itself can be light while carrying a heavy message.

Gifts reflect those who give them.

It is difficult to repay the gifts you get at a wedding or a funeral.

China

A girl receives, a widow takes her husband.

A girl that blushes too much, knows too much.

Beautiful girls are seldom happy, intelligent boys are seldom beautiful.

Even when a girl is as shy as a mouse, you still have to beware of the tiger within.

God and fairies can be wrong as well.

Real gold is not afraid of the melting pot.

The miser does not own the gold, it is the gold that owns the miser.

The pleasure of doing good is the only one that will not wear out.

Do something good and your neighbor will never know, do something bad and they will hear about it a hundred miles away.

To do good for ten years is not enough; do bad things for one day and it is too much.

Make friends with what is good in a man and not his goods.

There's many a good man to be found under a shabby hat.

There is gossip every day, but if no one listens anymore the gossip will die.

It is easier to govern a country than a son.

The house with an old grandparent harbors a jewel.

A day of grief lasts longer than a month of joy.

The guest who outstays his fellow guests loses his overcoat.

He who is not friendly towards a good guest will never have one.

Great things can be reduced to small things, and small things can be reduced to nothing.

If you would be happy for a week, take a wife; if you would be happy for a month, kill a pig; but if you would be happy all your life, plant a garden.

Happiness is like a sunbeam, which the least shadow intercepts, while adversity is often as the rain of spring.

Happiness has its roots—sorrow has its womb.

You can never be happy at the expense of the happiness of others.

Happy is the man who knows he's happy.

Happy is the man without sickness. Rich is the man with no debts.

The happiest life ends before death.

After all, harming others means you first harm yourself.

The harvest of a whole year depends on what you sow in the spring-time.

The net of heaven is large and wide, but it lets nothing through.

When the heart is at ease, the body is healthy.

The heart is but the beach beside the sea that is the world.

He who knows his heart mistrusts his eyes.

A heart that is rotten—breath that smells.

The human heart is difficult to gauge.

The human heart is never satisfied, just like the snake that wants to swallow an elephant.

The winds of heaven change suddenly; so do human fortunes.

For each man produced by heaven, earth provides a grave.

If heaven above lets fall a plum, open your mouth.

It is often more difficult to come back home than it is to go away.

Four horses cannot overtake the tongue.

A horse with two masters is always skinny; the ship with two captains sinks.

The war horses are born on the frontiers.

The day your horse dies and your money's gone, your relatives change into strangers.

Whoever buys a house must examine the beams; whoever wants a wife must look at her mother.

The household with its own elder has indeed its own adornment.

To have saved one human life is worth more than to build a pagoda with seven stories.

To be human is easy, to be a human being is difficult.

Over a distance of a thousand miles only humanity works, not power.

He who is hungry is never a good civil servant.

China

If you are hunting for a red deer then ignore the hares.

If you are in a hurry, go via the roundabout.

When you are in a hurry, the horse holds back.

He who opens his heart for ambition, closes it for the rest.

To be for one day entirely at leisure is to be for one day an immortal.

Indulgences have more victims than swords.

Who is inferior and is ashamed of it proves that he really is inferior.

Choose your inn before dark, get back on the road before dawn.

It is better to save your innocence at the expense of your honor than your country at the expense of your life.

The wise man forgets insults as the ungrateful forget benefits.

Only one who can swallow an insult is a man.

He who takes revenge for a small insult, will have a bigger one thrown at him.

Never has a man more need of his intelligence than when a fool asks him a question.

Don't let your tongue or your paintbrush wag your tail when they are making up an inventory.

No iron is so strong that it cannot be melted down, and no business so dirty that can be fixed with money.

The itch that gives someone skill is difficult to scratch.

The jail is closed day and night and always full; temples are always open and still empty.

As soon as you have finished a job, you start appreciating the difficulties.

A journey of a thousand miles must begin with a single step.

One joy scatters a hundred griefs.

Justice is the result of public opinion.

Do not forget little kindnesses and do not remember small faults.

When a king makes a mistake, all the people suffer.

It is easy to govern a kingdom but difficult to rule one's family.

To know and know that you know, not to know and know that you
don't know, *that* is to know.

He who knows himself knows everybody.

Knowledge that is not replenished diminishes every day.

When the lamps in the house are lit it is like the flowering of lotus on
the lake.

The law is good, but people are not.

The maker of laws must be severe; who executes them must be generous.

Win your lawsuit and lose your money.

When there are two in a lawsuit only a third will profit from it.

Lazy people always want to do everything at the same time.

Learning is a treasure which accompanies its owner everywhere.

To learn about other people is science, to learn to know yourself is intelligence.

To learn what is good, a thousand days are not sufficient; to learn
what is evil, an hour is too long.

Every letter must be chewed before you can refresh yourself with its
juice.

One man tells a lie, dozens repeat it as the truth.

If life is fulfilled we go away with empty hands.

Life is like a candle in the wind; like frost on the roof; like the wrig-
gling of the fish in the pan.

Don't ask in this life for the three most difficult things: good sons,
long life and a long beard.

The most important thing in life is to be buried well.

Win a cat and lose a cow—the consequence of litigation.

Locks can not be made from good iron, soldiers are not made out of
good people.

Choose your lodging before dark and leave before the morning dew.

Don't look back when you are walking along the edge of a wall.

A louse cannot lift the eiderdown.

China

Love is an eye that doesn't see anything.

Love has its tides; before ebb tide you must take advantage of the flood.

Whoever tastes from the head of a poppy will not expect any thing from love.

For people who love even water is sweet.

Men see only the present; heaven sees the future.

You can chop a man's head off, but you can't keep him quiet.

A man thinks that he knows it, but his wife knows better.

A man is old when he takes the whole night to do what he used to do all night long.

Deep down all men are alike—and that is the problem.

No matter how worthless a man may be, kill him and see how much he costs you.

A well mannered man does not step on the shadow of his fellow man.

What is told into a man's ear is often heard a hundred miles away.

The man is heaven and earth in miniature.

A man combs his hair every morning—why not his heart?

Every man assumes the colors of his surroundings.

A man's greatest shortcoming is that he neglects his own field and weeds that of others.

Man's eyelids are transparent.

Good manners can be paid for with compliments, but only the sound of money will pay your debts.

He who is master of himself cannot tolerate another boss.

Just as a medicine may not cure a serious illness, wine will certainly not dispel your grief.

An accidental meeting is more pleasant than a planned one.

No melon peddler cries, "Bitter melons." No wine dealer says, "Sour wine."

A good memory is not so good as a little ink.

Merit and glory never adorn a nightcap.

China

A vacant mind is open to all suggestions, as a hollow building echoes all sounds.

Your best mirror is someone more beautiful than you.

You can mirror something from other people; you can only give out that which is your own.

Misfortune only comes in when the door is open.

He who covers up his mistakes intends to make some more.

Always leave a little room for a mistake.

You never are so easily mistaken as when you think you know the way.

To mock your elders is to wreck the house where you have to stay to-night.

Mockery is the flashing of slander.

With money, a dragon—without it, a worm.

With money one may command devils; without it, one cannot even summon a man.

Lend money to someone who won't pay you back and he'll hate you.

I have money, you have money; so we are friends.

With money you can make the dead speak; without it you can't even keep the deaf quiet.

He who hasn't a penny sees bargains everywhere.

When money is stolen you can only beat the dog.

Money can buy a lot that is not even for sale.

He who has a lot of money and no children is not rich; he who has many children and no money is not a pauper.

When a finger is pointing at the moon, the fool looks at the finger.

Even the most beautiful morning cannot bring back the evening.

If you don't scale the mountain, you can't view the plain.

There are many paths up the mountain, but the view from the top is always the same.

He who stands still in the mud sticks in it.

One can forgive a murder but not impoliteness.

Heavenly music is interpreted differently by everyone.

Who is narrow minded cannot be bighearted.

If you do without something for long enough, then you don't need it.

No needle is sharp at both ends.

Love your neighbors, but don't pull down the fence.

It never rains on your neighbors without you getting your feet wet.

When your neighbor walks through your orchard, the polite thing to do is to ignore it.

It's better to do good in the neighborhood than to burn incense far away.

A hundred "no's" are less painful than one insincere "yes."

Nobility is what is earned by those who have no other earnings.

An obscure style is a blind mirror.

If you have nothing else to offer me, offer me your smile.

The life of an old man can be compared with the flame of a candle in a drought.

It is only good when the old and the young respect each other.

Opinions are like nails: the more often you hit them the deeper they penetrate.

Pain is easier to endure than an itch.

To understand your parents' love you must raise children yourself.

Patience, and the mulberry leaf becomes a silk gown.

A moment of patience can prevent a great disaster and a moment of impatience can ruin a whole life.

Have patience, the grass will be milk soon enough.

Patience in the household is a real treasure.

He who loves peace minds his own business.

If the pedestal is beautiful the statue must be even more beautiful.

People live like birds in a wood: When the time comes, each takes flight.

People can be done without but a lot of us need a friend.

People fool themselves. They pray for a long life but fear old age.

A man can never be perfect in a hundred years; but he may become corrupt in less than a day.

A clever person turns great troubles into little ones and little ones into none at all.

There are three kinds of person that you must not challenge: civil servants, customers and widows.

There are two kinds of perfect person; one who is dead and the other one is not yet born.

A person without a smiling face must never open a shop.

Even an accomplished physician cannot cure himself.

A picture is worth ten thousand words.

While wrangling over a quarter of pig, you can lose a flock of sheep.

Last night I made a thousand plans, but this morning I went my old way.

If you must play, decide upon three things at the start: the rules of the game, the stakes, and when to stop.

Too much politeness conceals deceit.

The poorer you are, the more devils you meet.

The poor can only guess at what wealth is; the rich don't know what poverty means.

The poor ones give their alms in a humble way, the rich man throws them down with contempt. Great people give it with reproaches.

Poverty and ugliness are difficult to hide.

The powerful are never faithful.

If a man becomes powerful even his chicken and his dog go to heaven.

Some people want to be praised for the rest of their lives for what they have done well for one day.

Don't try to make predictions—especially those concerning the future.

He who was presented with an ox must give in return a horse.

To serve a prince is like sleeping with a tiger.

China

A man of high principles is someone who can watch a chess game without passing comment.

Don't buy someone else's problems.

Solve one problem, and you keep a hundred others away.

Procrastination is the thief of time.

Whenever there is profit to be made then think of honesty.

Don't promise something when you are full of joy; don't answer letters when you are full of anger.

You will never be punished for making people die of laughter.

If rain bothers you, you can always jump into the sea.

If a rat wants to die it bites a cat's tail.

A red-nosed man may not be a drunkard, but he will always be called one.

Repentance is the spring beneath our virtues.

Never eat in a restaurant where the chef is thin.

It's better for people to wait for rice, than rice for people.

Talking doesn't get your rice cooked.

The rich man plans for tomorrow, the poor man for today.

The only thing that was missing at the rich man's funeral was mourners.

He who has nothing to lose is rich.

Being in the right does not depend on having a loud voice.

Do not insult the river god while crossing the river.

Quiet rivers have flowery banks.

It is no good going to the river just wanting to catch a fish; you have to take a net as well.

To find out about the road ahead, ask those coming back.

All roads lead to Beijing.

Beautiful roads never go far.

The main road is an easy way, but everyone loves the side streets.

The scent of a rose will always stay on the hand of the giver.

The rose has thorns only for those who want to pick it.

You cannot pick up salt with dry fingers.

A satisfied man is happy even if he is poor; a dissatisfied man is sad even if he is rich.

When you say one thing, the clever person understands three.

You always win by not saying the things you don't have to say.

Be skeptical; long garments can also hide big feet.

The scholar builds the cities, the woman knocks them down.

The real scholar is not afraid to ask questions of his pupil.

The great scholar forgets about fame, the average scholar works for it, and the unworthy scholar steals it.

Rivalry between scholars improves science.

No matter how big the sea may be, sometimes two ships meet.

Within the four seas all man are brethren.

Though all rivers flow into it, the sea never overflows.

Never do anything that you want to remain a secret.

Believe your servants but do not listen to them.

To have beautiful servant girls is a threat to good marriages.

Shadows are formed all along the wishes of the sun.

Shame is forgotten, debts are not.

Even a sheep with the skin of a tiger is afraid of the wolf.

Big ships often sail on big debts.

Why jump in the water before the ship turns over.

To open a shop is easy—the hard part is keeping it open.

Slander piles itself before the door of a widow.

The loss of one night's sleep is followed by ten days of inconvenience.

Be not afraid of going slowly, be afraid only of standing still.

A man who cannot tolerate small ills can never accomplish great things.

The main thing is that we can smile at our duties—yes even at our suffering.

The fangs of the green snake and the sting of a wasp don't really make poison—that is only to be found in a woman's heart.

If you walk on snow you cannot hide your footprints.

He who does not regularly put on clean socks will never get used to circus life.

It is easy to get a thousand soldiers, but difficult to get one general.

It is a sad situation for a son-in-law when his mother-in-law praises him.

A dead songbird gives us no meat.

The more souls the more gossip.

The one who understands does not speak; the one who speaks does not understand.

The spirit goes on foot.

Too much spirit shows a lack of it.

Respect spiritual beings but keep your distance.

Spouses that love each other say a thousand things without speaking.

Spring is sooner recognized by plants than by men.

You can't look at the stars while you are walking if you have a stone in your shoe.

He who steps aside for someone broadens the way.

Long or short, a stick is always a stick; tall or short, people are always people.

A good storyteller must be able to lie a little.

If you are not so strong, don't carry heavy burdens. If your words are worthless, don't give advice.

Don't draw a sword against a louse.

If you wish to succeed, consult three old people.

The key to success isn't much good until one discovers the right lock to put it in.

Not only those who can talk the best tell you the most interesting things.

When people only talk about things they understand then a great silence will descend upon the world.

Talking without thinking is shooting without aiming.

Though talking face to face, their hearts are a thousand miles apart.

A teacher is someone who ploughs with his tongue to fill his little bowl with rice.

Those who have free tickets to the theater have the most criticism to make.

A thief has more than two hands.

Look not at thieves eating meat, but look at them suffering punishment.

He who thinks too much about every step he takes will stay on one leg all his life.

He who is thirsty dreams that he is drinking.

If you wish to know what most occupies a man's thoughts, you have only to listen to his conversation.

Treat thoughts as guests and wishes as children.

The thoughtless person buries a well when he is thirsty.

Thrift is independence.

Measure your throat before you swallow a bone.

While keeping a tiger from the front door, the wolf comes in at the back.

A tiger cannot beat a crowd of monkeys.

He who rides on a tiger can never get off.

Learn to paint a tiger and you only paint his skin; learn to know a human being and you only know his face.

If the main timbers in the house are not straight, the smaller timber will be unsafe; and if the smaller timbers are not straight, the house will fall.

You can't buy an inch of time with an inch of gold.

As long as time is not pressing one does not burn incense; when it becomes urgent one kisses the feet of Buddha.

Too often do we waste time chasing a gust of wind or grasping at shadows.

The tongue that concedes will not wear out; obstinate teeth fall out.

One measures the towers by their shadows and great people by those who envy them.

Even a tower a hundred yards tall has still its foundations on the ground.

The loftiest towers rise from the ground.

When traveling do not calculate the distance, at dinner don't think of how much.

He who travels a lot becomes wise; he who is wise stays home.

A big tree attracts the wind.

No matter how tall the tree is, its leaves will always fall to the ground.

Keep a green tree in your heart and perhaps the singing bird will come.

Don't climb a tree to catch a fish.

There are only two ways to reach the truth—with literature and agriculture.

Do not trust a person who claims to be honest, and never trust exaggerated friendliness.

Sooner or later the day comes when the tumor can be lanced.

Even ugly faces are worth looking at—and that is a great comfort for most people.

What is not urgent must be done quickly in order to take care of the urgent things calmly.

The door to virtue is heavy and hard to open.

The greatest virtue is like water; good for everything.

He who is sure of his victory will not start a war.

There is no cure for vulgarity.

Do not tear down the east wall to repair the west.

The water that a ship sails on is the same water that swallows it up.

When the water falls the stone becomes visible.

When someone gives you a drop of water reward him with a never ending source.

Water can do without fishes, fishes cannot do without water.

Well water is not an enemy of spring water.

Flowing water never gets dirty.

Water does not stick to the mountain, and vengeance does not stick to a big heart.

Water from far away is no good for a fire close by.

When you drink water, remember where the mountain spring is.

Ill gotten gains are like snow that is sprinkled with hot water.

He who goes his own way does not deserve being received.

Weaklings never forgive their enemies.

Wealth is but dung, useful only when spread about.

Dig a well before you are thirsty.

It's not that the well is too deep, but rather the rope is too short.

Don't trust your wife until she has borne you ten sons.

Teach your son in the front garden and your wife on the pillow.

Great souls have wills; feeble ones have only wishes.

Wine lets secrets out.

Three glasses of wine end a hundred quarrels.

Better the cold blast of winter than the hot breath of a pursuing elephant.

A wise man adapts himself to circumstances, as water shapes itself to the vessel that contains it.

The palace leads to fame, the market to fortune, and loneliness to wisdom.

The wise man doesn't say what he does but he never does what can't be said.

No matter how much the wise man travels, he always lives in the same place.

The wise man and the tortoise travel but never leave their home.

The wise man asks questions of himself; the fool questions others.

A wise man takes his own decisions; the ignorant goes with the crowd.

The conversation of the wise concerns ideas; that of the intelligent is about ideas; the common folk talk about food.

A wise man will not rebuke a fool.

Wise men are never in a hurry.

Our wishes are like little children—the more you indulge the more they want from you.

You need your wits about you the most when you are dealing with an idiot.

It's not the beauty of a woman that blinds the man, the man blinds himself.

A woman gets thirty percent of her beauty from nature and seventy percent from makeup.

The virtue of a woman does not go deep but her passion knows no limit.

The spirit of women is made of quicksilver; their heart of wax.

The first decision of a woman is the most intelligent and the last decision most dangerous.

Of all the female qualities a warm heart is the most valuable.

The advice of a clever woman can ruin a strong town.

The most highly praised woman is the one about whom no one speaks.

When a man is crazy about a woman only she can cure him.

Women and fools never forgive.

A woman that always laughs is everybody's wife; a man that is always laughing is an idiot.

The tongue of a woman is the sword that is never allowed to rust.

The woman who deceives her husband makes her lover swear never to be unfaithful to her.

A young woman with an old man is really someone else's woman.

Women never praise without gossiping.

What is lighter than a feather? The wind!
  Lighter than the wind? The spirit!
  Lighter than the spirit? The woman!
  Lighter than the woman? Nothing at all!

When a woman talks to you, smile but do not listen.

A patient woman can roast an ox with a lantern.

A thriftless woman burns the entire candle looking for a match.

Never does a woman lie in a more cunning way than when she tells
  the truth to someone who doesn't believe her.

The unfaithful woman has remorse, the faithful one has regret.

A curious woman is capable of turning around the rainbow just to
  see what is on the other side.

Every kind of wood is grey when they are reduced to ashes.

If one word does not succeed, ten thousand are of no avail.

Words that come from the heart stay warm three winters long.

You can live with tea and cold rice but not with cold words.

A word once spoken, an army of chariots cannot overtake it.

Urge people to work, not to eat.

A thousand workers, a thousand plans.

If you want to go up in the world, veil ambition with the forms of humanity.

The world is our house. Keep it clean.

Killing a man to save the world, does not save the world.

Before you prepare to improve the world, look around your own
  house three times.

If you stay long enough in one place the whole world passes you by.

Yesterday, today and tomorrow—these are the three days of man.

Colombia

Even the candle seller dies in the dark.

He who gives away his belongings, slowly becomes a beggar.

Where there are stones the brook babbles.

The old dog barks while he is sitting down.

Congo

A pretty basket does not prevent worries.

When the bee comes to your house, let her have beer; you may want to visit the bee's house some day.

Two birds disputed about a kernel, when a third swooped down and carried it off.

The watched chicken never lays.

Children are the reward of life.

What is said over the dead lion's body, could not be said to him alive.

Great events may stem from words of no importance.

He who is free of faults, will never die.

The fly has no pity for the thin man.

Friendship does not need pepper to cry.

Little by little grow the bananas.

Lower your head modestly while passing, and you will harvest bananas.

A house with two keys is worth nothing.

One day of hunger is not starvation.

The iron never takes advice from the hammer.

If you tell people to live together, you tell them to quarrel.

Love is like a baby: it needs to be treated tenderly.

To love someone who does not love you, is like shaking a tree to make the dew drops fall.

Lovers do not hide their nakedness.

Man is like palm-wine: when young, sweet but without strength; in old age, strong but harsh.

Do not dispose of the monkey's tail before he is dead.

Congo

The mother-in-law shows you her thighs without shame, you are the
embarrassed one.

Mothers-in-law are hard of hearing.

No matter how long the night, the day is sure to come.

You do not teach the paths of the forest to an old gorilla.

Being well dressed does not prevent one from being poor.

No matter how full the river, it still wants to grow.

Where there is no shame, there is no honor.

A single bracelet does not jingle.

Sleep is the cousin of death.

The snake and the crab don't sleep in the same hole.

The son shoots a leopard; the father is proud.

Let him speak who has seen with his eyes.

A little subtleness is better than a lot of force.

The teeth are smiling, but is the heart?

Without war there can be no peace.

The white man never forgets Europe.

He who doesn't like chattering women must stay a bachelor.

Wood may remain ten years in the water, but it will never become a
crocodile.

The flesh of a young animal tastes flat.

A bald-headed man will not grow hair by getting excited.

Drink beer, think beer.

Don't buy a boat that is under water.

Woe to the high spirited bride whose mother-in-law is still alive.

I own a cow in heaven, but I cannot drink her milk.

He who is free of faults, will never die.

An idiot will cross an ox with an elephant.

The impotent man does not eat spicy foods.

You inherit from the dead, not from the sick.

Those who inherit fortunes are frequently more of a problem than those who made them.

One knife will not cut another knife; one cheat will not cheat another cheat.

To love someone who does not love you, is like shaking a tree to make the dew drops fall.

Love is like a baby: it needs to be treated tenderly.

If you are too modest you will go hungry.

Don't cut off the monkey's tail before it is dead.

The nuts from a palm tree don't fall without dragging a few leaves with it.

If you tell people to live together, you tell them to quarrel.

The portion that a man keeps for himself is usually not the smallest.

Pride goes only as far as one can spit.

No matter how full the river, it still wants to swell more.

Don't buy the salt if you haven't licked it yet.

Who sits down is a cripple.

Sleep is the cousin of death.

War ends nothing.

Prepare yourself for when the water comes up to your knees.

Corsica

A man without a woman is a tree without leaves and branches.

Night is the mother of advice.

Every source flows to the sea.

A Christian forgives, an idiot forgets.

Where there is a cock the chicken will not crow.

Better the head of a village than the tail of a town.

The worst kind of dog is the one who does not want to bite.

The dog barks, the pig eats.

Courage cannot be bought at the inn.

Everyone tries to make the water flow to his mill.

He who is born a mule can never be a horse.

A pound's worth of tears will not settle a penny's worth of debt.

If it's not your time, you won't be born and you won't die.

The barrel can only yield the wine that's in it.

Seamen learn to get to know each other during a storm.

Creole Proverbs
(Southern United States)

Don't call the alligator "big-mouth" till you have crossed the river.

The back dies for the shoulder and the shoulder knows nothing about it.

Bathe other people's children but don't wash behind their ears.

The beggar that begs near another beggar will never be rich.

Never let a boy do a man's work.

Firm breasts don't last long.

If you don't lift the skirt of a bride you don't know what she wears under it.

Be sure that the candle is lit before you throw away the match.

Never mistake chicken shit for an egg.

Don't hang all your clothes on one hook.

Better your own cod than another's duck.

Cowardly men, healthy bones.

It's by following his friends that a crab lost its hiding place.

When the crocodile says that the river crossing is deep you must believe it.

The crow may be caged, but its thoughts are in the cornfield.

You can hate the dog, but do not tell him that his teeth are dirty.

Creole Proverbs

If you make yourself into a doormat, people will wipe their feet on you.

If you see what the ducks eat then you eat no more duck.

The ear is only a door.

Ears have no covers.

Eat with your mouth, pay with your back.

What you lose in the fire, you will find in the ashes.

You may hide the fire, but what about the smoke?

When the big fish fight the shrimps must lie low.

A fisherman never says his fish stink.

Speaking French is no proof of intelligence.

The frog knows more about the rain than the calendar.

A beautiful funeral does not necessarily lead to paradise.

The goat that climbs up the rock also has to go down.

Good looking and good luck don't always walk the same road.

Never hang your hat higher than you can reach.

What you don't know is bigger than you.

The monkey knows which branch to swing on.

The higher the monkey climbs, the more it is exposed to danger.

You never meet your mother-in-law on the day that you are well-dressed.

Never dress in mourning before the dead man is in his coffin.

You can make a mule cross the river but you can't make him drink the water.

Cutting off a mule's ears doesn't make it a horse.

The tail of an ox says, "Time goes, time comes."

The parson christens his own child first.

The pumpkin vine never bears watermelons.

Laugh at the rice and you will weep for the lentil.

The sea breeze blows the pelican where he wants to go.

Sick people have no friends.

Crete

If there were no sighing in the world, the world would stifle.
You must have slept with Jean to know how he snores.
Thanks cost nothing.
The mouth of a woman takes no holiday.

Crete

If you are a fast talker at least think slowly.

Croatia

Where the army goes there is no grass.
With a full belly it is easy to talk about fasting.
Every bird has a hawk above it.
It is better to be a bull for a year than a cow for a hundred years.
Better be in debt than in shame.
A guest will not know what fasting means.
Better a bad harvest than a bad neighbor.
Without money one cannot go anywhere, not even to church.
You may boast to strangers, but tell the truth to your own people.
Polite words open iron gates.
Check before you bite if it is bread or a stone.
The drunkard thinks of only one thing and the barman of something
   else.
The devil can make a pot but he can't make a lid.
The hunchback sees the hump of others—never his own.
The more eggs, the thicker the soup.
God does not love those who have not suffered.
Even a dog will not eat a leg without flesh.
The udder of a neighbor's cow is always bigger.

Cuba

It is better to work in your own land than to count your money abroad.

Lies never pay the toll.

If you take too long to choose, you will end up with the leftovers.

An empty barrel sings in the wind.

No solutions without discussions.

A good horse has many faults; a bad one has hardly any.

Feed your horse as a friend, mount him as an enemy.

Save three pieces of gold and the fourth one will fall into your lap.

Woe to him who sits upon a branch.

Much more than you have sown will grow in your garden.

The starving man will never burn his bread.

To follow everyone is wrong, to follow no one is worse.

Truth's violinist is always beaten with his own bow.

His whole life he carried his wife on his back. As soon as he set her down she said that she was tired.

Where right has no power—there power likes to be.

Cuba

Every head is a world.

Listen to what they say of the others and you will know what they say about you.

Believe only half of what you see and nothing of what you hear.

Life is short but a smile takes barely a second.

What is new is pleasing and what is old is satisfying.

Cyprus

We must convince by reason, not prescribe by tradition.

The children eat the fruit and the father sleeps on the peel.

Czech Republic

All rivers do their best for the sea.

The world at large doesn't lead to hell nor does the monastery lead to heaven.

Laws without punishment are like bells with no clackers.

There is no point in showing the way to an old hare.

It is better not to begin than, having begun, leave unfinished.

Do not buy with your ears but with your eyes.

Even in the tiniest little chapel there are some prayers said once a year.

He who doesn't know the church worships the stove.

He who covets the belongings of someone else loses his own.

He who has not been given brains from above will not buy them at the apothecary.

Consider each day of your life to be the best.

Doubts mean losing half of one's case beforehand.

Nothing seems expensive on credit.

Warm food, warm friendships.

The fool never undertakes little.

When the fool knows when to be silent, he would be sitting among the wise.

Many a friend has been lost by a jest, but none has ever been got by one.

Gentlemen don't want to give much and are ashamed to give little.

The Germans in the stable, the Czech in the kitchen and the French in bed.

If the goat had a longer tail he could wipe the stars clean.

The God who gave us teeth will also give us bread.

When we are at our happiest, then it is best to leave and go home.

He who looks only at heaven may easily break his nose on earth.

Even in hell it is good to have friends.

Hope is a great breakfast but a poor dinner.

Against the beastly human being even the gods are powerless.

Joy and sorrow sleep in the same bed.

Joyfulness is half your health.

There can be no judge without an accused.

Don't jump high in a room with a low ceiling.

The law has a nose of wax.

Better a lie that heals than a truth that wounds.

Don't be a lion in your own house.

When a man is not a lover in his twenties, not strong in his thirties,
    not rich in his forties and not wise in his fifties he will never be so.

Good memories last long, bad ones last longer.

Better to have a handful of might than a sack of justice.

The moon does not care if the dog barks at it.

A good neighbor increases the value of your property.

Our parents taught us to speak and the world taught us to be silent.

Politeness pleases even a cat.

Do not protect yourself by a fence, but rather by your friends.

Morning rain and women's tears dry as fast as each other.

The first sin makes the bed for the second.

The big thieves hang the little ones.

Long tongue—short hands.

If you want to hear the truth about yourself—offend your neighbor.

If you wake up in the morning and feel no pain it is to be feared that
    you died in the night.

Do not choose your wife at a dance, but in the field among the har-
    vesters.

Wisdom is easy to carry but difficult to gather.

If a woman doesn't know what she has to answer then the sea is dry.

A custom wears a shirt of iron.

The wedding lasts for two or three days, but the trouble stays longer.

If you do good to the Devil, out of gratitude he will deliver you to hell.

As long as a language lives, the people will not perish.

I am a gentleman and you are a gentleman; who, then, should look after the pigs?

Wait for a month before you praise a horse, and for a year before you praise a woman.

Wars are caused by women and priests.

Extol the virtue of water, but drink wine.

Choose your woman with a velvet glove, but control her with a fist of iron.

A sweaty foot seldom comes alone.

Do not blow in the bear's ear.

No church without a sermon.

There were once three brothers: a lie, theft and the gallows.

Denmark

Not everybody is as bad as he is dressed.

Death does not look at your teeth.

Advice after injury is like medicine after death.

He who builds according to every man's advice will have a crooked house.

Age is a sorry travelling companion.

The air is no less blue because the blind man doesn't see it.

"If 'almost' did not exist," said the woman, "than I would have shot a hare."

Ambition and revenge are always hungry.

No answer is also an answer.

Art finds its food everywhere.

One who is afraid of asking is ashamed of learning.

Better ask twice than to lose your way once.

Denmark

Bad is never good until worse happens.

If the beard meant everything, the goat would preach.

Beauty without honesty is like a rose without perfume.

A beautiful face is admired even when its owner doesn't say anything.

He that doesn't know his bed is too hard sleeps well.

If a bird knew how poor he was it wouldn't sing so beautifully.

Better to be a free bird than a captive king.

No matter how high a bird can fly, it still has to look for food on the ground.

Better a bite from a friend than a caress from an enemy.

The nobler the blood, the less the pride.

A boor remains a boor even if sleeping on silken pillows.

The branch is seldom better than the stem.

It is hard to pay for bread that has already been eaten.

If your head is made of butter, don't be a baker.

It's possible to light another man's candle without damaging your own.

When the cat and the mouse agree the farmer doesn't stand a chance.

If the cat had wings all sparrows would die.

If you hunt with cats you'll catch mice.

No one can be caught in places he does not visit.

A chain is as strong as its weakest link.

The chair on which a Dane is sitting is beautifully decorated.

They are most cheated who cheat themselves.

He who eats cherries with gentlemen risks getting the pips in his nose.

Who takes the child by the hand, takes the mother by the heart.

Better the child cry, than the mother sigh.

Children are a poor man's wealth.

A small cloud may hide both sun and moon.

He who comforts never has a headache.

To give counsel to a fool is like throwing water on a goose.

Frequent washing makes not the crow whiter.

The crust is part of the loaf.

Better a daughter that has been slept on than a son who has been hanged.

A deaf husband and a blind wife will always make a happy couple.

Death does not blow a trumpet.

"Virtue in the middle," said the Devil when seated between two lawyers.

The dog's kennel is no place to keep a sausage.

A donkey that carries a lot of books is not necessarily learned.

Donkeys only come to the court to carry bags.

A drunkard can be a sheep, a monkey or a lion.

Eggs and oaths are easily broken.

Everything has an end—except a sausage, which has two.

Though your enemy is the size of an ant, look upon him as an elephant.

If envy were a fever, all the world would be ill.

Envy does not enter empty houses.

An old error has more friends than a new truth.

A good example is like a bell that calls many to church.

One eye is a better witness than two ears.

He who doesn't open his eyes when he buys must still open his purse to pay.

He who has no falcon must hunt with an owl.

Faults are thick where love is thin.

The fire doesn't care about the owner of the coat that is burning.

Flattery is sweet food for those who can swallow it.

Food tastes best when you eat it with your own spoon.

Fools are like other folks as long as they are silent.

A fool only wins the first game.

He who wants to catch foxes must hunt with geese.

Denmark

Fresh air impoverishes doctors.

Go often to the house of a friend; for weeds soon choke up the unused path.

To a friend's house the road is never long.

He who gives to me teaches me to give.

God gives all birds their food but does not drop it into their nests.

God feeds the birds that use their wings.

The goose goes so often into the kitchen till at last she sticks to the spit.

When the government has no ears to listen with, then she has no head for governing.

Great men's requests are commands.

Grey hairs are death's blossoms.

Happiness does not give, it only lends.

Happiness and glass break easily.

Take off your hat quickly but slowly take hold of your purse.

If there is room in your heart there is room in your house.

Let no one look into your heart or into your purse.

Heaven dries what it has made wet.

They must stand high who would see their own destiny.

"Almost a hit," said the boy as he threw the stone at his dog and hit his stepmother's leg.

An honest man does not make himself a dog for the sake of a bone.

Hope is an egg, of which one man gets the yolk, another the white, and a third the shell.

Better one poor horse than an empty stall.

The horse that you love draws more than four oxen.

He who wants to jump high must take a long run.

A lazy boy and a warm bed are difficult to part.

The ground is always frozen for the lazy swine.

The fall of a leaf is a whisper to the living.

Denmark

If you want some lies to be believed wrap them up in truths.

Love is one-eyed, hate is blind.

Love is blind and thinks that others don't see either.

Love has produced some heroes but many idiots too.

No man is so tall that he need never stretch and none so small that he need never stoop.

As the man is, so is his language.

The man loves with his head, the woman thinks with her heart.

Many men are like clocks that show one hour and strike another.

A man has two ears and one mouth; he therefore should listen more than he talks.

When the master hurts his foot the servants limp.

The eye of the master does more than his two hands.

Mine and thine are the sources of all quarrels.

Misfortune sits on a rich man's lap but grabs the throat of the pauper.

Old mistakes need more friends than new truths.

If you have no money, be polite.

Money is more eloquent than twelve members of parliament.

One bag of money is stronger than two bags of truth.

The most difficult mountain to cross is the threshold.

It is a bold mouse that makes her nest in a cat's ear.

No one is so rich that he can do without a good neighbor.

If there are no nightingales one must settle for owls.

He must have clean fingers who wants to blow another's nose.

Onions, smoke and women bring tears to your eyes.

The herb patience does not grow in every man's garden.

Young pigs grunt as old pigs grunted before them.

Give to a pig when it grunts and a child when it cries, and you will have a fine pig and a bad child.

It's no disgrace to be poor, but it can be inconvenient.

Presents make women affable, priests indulgent, and the law crooked.

Denmark

Quick and well seldom go together.

A rich child often sits in a poor mother's lap.

Don't sail out farther than you can row back.

There are simple remedies for sausages that are too long.

After pleasant scratching comes unpleasant smarting.

Do not keep secret from your friend what your enemy already knows.

He who lets another sit on his shoulder will soon have him on his
    head.

All who snore are not asleep.

What the sober man has in his heart, the drunkard has on his lips.

Who leaves a son isn't really dead.

The person who loves sorrow will always find something to moan
    about.

Don't stop sowing just because the birds ate a few seeds.

One should speak a little with others and a lot with oneself.

Even a small star shines in the darkness.

The stone that is not in your way does not bother you.

The stone that everybody spits on will eventually be wet.

The strongest among the weak is the one who doesn't forget his weak-
    nesses.

It is better to suffer for truth than to prosper by falsehood.

You have either to suffer a lot or die young.

What is sweet in the mouth is not always good in the stomach.

It is too late to learn to swim when the water is up to your lips.

The teeth often bite the tongue, still the two stay together.

To tell the truth is dangerous; to listen to it is boring.

He who wants to tell the truth will always stand before closed doors.

Truth is always homeless.

Unanimity is the strongest fortress.

Act so in the valley that you need not fear those who stand on the hill.

He that feeds himself from waiting could die of hunger.

Don't throw away dirty water before you have more clean water.

All water flows into the ocean or into the purse of the rich.

He who marries a widow with three children marries four thieves.

To have a woman is bad; to lose her is worse.

Silence is a wonderful jewel for a woman but she seldom wears it.

A silent man's words are not brought into court.

A wound never heals so well that a scar cannot be seen.

The year has a wide mouth and a big belly.

Don't praise the bread that is not out of the oven.

Half a nose is quickly blown.

East Asia

If you owe a dog anything, call him "sir."

Ecuador

Every donkey has its own saddle.

Hands that give also receive.

Egypt

When the angels appear, the devils run away.

He who has a back is not beaten on the belly.

A back does not break from bending.

A beautiful thing is never perfect.

A blow to another's purse is like a blow to a mountain of sand.

A borrowed coat does not keep one warm.

Rather a piece of bread with a happy heart than wealth with grief.

He who chatters with you will chatter about you.

Egypt

More precious than our children are the children of our children.

Old countries don't disappear overnight; they stay for breakfast.

I am talking to you, daughter-in-law, so that you could hear it, neighbor!

The day cuts off the promise of the night.

Better half a donkey than half a camel.

Yesterday's drunkenness will not quench today's thirst.

Pass by your enemy hungry but never naked.

For the benefit of the flowers, we water the thorns, too.

Your friend chooses pebbles for you and your enemy counts your faults.

Friendship doubles joy and halves grief.

The glow soon becomes ashes.

Cover up the good you do—do like the Nile and conceal your sources.

Everything is formed by habit, even praying.

Whoever lets himself be led by the heart will never lose his way.

A small house can lodge a hundred friends.

The idiot who has his eye on your wife is like a blood sucking fly.

Believe the liar up to the door of his house and no further than that.

If you love, love the moon; if you steal, steal a camel.

Love and let the world know, hate in silence.

A man with two ears can be supported by two words.

One who marries for love alone will have bad days but good nights.

The miser destroys what he collected.

Money is sweet balm.

Making money selling manure is better than losing money selling musk.

Be patient with a bad neighbor: he may move or face misfortune.

In his own nest a beetle is a sultan.

An onion shared with a friend tastes like roast lamb.

Pride and dignity would belong to women if only men would leave them alone.

Put a rope around your neck and many will be happy to drag you along.

Follow the saint no further than his doorstep.

The heart of a servant that is not beaten is full of curses.

He who knows not shame does whatever he likes.

Silence is the best answer to the stupid.

Silence is more than just a lack of words.

When a slave mounts a camel he wants to ride on both humps.

Because we focused on the snake, we missed the scorpion.

The tears of the adulteress are ever ready to be shed.

The tyrant is only the slave turned inside out.

When a whore repents she becomes a matchmaker.

Whoever is ashamed to sleep with his wife will never have children.

The woman who does not covet the possessions of her husband is in love with another man.

When a woman is not singing, she is not working much either.

A woman will be twice bound when her chains feel comfortable.

A person with a wound on his head keeps touching it.

If there were no wrongdoing, there would be no forgiveness.

Youth is beauty, even in cattle.

England

Absence makes the heart grow fonder.

Actions speak louder than words.

Advice is least heeded when most needed.

All for one and one for all.

All's well that ends well.

Appearances can be deceiving.

An apple a day keeps the doctor away.

An apple never falls far from the tree.

One rotten apple spoils the whole barrel.

April showers bring May flowers.

What will be, will be.

Beauty is only skin deep.

Early to bed and early to rise makes a man healthy, wealthy, and wise.

Beggars can't be choosers.

Well begun is half done.

The bigger they are the harder they fall.

A bird in the hand is worth two in the bush.

Birds of a feather flock together.

Once bitten, twice shy.

Don't judge a book by its cover.

Beware of a man of one book.

Never fall out with your bread and butter.

Let bygones be bygones.

Don't put the cart before the horse.

There's more than one way to skin a cat.

Don't count your chickens before they hatch.

He that hath no children doth bring them up well.

Every cloud has a silver lining.

Don't cry over spilt milk.

A full cup must be carried steadily.

First deserve, and then desire.

The devil dances in empty pockets.

Do unto others as you would have them do unto you.

A dog is a man's best friend.

You can't teach an old dog new tricks.

The early bird catches the worm.

Don't put all your eggs in one basket.

You have to break a few eggs to make an omelette.

Experience is the best teacher.

Don't fall before you're pushed.

A fool and his money are soon parted.

A fool may ask more questions in an hour than a wise man can answer in seven years.

A friend in need is a friend indeed.

You get what you pay for.

You have to take the good with the bad.

A goose quill is more dangerous than a lion's claw.

The grass is always greener on the other side.

Don't dig your grave with your own knife and fork.

Beware of Greeks bearing gifts.

Many hands make light work.

Haste makes waste.

Make hay while the sun shines.

Two heads are better than one.

The road to hell is paved with good intentions.

He who hesitates is lost.

Hope for the best, but prepare for the worst.

Don't look a gift horse in the mouth.

You can lead a horse to water, but you can't make him drink.

Do not be in a hurry to tie what you cannot untie.

Let him make use of instinct who cannot make use of reason.

It's never too late to mend.

Better late than never.

Laugh, and the world laughs with you; weep, and you weep alone.

He laughs best who laughs last.

The leopard cannot change its spots.

England

Lightning never strikes twice in the same place.

Little strokes fell great oaks.

Live and learn.

Live and let live.

Half a loaf is better than none.

Look before you leap.

Whom we love best, to them we can say least.

A man's first care should be to avoid the reproaches of his own heart, his next to escape the censures of the world.

Misery loves company.

A miss is as good as a mile.

Money is the root of all evil.

In the morning be first up, and in the evening last to go to bed, for they that sleep catch no fish.

Necessity is the mother of invention.

Don't cut off your nose to spite your face.

Great oaks from little acorns grow.

Mind your p's and q's.

A penny saved is a penny earned.

One picture is worth a thousand words.

A place for everything and everything in its place.

There's no place like home.

The best laid plans of mice and men often go awry.

Practice makes perfect.

Practice what you preach.

An ounce of prevention is worth a pound of cure.

The proof of the pudding is in the eating.

In times of prosperity friends will be plenty, in times of adversity not one in twenty.

Never put off to tomorrow what you can do today.

When it rains, it pours.

A rolling stone gathers no moss.

Rome wasn't built in a day.

When in Rome, do as the Romans do.

Better safe than sorry.

Seeing is believing.

The show must go on.

Out of sight, out of mind.

Silence is golden.

Don't lock the stable door after the horse is stolen.

A stitch in time saves nine.

Strike while the iron is hot.

If at first you don't succeed, try, try again.

Spread the table and contention will cease.

There is no accounting for tastes.

If it's not one thing it's another.

Time heals all wounds.

Truth is stranger than fiction.

Waste not, want not.

A watched pot never boils.

If wishes were horses then beggars would ride.

Use soft words and hard arguments.

Many a true word is spoken in jest.

Two wrongs don't make a right.

Eskimo Proverbs

Never pet a bear unless it is a rug.

You never really know your friends from your enemies until the ice
breaks.

Estonia

One cannot make soup out of beauty.

The new boat will find the old stones.

If the bread in the oven is a failure you lose a week; if the harvest is a failure you lose a year; if marriage is a failure then you lose a life.

Coal that does not burn gives little heat.

The cork is always bigger than the mouth of the bottle.

When death comes, the rich man has no money and the poor man no debt.

A debt is always new.

A good deed bears interest.

A good deed is written on snow.

The devil does not always wear boots—he sometimes comes barefoot.

Barking dogs don't catch hares.

Earth is dearer than gold.

Where there is no fear, there is no pity.

In a garment made of silk there are no fleas.

Better a goat that can give milk than a cow that cannot.

When God gives a child, he also gives the clothing.

Give good and get good.

Who never built a house thinks that the walls grow out of the ground.

Justice knows no friendship.

Little kettles soon boil over.

There is no room for two kings in one castle.

The law is three days older than the earth.

Old love does not rust.

They are not all men who wear trousers.

Manure is the farmer's gold.

Happy the marriage where the husband is the head and the wife the heart.

The mistakes of others are good teachers.

A girl without a needle is like a cat without a claw.

The old man looks death in the eye, the young man keeps him behind his back.

The pipe is nearer than the wife.

A much-used plow shines; stagnant waters stink.

Silence is sometimes the answer.

The stomach never gets full with licking.

The summer comes and kisses the child, the winter comes and kills it.

Who does not thank for a little will not thank for a lot.

Wasting time is stealing from oneself.

The town is new every day.

It is better to be without a wife for a minute than without tobacco for an hour.

Do not choose your wife on your way to the church.

If you go only once round the room, you are wiser than he who sits still.

The wood is the poor man's coat.

The work will teach you how to do it.

Ethiopia

The heart of a fool is in his mouth and the mouth of the wise man is in his heart.

Do not blame God for having created the tiger, but thank Him for not giving it wings.

Only the man who is not hungry says the coconut has a hard shell.

The little stars will always shine while the great sun is often eclipsed.

Mock the palm tree only when the date harvest is over.

A good conversation is better than a good bed.

If you are planning to travel where corn grows, you should take a sickle with you.

Ethiopia

Men fear danger, women only the sight of it.

You travel on until you return home; you live on until you return to earth.

Regret, like a tail, comes at the end.

Advise and counsel him; if he does not listen, let adversity teach him.

He who lives with an ass, sounds like an ass.

He who wants to barter, usually knows what is best for him.

A blade won't cut another blade; a cheat won't cheat another cheat.

What has been blown away, cannot be found again.

One is born, one dies; the land grows.

A partner in the business will not put an obstacle to it.

Cactus is bitter only to him who tastes it.

A cat may go to a monastery, but will always remain a cat.

The cattle is as good as the pasture in which it grazes.

Saying that it's for her child, she gets herself a loaf of bread.

Even if Christ's death could have been prevented, Judas would still be a traitor.

Clothes put on while running come off while running.

The cow knows the cowherd but not the owner.

A cow gave birth to a fire; she wanted to lick it, but it burned; she wanted to leave it, but she could not because it was her own child.

I have a cow in the sky, but cannot drink her milk.

Even over cold pudding, the coward says: "It will burn my mouth."

There is no cure for him who hides an illness.

A silly daughter teaches her mother how to bear children.

No one knows what the dawn will bring.

What one desires is always better than what one has.

Dine with a stranger but save your love for your family.

The dog I bought, bit me; the fire I kindled burned me.

Unless you call out, who will open the door?

Eat when the meal is ready, speak when the time is ripe.

Ethiopia

Better an egg this year than a chicken next year.

Evil enters like a needle and spreads like an oak tree.

An eye and a friend are quickly hurt.

He who digs too deep for a fish, may come out with a snake.

The fool is thirsty in the midst of water.

A fool will pair an ox with an elephant.

A fool looks for dung where the cow never grazed.

The fool speaks, the wise man listens.

A fool and water will go the way they are directed.

When a fool is cursed, he thinks he is being praised.

Restless feet may walk into a snake pit.

A close friend can become a close enemy.

A powerful friend becomes a powerful enemy.

If a friend hurts you, run to your wife.

To one who knows no better, a small garden is a forest.

Anticipate the good so that you may enjoy it.

Great men have big hearts.

If the heart is sad, tears will flow.

Horns are not too heavy for the cow.

If one is not in a hurry, even an egg will start walking.

When the hyena is gone, the dog begins to bark.

"O, sheep if I do not eat you, you will eat me," said the hyena.

What is inflated too much, will burst into fragments.

He who learns, teaches.

You may well have two legs but you still can't climb two trees at the same time.

Try not to get hold of a leopard's tail, but if you do—don't let go.

Living is worthless for one without a home.

When one is in love, a cliff becomes a meadow.

With man comes the quarrel.

Ethiopia

A melancholic look is visible but not a melancholic heart.

An overly modest man goes hungry.

It is easy to become a monk in one's old age.

Move your neck according to the music.

The point of the needle must pass first.

When the Nile knows a secret the desert will soon know it too.

Don't demand that what you write in the Nile will be read in the desert.

If you offend, ask for pardon; if offended, forgive.

What is taken for oneself is usually not a small piece.

Singing "Alleluia" everywhere does not prove piety.

The witness of a rat is another rat.

If relatives help each other, what harm can be done to them?

There is no one who became rich because he broke a holiday, and no one who became fat because he broke a fast.

One who runs alone cannot be outrun by another.

When he looked under the saddle he lost his horse.

One scoops with a scoop.

Sharing a secret with a rogue is like carrying grain in a bag with a hole.

Where there is no shame, there is no honor.

One who recovers from sickness, forgets about God.

Sitting is being crippled.

Snake at your feet—a stick at your hand!

When spiders' webs unite, they can tie up a lion.

A single stick may smoke, but it will not burn.

You cannot build a house for last year's summer.

A coward sweats in water.

Termites live underground.

A loose tooth will not rest until it's pulled out.

If you see that a town worships a calf, then cut the grass and feed it.

Who cannot yet walk, cannot climb a ladder.

Because he killed his wife he took shelter with his in-laws.

No better witnesses than your own eyes.

Woman without man is like a field without seed.

A home without a woman is like a barn without cattle.

As the wound inflames the finger, so the thought inflames the mind.

Fiji Islands

The white flower has bloomed—it is time to sleep outside.

Idleness is to be dead in the limbs but alive within.

Listen to the wisdom of the toothless ones.

Don't do today what you probably can leave undone tomorrow as well.

Finland

Be always a little afraid so that you never will be much afraid.

Age does not give you good sense, it only makes you go slowly.

A good bell is heard from far, a bad one still further.

He needs a long candle who awaits the death of another.

The echo knows all languages.

God did not create haste.

In heaven you won't hear the mosquitoes.

With a walking-stick you reach many lands; you reach many more with words.

The lazy sweat when they eat and complain of the cold when they work.

One cannot ski so softly that the tracks cannot be seen.

The winter does not leave without a backward glance.

The world is a good teacher, but it charges a huge fee.

If the bathroom and a brandy cannot help a man, then death is imminent.

All that glitters is not gold, nor all that sparkles silver.

Better ice that melts than fire that extinguishes.

The old cow forgets that she was once a calf.

If you borrow some chaff from the rich man you have to repay him with wheat.

Love is a garden full of flowers and marriage is a field of stinging nettles.

Praise your horse tomorrow, your son when he has a beard, your daughter when she is married and yourself never.

You are not a man until you have plowed a field.

To an optimist every weed is a flower; to a pessimist every flower is a weed.

The back has to pay for what the ears didn't hear.

As we grow older our bad qualities make us younger.

Rain does not stay in the sky.

Never judge a reindeer from close by when you got it from a rich man because you may find that some of the antlers are missing.

Even a small star shines in the dark.

A married man has many sorrows—an unmarried man has one more.

Do it today! Tomorrow it might be forbidden.

Happiness does not come from happiness itself, but from the journey towards achieving it.

He who cannot light a fire knows nothing about love.

A widow, like a widower, is a house without a roof.

France
(Alsace, Auvergne, Béarn, Burgundy, Champagne, French-Comté, French Flanders, Normandy, Savoye)

Loving with the eyes only, has blinded a lot of fools.

He who has two women loses his soul; he who has two houses loses
his mind.

Only a fool gets drunk from his own bottle.

There is many a slip twixt cup and lip.

A good bottle of wine does not need a cork.

Whoever rubs himself with garlic will not smell of cloves.

Better a small fire that warms you than a big one that burns you.

Fields have eyes and woods have ears.

Choosy pigs never get fat.

What you keep rots; what you give flourishes.

Even the best mule still saves a kick for his master.

There are no beautiful prisons or ugly loved ones.

The world is a barrel, for all to draw from.

Not until the tree is felled can you see how tall it was.

Better bread in the basket than a feather in your cap.

Every doctor thinks his pills are the best.

Half an egg is better than an empty eggcup.

To be a fool at the right time is an art.

Where love sets the table food tastes at its best.

A mother can more easily feed seven children than seven children can
feed one mother.

When the miller is also the mayor, there are two thieves in one pair
of trousers.

Every mother-in-law is a piece of the devil's pants.

Don't slaughter more pigs than you can salt.

A beautiful maxim in the memory is like a piece of gold in the purse.

He who spits in the air pollutes himself.

He who sows the seed of discord works in the devil's barn.

What you lose in the fire, you will find amongst the ashes.

Sickness comes in like a horse and leaves like a snail.

A little absence does a lot of good.

Those who are absent are always wrong.

Absent people do not inherit.

Good advice is often annoying—bad advice never is.

They who come from afar have leave to lie.

Africa is a cold land where the sun is warm.

Every age wants its playthings.

Nothing ages more than a good deed.

"Almost" and "about" prevent lying.

Better alone than in bad company.

Anger is a bad adviser.

An old ape never made a pretty grimace.

One good argument is worth more than ten better ones.

A good armchair makes the backside soft and the heart hard.

Every art requires the whole person.

Seekers of art; finders of the beggar's bag.

He that does not ask will never get a bargain.

The attack tames the beast.

Authority has no partner.

The bad man thinks that everybody looks like him.

The ball always looks for the best player.

A beggar on his feet is worth more than an emperor in his grave.

You do not always have to believe what you see.

Better beloved than admired.

Flying birds have no master.

A black hen lays a white egg.

It is only the first bottle that is expensive.

There is no old bread that cannot find its cheese.

Bread and wine start a banquet.

Small brooks make big rivers.

The burden tames the beast.

Everyone thinks his own burden heavy.

Even the smallest little bush casts some shadow.

There are more foolish buyers than foolish sellers.

There are more buyers than connoisseurs.

You can cage a bird but you can't make it sing.

A fine cage won't feed the bird.

When the cage is ready the bird is flown.

He who carries nothing loses nothing.

The cart ruins the road, the woman the man, the water the wine.

A good cat deserves a good rat.

Old cats love young mice.

You pull chestnuts from the fire with a cat's paws.

The ugliest tomcat always has the most beautiful mate.

Even the tiniest little chapel has its saint.

Bad charcoal only makes smoke.

The chicken sings what the cock teaches him.

You don't have to kill the chicken to get eggs.

Who is born a chicken loves scratching.

The chicken that crows the loudest does not always give the biggest
  eggs.

Tasty is the chicken that is fed by someone else.

Children have more need of models than critics.

He who is near the Church is often far from God.

It is easier to climb down than up.

No clock is more regular than the belly.

A good cock is always slim.

Let him who is cold blow the fire.

Common sense is not so common.

In your own company no one is boss.

A bad compromise is better than a good lawsuit.

In a conclave many go in as a pope but come back out as the cardinal they were when they went in.

A clear conscience is a good pillow.

To contradict means sometimes to knock at the door to see if anyone is at home.

What is learned in the cradle lasts to the grave.

If you want to keep your credit you must use it as little as possible.

You must give credit to coincidence.

Sometimes the cry of the animal is worse than the animal itself.

I cried when I was born and each day now I realize why.

You dance better with a full belly than with a new dress.

When the daughter dies, the son-in-law is dead as well.

It is a long day, a day without bread.

A day is lost if one has not laughed.

We are all a long time dead.

There is a remedy for everything except death.

Deceit always returns to its master.

If you don't want to be deceived, then marry on February 30th.

It is a double pleasure to deceive the deceiver.

After us the deluge.

You often meet your destiny on the road you take to avoid it.

The devil sweetens another man's wife with a spoonful of honey.

The servant of the devil does more than is asked for.

You can sell the devil if he is well cooked.

When he was fifteen the devil was a good looking boy.

You only die once.

There is no dying by proxy.

One dish does not feed two gluttons.

He who dispraises a thing wants to buy it.

The doctor is often more to be feared than the disease.

Too many doctors too few medicines.

A living dog is better than a dead lion.

A dog with a docked tail is not afraid that its backside can be seen.

Dogs that always fight always have bleeding ears.

It's difficult to chain up an old dog.

No good dog barks without reason.

The communal donkey gets the heaviest burden.

Don't harness the donkey and the horse together.

When in doubt, Gallop! (Proverb of the French Foreign Legion)

You hear little from the drummer that is paid in advance.

There are more old drunkards than old doctors.

Nothing dries so fast as tears.

The ear is the road to the heart.

All the treasures of the earth can't bring back one lost moment.

The long awaited Easter feast is over in one day.

Eat with pleasure; drink with measure.

Economy is the wealth of the poor and the wisdom of the rich.

What was hard to endure is sweet to recall.

The enemy never sleeps.

Build a golden bridge for the fleeing enemy.

There is no little enemy.

Those who envy die, but envy stays alive.

He who has everything is content with nothing.

He who seeks evil will find it.

You always fall down in the direction of where you bend over.

A father is a banker provided by nature.

Some fathers love another man's daughter most.

Mean fathers, wasteful sons.

Fear and restlessness kill more than do illnesses.

What comes from the fife goes back to the drum.

A good figure is better than a reference letter.

If the fire does not burn you the smoke will blacken you.

Fish must swim three times: once in the water, a second time in the sauce, and a third time in wine in the stomach.

You don't find good flesh next to the bone.

You never get clean flour from a coal sack.

Don't try to fly before you have wings.

You cannot clear fog with a fan.

The shortest follies are the best.

He who fondles you more than usual has either deceived you or wants to.

The fool's mother is always pregnant.

Fools never get grey hair.

Fools are more useful to the wise than wise are to fools.

To want to forget something is to remember it.

Every fox carries his tail his own way.

They are not free who drag their chains behind them.

The friends of our friends are our friends.

I love my friends, but myself better.

Better to have a friend on the road than gold and silver in your purse.

It is more disgraceful to suspect our friends than to be deceived by them.

Friendship is love without wings.

Do not let grass grow on the path of friendship.

The friendship of a great man is like the shadow of a bush—soon gone.

There is no lock on the purse of a gambler.

He who leaves the game, loses.

No one is so generous as he who has nothing to give.

If you give a gift to a rich man, the devil sniggers.

Small gifts maintain friendship, big ones maintain love.

A girl without a friend is like the spring without roses.

When glory comes, memory departs.

Glow worms are not lanterns.

God often visits us, but most of the time we are not at home.

Why hide from God what the saints already know?

Gossipers are the devil's trumpeters.

Grass will not grow on a volcano.

Gratitude is the heart's memory.

The graveyards are full of young lawyers, lost inheritance and young doctors.

Our hairs are numbered.

A man is no happier than he thinks himself.

For some of us happiness comes while we sleep.

You cannot make a hawk of a buzzard.

The head and feet keep warm; the rest will take no harm.

If you do not have a head, you must have legs.

He who has no health has nothing.

The same heat that melts wax, bakes clay.

To heaven for the music but to hell for a good conversation.

The best herbs are in the smallest bags.

You sell more herrings on the market than sole.

Honey in the mouth, bile in the heart.

It is easy to go on foot if you are holding your horse by the rein.

Where the hostess is beautiful the wine is tasty.

He that wants to keep his house clean must not let priest or pigeon into it.

It is a sorry house in which the cock is silent and the hen crows.

If you want to love your household as much as your bread then you will have to knead your wife like dough.

Everybody has a hump when he stoops.

All are not hunters who blow the horn.

With the help of an "if" you might put Paris into a bottle.

To believe a thing impossible is to make it so.

It is always the impossible that happens.

One finds little ingratitude so long as one is in a position to grant favors.

For most people love of justice is no more than the fear to suffer injustice.

Even the king does not dine twice.

When the kitchenmaids are together the roast burns.

You always knock yourself on the tenderest places.

To wish to know is to wish to doubt.

The law says what the king pleases.

A good lawyer is a bad neighbor.

A lawyer needs three bags: one full of papers, one full of money, and one full of patience.

Unless Hell is full, no lawyer will ever be saved.

Lazy people are always eager to be doing something.

He who wants to conquer lechery must flee from it.

He who lends to a friend loses twice.

If you lend something you may lose it, but not if you give it.

You only lend to rich people.

You easily lend bread to the one who has flour.

He who can lick can bite.

Life is an onion that you peel crying.

Life is half spent before one knows what life is.

The first half of life is spent in longing for the second, the second half in regretting the first.

To enjoy life is worth so much more than it costs.

Life is a dung pie from which you take a bite every day. The art is to eat it with taste.

When you have not what you like, you must like what you have.

Dead lions do not roar.

Love is often the fruit of marriage.

Love makes the time pass. Time makes love pass.

Love never dies of starvation, but often of indigestion.

Try to reason about love, and you will lose your reason.

Love does wonders, but money makes marriages.

In love, there is always one who kisses and one who offers the cheek.

He who marries for love has good nights and bad days.

Love teaches even asses to dance.

Being loved is the best way of being useful.

When we cannot get what we love, we must love what is within our reach.

What you love is always beautiful.

The love that you die from is too big.

The torch of love is lit in the kitchen.

Love me, love my dog.

Real love is when you don't have to tell each other.

The first love letters are written with the eyes.

There is a pinch of the madman in every great man.

Man is the only mammal that can be skinned more than once.

One man alone is prey to the wolf.

When a man stops thinking he stops feeling.

If you want to understand men, study women.

Men make laws; women make morals.

Marriage teaches you to live alone.

Marriages sealed with rings end with drawn knives.

He who marries a widow also marries her debts.

He who marries on a rainy day will be happy for the rest of his life.

The eye of the master fattens the steed.

So many mates; so many enemies.

A good meal ought to begin with hunger.

Everyone blames his memory, but never his judgement.

Bad merchandise is never cheap.

Only he who does nothing makes a mistake.

Mistrust is the mother of certainty.

Money makes even dogs dance.

No money, no Swiss.

A man without money is like a wolf without teeth.

Ready money works great cures.

Money knows no jurisdiction.

Nothing speaks more eloquently than money.

Loaning money causes loss of memory.

The monk responds to the abbot's chants.

The cassock does not make the monk.

One must bless the new moon when it is visible in the sky.

There once was a good mother-in-law but the wolf gobbled her up.

Mother-in-law and daughter-in-law can be cooked together but they
    will never be tender.

He who has much, wants more.

Too much is never good; too little is never enough.

If there isn't too much, there is too little.

Everything comes to the man who does not need it.

The city that negotiates is half conquered.

Bad news has wings.

You know a person by his nickname.

Wait until it is night before saying that it has been a fine day.

A big nose never spoiled a handsome face.

The one with a running nose always wants to blow someone else's.

What orators lack in depth, they make up for in length.

He who sells the ox sets its price.

Paris is owned by the early risers.

A party of one alone is not a party. A party of two is that of God; of three of the king; of four is of the devil.

There is no science without patience.

Patience is the virtue of the donkeys.

Patience is bitter but its fruits are sweet.

The patient one always wins.

When you can't find peace within yourself, it's useless to seek it elsewhere.

A person is unlucky who falls on his back and breaks his nose.

You do not fatten pigs with pure water.

You cannot have the bacon and the pig at the same time.

There is no pillow so soft as a clear conscience.

The art of pleasing is the art of deceiving.

One pleasure, a thousand pains.

No one became poor by giving alms.

I know by my own pot how the others boil.

Where power reigns there is no room for reason.

Pray, pray very much; but beware of telling God what you want.

Who can't pretend cannot govern.

Prices are forgotten, quality remains.

Pride can only lose.

Every priest recommends his relics.

Small profits are good if they come often.

We make big promises to avoid little presents.

He who is too proud to ask is too good to receive.

That which proves too much, proves nothing.

If it rains on the pastor it drops on the vicar.

The rich man has more relations than he knows about.

When you are rich you suffer in a more comfortable way.

Rich people eat gold and shit lead.

Rich people never know who their friends are.

You have to be rich to be able to live like a poor man.

He is rich who owes nothing.

Ridicule kills.

No river swells without getting muddy.

If you live in Rome, don't quarrel with the Pope.

It is the belief in roses that makes them flourish.

It is not enough to run; you must start on time.

You recognize the saint by his miracle.

A saint that cannot cure anyone has few disciples.

Young saints, old devils.

You cannot satisfy the whole world and your father.

However treacherous the sea may be, women are still more so.

If the seawater were hotter we could catch boiled fish.

The secret of two people is God's secret, the secret of three people is everybody's secret.

Nothing is such a heavy burden as a secret is.

Self-love is the worst of all flattery.

You are never better served than by yourself.

When sheep get angry they are worse than wolves.

Silence is the soul of all things.

When all other sins are old, greed still stays young.

Old sins, new shame.

A sin that is hidden is half forgiven.

Small people always cast big shadows.

You cannot be very smart if you have never done anything foolish.

A smile shortens the distance.

Snakes prefer to hide under flowers.

A healthy soul cannot live in a dry body.

The soup makes the soldier.

The best soup is made of old meat.

He who sows everywhere harvests nowhere.

Two sparrows on the same ear of corn are not long friends.

Starlings are skinny because they fly in a group.

He who has a stepmother has the devil at his hearth.

A stingy man is always poor.

Even the strongest person will find his master.

A man who is afraid of suffering suffers from fear itself.

Put something sweet in his mouth and send good news to the heart.

He who teaches, learns.

Set a thief to catch a thief.

There are more thieves than gallows.

Think much, say little, write less.

He who is master of his thirst is master of his health.

Not every thunderclap is followed by lightning.

Everything in time comes to him who knows how to wait.

You have to give time some time.

Why kill time when one can employ it.

The tiredness of the body is the health of the soul.

The tongue goes to where the tooth aches.

What is true by lamplight is not always true by sunlight.

Trust is the mother of exasperation.

Only the truth hurts.

Two times good—one time stupid.

Vice hides under a cloak of virtue.

The villain that becomes rich knows neither friends nor family.

Nothing looks more like an honest man than a villain.

People count up the faults of those who are keeping them waiting.

He who is waiting for someone else's bowl often dines late.

We never know the worth of water till the well is dry.

Muddied water does not reflect.

He who has a head of wax must not go near the fire.

The longer the way, the more tired the man.

The weather, fleecy clouds, and a made up woman don't last long.

Small wells are better to quench your thirst.

Whores and thieves are always very pious.

Widows comfort themselves when they remarry, widowers take revenge.

Better the second husband of a widow than the first.

He who believes his wife too much will regret it in the end.

If you lose your wife and fifteen pennies—oh ! what a pity about the money.

To be willing is to be able.

Big winds, small showers.

Where wine appears the doctor disappears.

If the wine bothers you while you work, stop working.

Beautiful grapes often make poor wine.

They forgive the wine but they hang the bottle.

A good burgundy does a lot for women, especially when men drink it.

It is a hard winter when one wolf eats another.

Every wise man is afraid of a fool.

For a wise man a fool is a good advisor.

So long as the wolf is captured the dog will bite his leg.

A woman like a horse needs spurs.

A woman would rather swallow her teeth than her tongue.

A woman who dances too much gets ill from little work.

There are no women or horses without shortcomings.

It is more difficult for beautiful women to stay chaste.

A silent woman is a gift from God.

When the woman wants something God quakes.

As changeable is the moon so is the opinion of the woman.

With money you can comfort any woman.

Tell a woman once she is beautiful and the devil will repeat it ten times.

The world is the book of women.

Women believe the strangest of lies as long as they are wrapped up in praise.

All good women are in the graveyard.

The beauty of a woman does not make a man richer.

Where the woman goes the devil follows.

A woman's heart dries quicker than her tears.

Every woman needs two men—one to be married to and the other to compare.

The word of a woman is as a little feather on the water.

Never trust a woman who mentions her virtue.

A woman and a melon are hard to choose.

Many enter the wood without an axe.

Words are feminine, deeds masculine.

A bad workman never finds a good tool.

We know the worth of a thing when we have lost it.

When everybody is wrong then everybody is right.

If youth knew! If age could!

Better ten people hurt than one dead.

Between saying and doing many a pair of shoes is worn out.

Who is known as an early riser may sleep longer.

Nothing is more expensive than the first beer.

It is good to dance on another man's floor.

In a good family the husband is deaf and the wife blind.

Men eat fish—thanks to the sauce.

Men will only throw stones at trees that are laden with fruit.

It's a big wind that blows on small doors.

A good fox does not eat his neighbor's chickens.

He who is hopeless is capable of everything.

You are either hammer or anvil.
The urine of one dog will not pollute the ocean.
You cannot make a beautiful plumage out of a pig's tail.
I have so much to do that I am going to bed.

French Guyana

If you see your neighbor's beard burning then wet your own.
Most insects are to be found near the blossoms.
He who did evil expects evil.

Gabon

The feathers of a dead eagle would cover you all over.
He who has an egg in his pocket does not dance.
You cannot climb a tree with one hand.
You don't refuse your mother's breast for fear of scabies.
What comes out of the mouth has lost its master.
A mousetrap cannot kill an elephant.
Bad friends prevent you from having good friends.
It is better to work and be free than to be fed in captivity.

Gaelic Proverbs

Don't give cherries to pigs or advice to fools.
Avoid the evil, and it will avoid thee.
Nothing is easy to the unwilling.
The fated thing will happen.
Even God cannot make two mountains without a valley in between.
Self-assurance is two-thirds of success.

Keep a thing seven years and you'll find a use for it.

A wild goose never laid a tame egg.

Gambia

Before healing others, heal yourself.

Not to know is bad, not to want to know is worse.

Even the best words bring no food.

He who cannot do anything does nothing.

Georgia

The right balance depends on the weigher.

Catch the bird before you build a cage.

Give a blind man eyes and he will ask for eyebrows.

One blind man followed the other and they both fell into the ditch.

Beware of the front of a bull, the back of a horse and both sides of a blind man.

Blood vessels are not cleaned with blood.

Mewing cats catch no mice.

A church without a leader is prey for the devil.

A communal field is ruined by the bears.

Better your own copper than another man's gold.

In a place without dogs they teach the cats to bark.

You can better drink from a small well with soft water than from the salty sea.

When three people say you are drunk, go to sleep.

Only the dumb can silence the chatterer.

"I have a lot to say," said the fish, "but my mouth is full of water."

The buzzing of the flies does not turn them into bees.

If you forgive the fox for stealing your chickens, he will take your sheep.

God is the comfort of the poor.

A golden plate is worth nothing to me when my blood is spilled on it.

He who is in a hurry always arrives late.

The lucky fellow loses his wife, the unlucky fellow loses his horse.

Whoever I love is the most beautiful.

If the moon helps me I will scoff at the stars.

Men prefer the wife of another but love their own sons more.

God laughs at man's proposal.

If you give a man nuts then give him something to crack them with.

Thousands of men were murdered because of their beautiful wives.

A mother will understand what her dumb son says.

When you put your nose into the water your cheeks get wet as well.

One dirty pig pollutes others.

The rich eat when they want, the poor when they can.

The smile of a rose uplifts the nightingale.

Do not blame the sun for the darkness of the night.

The tall one wouldn't bend; the short one wouldn't stretch and the kiss was lost.

Whatever the wind brings he takes away with him.

If women were really good, God would be married.

You can conquer the whole world with words, but not with drawn swords.

Germany

Never give advice unless asked.

Never listen to these three advisers: wine, the night, and love.

A lean agreement is better than a fat lawsuit.

Ambition and fleas jump high.

In America an hour is forty minutes.

Street angel, house devil.

To act in anger is like tying up a ship in a storm.

The anvil fears no blow.

If you fail to practice your art, it will soon disappear.

The ass bedecked with gold still eats thistles.

The bachelor is a peacock, the engaged man a lion, and the married man a jackass.

If bad luck is asleep you must not awaken it.

In bad luck, hold out; in good luck, hold in.

The heaviest baggage for a traveller is an empty purse.

Who stands bail for someone is being teased by the devil.

The bait tastes first the fish.

Good bargains empty your pockets.

Never tickle the nose of a sleeping bear.

Beard and cloak do not make one a philosopher.

One beats the bush, another catches the bird.

Beauty is a good letter of introduction.

Beauty is the eye's food but the soul's sorrow.

No bed is big enough to hold three.

Who makes his bed on the morrow; goes all day without sorrow.

He who sleeps in a silver bed has golden dreams.

Begged bread has a hard crust.

Who begins too much accomplishes little.

Shake hands at the beginning and at the end.

To believe everything is too much, to believe nothing is not enough.

The belly is a bad adviser.

The belly has no conscience.

So long as the belly is silent all whores are virgins.

Better is better.

As the old birds sing, so the young ones twitter.

It is hard to catch birds with an empty hand.

Birds of prey do not sing.

He who has not tasted bitter things, knows not what sweet is.

A man trying to sell a blind horse always praises its feet.

Both noble and common blood are the same color.

Who bathes his hands in blood will have to wash them with tears.

A good book praises itself.

Boredom is the father of all sins.

He who is quick to borrow, is slow to pay.

Brandy is as lead in the morning, silver at noon, and gold at night.

Where God gives hard bread He also gives sharp teeth.

He who cries today that he has no bread will cry again tomorrow because he isn't hungry.

When I eat your bread, I sing your song.

It's a bad bridge that is narrower than the stream.

He who has burned his mouth blows his soup.

Buying is cheaper than asking.

The narrower the cage, the sweeter the liberty.

A pack of cards is the devil's prayer book.

What is sport to the cat is death to the mouse.

To catch rats the cats take off their gloves.

The cat's play is the mouse's death.

A bad cause requires many words.

Who mocks his chains will not be free.

To change and to improve are two different things.

People show their character by what they laugh at.

Charity looks at the need and not at the cause.

Cheerful company shortens the journey.

Cheese and bread make the cheeks red.

He who likes cherries soon learns to climb.

The chickens don't mourn when the poulterer dies.

You can do anything with children if you only play with them.

Old churches have dark windows.

In the visible church the true Christians are invisible.

To claim is not to prove.

High climbers and deep swimmers never grow old.

Compliments cost nothing, yet many pay dearly for them.

Better a good conscience without wisdom than wisdom without a good conscience.

For a lot of people their conscience lives in the middle of the street.

Everybody knows good counsel except he who has need of it.

Even ill-natured cows give milk.

The cow does not lick a strange calf.

Crime is cunning; it puts an angel in front of every devil.

In the land of the cripple everyone thinks he walks straight.

To criticize is easy, to do is difficult.

If you don't want to be deceived, you must have as many eyes as hairs on the head.

Better a friendly denial than unwilling compliance.

The devil catches most souls in a golden net.

Even the devil is beautiful when he is young.

Even the devil's grandmother was a nice girl when she was young.

In times of emergency the devil eats flies.

When the devil reigns today God will be master tomorrow.

"Age before beauty," said the devil as he threw his grandmother off the stairs.

Let the devil get into the church, and he will mount the altar.

No diadem can cure a headache.

Dying is not child's play.

A lot will stick to dirty hands.

A young doctor means a new graveyard.

Doctors are the signposts to heaven.

I would rather have a dog as a friend than an enemy.

The silent dog is the first to bite.

The skinnier the dog, the more fleas he has.

Timid dogs bark most.

The king of the dreamers lies in the hospital.

Drink makes you forget your sorrow; but only, alas, until tomorrow.

He who drinks no more still likes to see the beer pulled.

Young drinkers, old beggars.

He who drinks a little too much drinks much too much.

More people drown in glasses than in rivers.

Drunk sweetly, paid sourly.

Dwarfs see giants everywhere.

Eagles do not breed doves.

Eat less, live longer.

There's no eel so small but it hopes to become a whale.

They quarrel about an egg and let the hen fly.

When there is no enemy it is safe to fight.

He who has no enemies has no friends either.

One enemy is too much, and a hundred friends are not enough.

Enough is better than too much.

Envy eats nothing but its own heart.

Before God and the bus driver we are all equal.

If you want equality, then go to the graveyard.

One does evil enough when one does nothing good.

He who does not punish evil invites it.

Experience is the teacher of jesters and the intelligence of the wise.

Eyes trust themselves, ears trust others.

He who does not open his eyes must open his purse.

You can eat and drink with your family but not count and measure.

What the farmer does not know he doesn't eat.

He who blows on the fire will get sparks in his eyes.

Fire in the heart sends smoke to the head.

He who wants a fire must be able to bear smoke.

Eat your fish while it is still fresh and marry the girl while she is still young.

A flatterer has water in one hand and fire in the other.

Fair flowers do not remain long by the wayside.

Nothing looks more like a sensible man as a fool who holds his tongue.

The biggest fools are those who are paid to be wise.

Fortune and misfortune are two buckets in the same well.

Set a fox to catch a fox.

When the fox preaches, look to the geese.

The best friends are in one's purse.

To get to know a friend, you must share an inheritance with him.

He who is the judge between two friends loses one of them.

Friendship is love with intelligence.

True friendship does not freeze in the winter.

Friendship with the French is like their wine; exquisite but short lived.

When friendship goes with love it must play the second fiddle.

Friendship is a plant we must often water.

Though you seat the frog on a golden stool, he'll soon jump off it into the pool.

The better the fruit, the more wasps to eat it.

All the fruit is not found in just one field.

Rich gamblers and old trumpeters are rare.

When the giver comes, the gate opens by itself.

Where God builds a church, the devil builds a chapel.

God forgives sinners, otherwise His heaven would be empty.

When God says "today," the devil says "tomorrow."

God gives us nuts but he does not crack them for us.

God gave us hands but He doesn't build bridges with them.

God will help a seaman in a storm but the pilot must still remain at the wheel.

The gold of the new world has ruined the old one.

He who would make a golden door must add a nail to it daily.

Good will gives wings to the feet.

Even a fool can govern if nothing happens.

Grain and graciousness grow on good ground.

What grows makes no noise.

Habit is the intelligence of the crowd.

How easily a hair gets into the butter.

You cannot hang a man twice.

You cannot hang a man for what he thinks.

Better a good hanging than a bad marriage.

If you don't want to be hung yourself, blame the dog for stealing the sausage.

Happiness opens the arms and closes the eyes.

Where you are not—there is happiness.

No one is happier than he who believes in his happiness.

A happy man does not hear the clock strike.

Were I a hatter, men would come into the world without heads.

Let your head be more than a funnel to your stomach.

Fire in the heart sends smoke into the head.

A hedge between keeps friendship green.

Take one step to hell and you are already half way there.

Fat hens lay few eggs.

One time "here you are" is better than ten times "heaven help you."

Honesty makes you rich, but she works slowly.

Honey is never far away from the sting.

Hobby horses are more expensive than Arabian stallions.

Only when the horses have escaped do men repair the stable.

The fingers of the housewife do more than a yoke of oxen.

The Hungarian is far too lazy to be bored.

Hunger is the best cook, but he has nothing to eat.

Hussars pray for war and doctors for fever.

Never to forsake your ideals is better than dreaming of great things.

He who inherits a penny is expected to spend a dollar.

The nearer the inn, the longer the road.

Intelligence is the best capital.

Jealousy is a pain that seeks what caused it.

Where there is no jealousy there is no love.

The bridge between joy and sorrow is not long.

He who wants to do a good jump must sometimes take a step back.

He that wants to eat the kernel must crack the nut.

A refined kitchen leads to the pharmacy.

To know is easier than to do.

He who holds the ladder is as bad as the thief.

The last shuts the door.

The more laws the less justice.

Few laws, good nations.

A lawyer and a cartwheel must be well greased.

The acre of laziness is full of thistles.

Lazy men get active when it's time to sleep.

What little Hans didn't learn, big Hans doesn't know.

A person has learned much who has learned how to die.

He who does not want to lend loses friends; he who lends gains enemies.

A good lie finds more believers than a bad truth.

A lie becomes true when one believes it.

Germany

It is little honor to the lion to seize the mouse.

Even the lion has to defend himself against flies.

If you want to live long, be healthy and fat, drink like a dog and eat like a cat.

Long is not forever.

Love can turn a cottage into a golden palace.

Loving and singing are not to be forced.

Love talks, even with closed lips.

Love sees roses without thorns.

He who writes love letters must have clammy hands.

Luck sometimes visits a fool, but never sits down with him.

A marriage in later years sends a letter to the grave digger.

Marriage is the opposite to a fever attack; it begins very hot and ends very cold.

If something happens to the master the servants will get his share too.

Meekness is the pride of the humble.

Where might is master, justice is servant.

A millstone gathers no moss.

The misery is that you have to ruin your day with work.

When money is talking, the rest of the world shuts up.

The monk's habit is never so blessed that the devil can't hide in it.

An ounce of a mother's wit is worth a pound of schoolgirl's wit.

I give a present to the mother but I think of the daughter.

The husband's mother is the wife's devil.

It's a poor mouse that sits on the sack and doesn't gnaw.

You catch the mice with bacon.

Mules make a great fuss about their ancestors having been donkeys.

"Must" is a bitter herb.

There is no nail varnish that can make old hands look younger.

A good name is a second inheritance.

Sometimes the whole nation has to pay for the foolish deed of one man.

Where Nature stops folly begins.

Nature hangs out her sign everywhere.

Necessity teaches all things.

Our neighbor's children are always the worst.

Love your neighbor, but don't tear down your fence.

He who puts his nose in a turd does not know what he is smelling.

The old one who is loved is like a winter flower.

When an old man marries, death laughs.

Old age is a disease that you die from.

Old age is no protection against foolishness.

Patience is often better than medicine.

Good pay makes happy workers.

A ripe pear is more likely to fall in the shit than onto the clean ground.

Where philosophy ends medicine begins.

Poor or rich, death makes us all equal.

Those in a high position can be seen from far away.

If you heat an empty pot it bursts.

Everyone wipes his feet on poverty.

Undeserved praise is mockery disguised.

The praise of a thousand jesters counts for nothing against the reprimand of one wise man.

Pray as though no work could help, and work as though no prayer could help.

The fewer the words, the better the prayer.

Most people like short prayers and long sausages.

The preacher must be like a chicken who always has an egg in reserve.

Priests and road signs show you the way but don't go with you.

A prince without ears to listen has no head to govern.

Promises have legs. Only a gift has hands.

He who listens to a proposition is already half sold.

Better an empty purse than an empty head.

Today red, tomorrow dead.

Better a friendly refusal than an unwilling promise.

Better twice remembered than once forgotten.

Rent and taxes never sleep.

Rhubarb and patience can work wonders.

The rich have medicines the poor have health.

For rich and poor alike the womb is equally warm.

The best way to learn to ride is on an old bike.

The most beautiful roses grow on graves.

What is the use of running when you're on the wrong road?

Running and buying don't go together—running and selling do.

Salt and bread make the cheeks red.

Whatever you save is also earned.

It is difficult to scare people who think they will profit from dying.

The salary of a good servant is never too high.

Turn yourself into a sheep and the wolves will eat you.

The more shepherds there are, the worse the flocks are watched.

When shepherds quarrel, the wolf has a winning game.

Don't throw away your old shoes until you have a new pair.

He who has no shoes dances in his socks.

Sin when you are drunk, pay the fine when you are sober.

He who starts singing too high will never finish the song.

You are still a slave if only your limbs are free.

A good soldier has only three things to think about; the king, God, and nothing.

Sorrow does not pay any debts.

When the sow is satisfied she throws the trough away.

Germany

Better no spoon than no soup.

Criticism of the state is all right, but don't forget the nation is you.

If I am seen I am joking; if I am not seen I steal.

He who invites storks must have frogs in the house.

The stubborn man is ruled by a fool.

Where there are no swamps there are no frogs.

It is good to swim near a boat.

Who talks a lot at the table will leave it hungry.

People talk about something until it actually happens.

He who is his own teacher has a fool for a pupil.

Petty thieves are hanged, you take off your hat to the big ones.

A thief who steals from a thief is not a thief.

However long the sun shines upon a thistle, it will never become a rose.

Those who tickle themselves may laugh when they please.

Time is anger's medicine.

Time chases love away and love chases the time away.

Don't let your tongue say what your head may have to pay for.

Big trees cast more shadow than fruit.

The oldest trees bear the softest fruits.

A good tree bears good fruit.

Truth is for the ears what smoke is for the eyes and vinegar for the tongue.

A truth that comes too early or too late is just like a lie.

Two is an army against one.

Who loves ugliness will not encounter beauty.

No one is unhappier than the one who believes in happiness.

Three things come into the house uninvited: debts, age, and death.

Vice often rides triumphantly in the coach of virtue.

On the day of victory no fatigue is felt.

In time of war the devil makes more room in hell.

144

Water quenches the thirst but does not teach you how to sing.

Weapons, women, and locks must be guarded at all times.

If you let the weeds grow for a year you will need seven to clear them.

You don't need a teacher of wickedness.

The one who wins plays best.

Wine makes secrets float to the surface.

To question a wise man is the beginning of wisdom.

The wise man has long ears and a short tongue.

A smart witch can also dance without a broomstick.

Howling makes the wolf bigger than he really is.

Hunger leads the wolf to the village.

Wolves never gossip about each other.

A woman's first advice is her best.

Women prefer to be beautiful rather than good.

Women only keep quiet about their age.

Women and fishes are best in the middle.

A second woman has golden thighs.

Only believe in the faith of a woman as you would believe in miracles.

Whenever women say good-bye they always hang around for a while.

A woman and a stove may not leave the house.

Green wood gives more smoke than heat.

Better one living word than a hundred dead ones.

Working on the land is better than praying in the desert.

Work paid for in advance has feet of lead.

The world could have been great if only people had been more useful.

O foolish world, why are you scratching around in the dark?

Not all people who have yawned together must get married.

If you want to be old, hang yourself when you are young.

If you've enjoyed the dance, pay the musicians.

Nobles and dogs leave the door open.

Ghana

God gives us milk but no jug.

A donkey in Saxony is a professor in Rome.

Small molehills can turn carriages over.

The mountains make the mist and the valleys must consume them.

All men are baked in the same clay.

Wherever the ram goes the sheep will follow.

Ghana

Two small antelopes can beat one big one.

An army is driven back by courage and not by insults, however many.

What is bad luck for one man is good luck for another.

By going and coming, a bird weaves its nest.

No one boasts of what belongs to another.

The chicken also knows when it's morning, but still watches the mouth of the cock.

When someone is already approaching, there is no need to say "Come here."

When the cock is drunk, he forgets about the hawk.

Only when you have crossed the river, can you say the crocodile has a lump on his snout.

Death has the key to open the miser's chest.

If we knew where death resided, we would never stay there.

You cannot kill an elephant with bullets of wax.

One falsehood spoils a thousand truths.

One cannot both feast and become rich.

When you follow in the path of your father, you learn to walk like him.

Fire and gunpowder are not bedfellows.

By the time the fool has learned the game, the players have dispersed.

Do not call the forest that shelters you a jungle.

He who is guilty has much to say.

If the hunter comes back with mushrooms, don't ask him how his hunt was.

A knife does not know who is its master.

There is no medicine to cure hatred.

If you are in hiding, don't light a fire.

Hunger is felt by slave and king alike.

When a king has good counsellors, his reign is peaceful.

Rain beats on a leopard's skin, but it does not wash out the spots.

Money is sharper than a sword.

The monkey says there is nothing better than poverty to unlearn man of his conceit.

The moon moves slowly, but it gets across the town.

It is Mr. Old-Man-Monkey who marries Mrs. Old-Woman-Monkey.

Even though the old man is strong and hearty, he will not live forever.

The poor man and the rich man do not play together.

When you are rich, you are resented; when you are poor, you are despised.

The rich man may wear old clothes.

No one tests the depth of a river with both feet.

The ruin of a nation begins in the homes of its people.

A slave does not choose his master.

If you take your tongue to the pawnshop, you can't redeem it later.

The surface of the water is beautiful, but it is no good to sleep on.

It's the fool's sheep that breaks loose twice.

It is the calm and silent water that drowns a man.

The white man lives in the castle; when he dies, he lies in the ground.

It is the wife who knows her husband.

When a woman is hungry, she says, "Roast something for the children that they may eat."

A woman is like a blanket: If you cover yourself with it, it bothers you; if you throw it aside you will feel the cold.

Wood already touched by fire is not hard to set alight.

It is no shame at all to work for money.

A man with too much ambition cannot sleep in peace.

Don't expect to be offered a chair when you visit a place where the chief himself sits on the floor.

A crab does not beget a bird.

If you find no fish, you have to eat bread.

Nature gave us two cheeks instead of one to make it easier to eat hot food.

There is bound to be a knot in a very long string.

One lie ruins a thousand truths.

If power can be bought then sell your mother to get it. You can always buy her back later.

Misfortune does not restrict his visits to one day.

You cannot hide behind your finger.

If a woman gets rich she changes into a man.

Nobody is shamed twice.

Greece
(including Naxos)

Alexander the Great was not very tall.

One word spoken in anger may spoil an entire life.

Empty barrels and insignificant people always make the most noise.

When you go to bed with a clear head, you will not get up with a headache.

The beginning is the half of every action.

A fat belly did not invent gun powder.

A good bird begins chirping while in the egg.

Better a sick body than an ignorant mind.

In business you need two Jews for one Greek, two Greeks for one Syrian and two Syrians for one Armenian.

A cat with gloves never catches mice.

An old cat likes young mice.

Nothing will content him who is not content with a little.

Every country is a fatherland.

Curses are like chickens; they come home to roost.

It is useless to knock at the door of a deaf man.

Deeds are fruits, words are only leaves.

When the devil grows poor he becomes a tax collector.

To deceive a diplomat speak the truth, he has no experience with it.

Don't forget to distrust.

Never consult a doctor who has never been ill himself.

My donkey is dead; let no more grass grow.

To have five drachmas in the hand is better than ten drachmas on paper.

A dove has no place amongst the crows.

A drowning man takes hold of his own hair.

No need to teach an eagle to fly.

An old enemy never becomes a friend.

Observe your enemies, for they first find your faults.

It is better to be envied than pitied.

Envy accomplishes nothing.

You easily forget the eyes that don't see you any more.

Those who fight with silver spears are sure of their victory.

Sometimes you have to throw yourself into the fire to escape from the smoke.

Fire does not extinguish fire.

Better the first of its kind than the last.

If you cannot catch a fish, do not blame the sea.

The best fish hook cannot catch limp cheese.

Many men know how to flatter, few men know how to praise.

The fly sat upon the axle of the chariot-wheel and said "What a lot of dust I raise!"

Do not compare a fly with an elephant.

The fox that waits until the chicken falls from the perch dies from hunger.

A fox is not caught twice in the same snare.

The frog wanted to be an ox and swelled up until he burst.

Swift gratitude is the sweetest.

We became gravediggers but nobody dies anymore.

Greeks only agree with each other about going to the toilet.

One hand washes the other and both wash the face.

He who wants to be happy must stay at home.

Who hunts two hares will catch neither.

Someone with an unrelenting heart is his own executioner.

The heart that loves is always young.

You cannot hide behind your finger.

Who wouldn't lick his fingers when they have been dipped in honey?

If it were not for hope, the heart would break.

They sowed the seed of an "if" but it didn't germinate.

First secure an independent income, then practice virtue.

He who is born in jail loves jail.

The knee is closer than the calf.

What is good to know is difficult to learn.

For lazy people it is always party time.

A library is a repository of medicine for the mind.

You learn to limp if you live with cripples.

Listen to that which is well said even if it is from the mouth of an enemy.

A lucky person is someone who plants pebbles and harvests potatoes.

Man is the measure of all things.

A young man should not marry yet, an old man not at all.

I hate a jovial table companion with a good memory.

No mill, no meal.

A miser and a liar bargain quickly.

The grumbling mother-in-law forgets that she once was a bride.

The more the mother-in-law drinks the more friendly is her greeting.

Mountains are used to snow.

A thousand people cannot undress a naked person.

Nature has given us two ears, two eyes, and but one tongue; to the
end we should hear and see more than we speak.

The old age of an eagle is better than the youth of the sparrow.

One minute of patience can mean ten years of peace.

The people make the town.

Pleasures are transient—honors immortal.

He who plunders with a little boat is a pirate; he who plunders with a
fleet is a conqueror.

A priest blesses his own bread first.

Son of a priest, grandson of the devil.

Nothing is so reckless as a blind horse.

Remorse is worse than a beating.

He who eats and drinks with the rich leaves the table hungry.

Where there is a sea there are pirates.

You know who the good seamen are when the storm comes.

Keep no secrets of thyself from thyself.

If you seek well, you will find.

Outside a sheep, inside a wolf.

You must keep quiet or say only things that improve silence.

No one loathes the smell of himself.

A society grows great when old men plant trees whose shade they
know they shall never sit in.

Not speech, but facts, convince.

Do not lean on a worm-eaten staff.

Under every stone sleeps a scorpion.

The style is the man himself.

Success has many friends.

It is not summer until the crickets sing.

Never give a sword to a fool or power to an unjust man.

Every tale can be told in a different way.

A lazy tailor finds his thread too long.

The thief shouts to frighten the hell out of his victim.

The second thought is the best.

Time is the best adviser.

Time is the soul of the world.

Give me today and you may keep tomorrow.

What is true is no more sure than the probable.

Truth lies at the bottom of a well.

Not to mention the truth is hiding gold.

From a broken violin do not expect fine music.

A wheel that turns gathers no rust.

Better a drop of wisdom than an ocean of gold.

Whoever feeds the wolf in the winter will be eaten by him in the spring.

A woman prefers a man without money to money without a man.

Take a young woman for the pleasure of possessing her until she is old.

Women are as changeable as the sea.

The rest of the world does not know what newlyweds know.

He who thinks the worst usually is right.

In the young, silence is better than speech.

You have to put a young girl onto an old man.

If all the bees made honey, there would be enough for even gypsies to eat.

Sharing the figs can leave you with none at all.

If the ox knew his own strength, God help us.

They throw stones at the walnut trees, but not at the maple.

A goat thief came along and they put him in jail. A real scoundrel turned up and they took off their hats to him.

Guadeloupe
(France)

The lid knows what is in the pot.

Do not count the eggs that are in the chicken's ass.

Guatemala

Everyone is as old as their heart.

Hearts, like thieves, never give back lost things.

Guinea

One camel does not make fun of the other camel's hump.

A cow that has no tail should not try to chase away flies.

A good deed is something one returns.

To have two eyes can be cause for pride; but to have one eye is better than to have none.

He who does not cultivate his field, will die of hunger.

Save your fowl before it stops flapping.

For news of the heart ask the face.

Knowledge is like a garden: if it is not cultivated, it cannot be harvested.

The man on his feet carries off the share of the man sitting down.

When a needle falls into a deep well, many people will look into the well, but few will be ready to go down after it.

Around a flowering tree, there are many insects.

To make preparations does not spoil the trip.

The toad likes water, but not when it's boiling.

When you wait for tomorrow it never comes. When you don't wait for it tomorrow still comes.

No matter how long the winter, spring is sure to follow.

Guyana

The devil tempts but doesn't force.

When the ear does not hear the eye will see better.

A good thief is the best guardian.

Gypsy Proverbs

You have to dig deep to bury your daddy.

You can count the apples on a tree but you can't count the trees from one apple.

Happiness you pay for is to be found everywhere.

You cannot stop a whore, not even with a hundred horses.

Children will tell you what they do, men what they think and older people what they have seen and heard.

Credit is better than money.

I have two masters—God and the devil; I work for the devil until lunch then I follow the Lord.

It is better to be the head of a mouse than the tail of a lion.

After bad luck comes good fortune.

Where rich people can make honest money, poor people have to steal.

The stick that breaks the window does not kill a dog.

A tear in the eye is the wound of the heart.

When do we have a day of fast? When there is no bread and ham in the larder.

There are such things as false truths and honest lies.

You don't kill a gypsy by cutting him in ten pieces—you only make ten more gypsies.

A gypsy only tells the truth once in his life but he regrets it afterwards.

The gypsy church was made of pork and the dogs ate it.

Stay where there are songs. Bad people don't sing.

Haiti

The crab that walks too far falls into the pot.

Eggs have no business dancing with stones.

The dog has four feet, but he does not walk in four roads at the same time.

If you want your eggs hatched, sit on them yourself.

To stumble is not to fall.

If they had cereal, they'd want gumbo.

The good white man dies, the bad one remains.

A single finger cannot catch fleas.

All food is fit to eat, but not all words are fit to speak.

Hang your knapsack where you can reach it.

Poor people entertain with the heart.

Better rags than nakedness.

Only the knife knows the heart of a pineapple.

Age and marriage tame the beast.

You don't know a man before he takes a woman.

Ignorance doesn't necessarily kill you but it makes you sweat a lot.

A monkey never thinks her baby's ugly.

If work were good for you, the rich would leave none for the poor.
The constitution is paper, bayonets are steel.
The pencil of God has not an eraser.
Beyond the mountain is another mountain.
To speak French doesn't mean you are smart.
The donkey sweats so the horse can be decorated with lace.

Hawaii

Those above are going down, those below are going up.
Do not allow sins to get beyond creeping.
Continue to do good, and heaven will come down to you.
No one is hurt by doing the right thing.
Love is like fog—there is no mountain on which it does not rest.
Don't ignore the small things—the kite flies because of its tail.
While the sun is still up, let people work that the earth may live.
A good surfer will not get wet. A bad one breaks his board.
Someone who speaks about "my inferiors" doesn't have them.
Sweet tongues buy horses on credit.

Hebrew Proverbs

An accuser may not act as a defender.
God detests a man who rushes to accuse a neighbor.
If you commence a good action, leave it not incomplete.
Beware of him who gives you advice according to his own interests.
He who follows advice from women will end up in hell.
Give me good advice but don't advise me not to do it.
Ask someone else for advice but keep your knowledge to yourself.
Ambition destroys its possessor.

Hebrew Proverbs

Do not eat before you have fed your animal.

There are three things that attract: a house for its inhabitants, a woman for her spouse, and a bargain for a customer.

Don't visit auctions if you have no money.

Clean bodies, pure morals.

If you are born an ass, you will die one.

A borrower may not lend the thing he borrowed.

Buttered bread always falls dry side up.

Breasts adorn a woman and make a man look ugly.

A change of name or place may sometimes save a person.

Until a child is one year old it is incapable of sin.

Do not confine your children to your own learning, for they were born in another time.

When you have no choice, mobilize the spirit of courage.

The city, whose physician has the gout, is in a bad state.

Courage is a kingdom without a crown.

Better be a cursed man than he who curses.

Customs are stronger than laws.

The day is short and work lasts a long time.

He who instigates good deeds is greater than the one who performs them.

More people die from overeating than from undernourishment.

When a divorced man marries a divorced woman, there are four people in that marital bed.

The best doctor is to be found in hell.

Don't live in a town where there are no doctors.

If the dog barks, go in; if the bitch barks you had better stay outside.

Two dogs can kill a lion.

A dream which has not been interpreted is like a letter unread.

Make sure to be in with your equals if you're going to fall out with your superiors.

Look for the good, not the evil, in the conduct of members of the family.

What you don't see with your eyes, don't witness with your mouth.

Two farmers each claimed to own a certain cow. While one pulled on its head and the other pulled on its tail, the cow was milked by the lawyer.

My fathers planted for me, and I planted for my children.

He is great whose faults can be numbered.

It is fitting for a great God to forgive great sinners.

Until your fortieth it is better to eat than to drink; afterwards it is vice versa.

Verbal fraud is worse than monetary fraud.

When two friends part they have to lock up each other's secrets and throw away the key.

One who looks for a friend without faults will have none.

Your friend has a friend and the friend of your friend has another friend. Learn how to keep quiet.

Gamblers do not contribute to the public welfare.

By the first glass a lamb, the second a lion, and the third a pig.

Gluttony has killed more people than famine has.

God could not be everywhere, that's why he made mothers.

Three things are good in small doses and bad in big ones: yeast, salt, and hesitation.

He who gossips and he who listens to it deserve to be thrown to the dogs.

Grapes picked too early don't even make good vinegar.

How great man would be were he not so arrogant.

Your health comes first—you can always hang yourself later.

A henpecked husband gets no support during a lawsuit.

He who puts up with insult invites injury.

No joy without wine.

He who is his own judge never finds a reason to condemn.

Do not judge your fellow man until you have stood in his place.

Judge a man not by the words of his mother, but from the comments of his neighbors.

Judgment delayed is judgment avoided.

If someone is coming to kill you, get up early and kill him first.

Leadership shortens life.

The punishment of a liar is that he is never believed, even when he speaks the truth.

Love and hate always exaggerate.

Love does not pay attention to dignity.

Men were born with bread in their hands women were born with empty hands.

A man without a woman cannot defend himself against seductions.

To save one man is like saving the world.

Whoever marries for money will have unworthy children.

No marriage contract is made without a quarrel.

There is no such thing as tasty medicine.

Who is mighty? One who makes an enemy into a friend.

Hope for a miracle, but don't rely on it.

Money purifies everything.

Two coins in a purse make more noise than a hundred.

He who prays for his neighbors will be heard for himself.

Better a night full of anger than a night full of repentance.

An old man in the house is a burden, but an old woman is a treasure.

If you can't go over, you must go under.

A pain that pricks the conscience is more effective than a lot of whip-lashes.

Approach the perfumer and thou wilt be perfumed.

The place honors not the man; it is the man who honors the place.

No one is so poor as an ignorant person.

Poverty runs after the poor, wealth after the rich.

When prices drop, buy.

Pride is the mask we make of our faults.

Promise little and do a lot.

When two men quarrel, the one who yields first displays the nobler character.

Repentance prolongs a man's life.

Respect flies away for the one who pursues it and hunts the person who is fleeing from it.

A rich man has no need of character.

Do not speak of secret matters in a field that is full of little hills.

What you don't see with your eyes, don't invent with your mouth.

Silence is a fence around wisdom.

Silence heals all ills.

Slander is more deadly than weapons; weapons wound from close range, slander hurts from a distance.

What soap is for the body, tears are for the soul.

The soldiers fight, and the kings are heroes.

With a good son-in-law you gain a son, with a bad one you lose your daughter, too.

To punish a student, use a shoe lace.

He has sold the sun to buy a candle.

Don't be too sweet lest you be eaten up; don't be too bitter lest you be spewed out.

Talking is silver, silence is golden.

The thief who has no opportunity to steal thinks he is an honest man.

Tread on thorns with your shoes on.

Teach your tongue to say: "I do not know."

Of what use is a torch at midday?

He who does not teach his son a trade teaches him to steal.

Never trust the man who tells you all his troubles but keeps from you all his joys.

If you add to the truth, you take something away from it.

You recognize the truth by its own sound.

The truth is a heavy burden that few care to carry.

Vinegar is the son of wine.

A visit is like rainwater; you pray for it when it stays away and its a problem when it rains too much.

Walls have ears.

A wedding is like a funeral, but with musicians.

The well that is most often used gives the purest water.

Whoever depends on his wife's earnings will not succeed.

Wine tops the list of all medicines.

If the wine comes in, good sense goes out.

Old wine is good for the stomach.

Where there is no wine, we need medicine.

The greatest wisdom of all is kindness.

When the wise man gets angry, he stops being wise.

Be careful not to make a woman weep. God counts her tears.

It is better to talk to a woman and think of God, than talk to God and think of a woman.

A woman prefers poverty with love to wealth without love.

A man dies when he stops working.

The world exists on three things: truth, justice, and peace.

The world is in the hands of fools.

The world is a tavern and the way hereafter is our home.

To do things wrong with best intentions is better than acting to the letter of the law with evil intentions.

Holland

Better lose the anchor than the whole ship.

Anger is a short madness.

Good looking apples are sometimes sour.

It is too late to cry "Hold hard!" when the arrow has left the bow.

When the ass is too happy he begins dancing on the ice.

It is a grief to one beggar that there is another at the door.

A bird never flew so high but it had to come to the ground for food.

Slowly but surely the bird builds his nest.

Cats don't catch the old birds.

He has the greatest blind side who thinks he has none.

Great boast, little roast.

Don't overstrain your bow—it may break.

All is well, for if the bride has not fair hair, she has a fair skin.

A sad bride makes a glad wife.

If it's not burning you why cool it?

If you eat someone's cake, you must also eat his lentils.

When the calf is drowned they cover the well.

The worse the carpenter, the more the chips.

The best cause requires a good champion.

Caution is the parent of delicate beer glasses.

In prosperity caution, in adversity patience.

No wheat without chaff.

He that chases another does not sit still himself.

Of listening children have your fears, for little pitchers have great ears.

He that has a choice has trouble.

Were everyone to sweep in front of his own house, every street would be clean.

Offer a clown your finger, and he'll take your fist.

An old coachman loves the crack of the whip.

A smart coat is a good letter of introduction.

Coffee has two virtues, it's wet and it's warm.

They who come from afar have leave to lie.

Little is done where many command.

Tell me the company you keep, and I'll tell you what you are.

When the cook and the steward fall out, we hear who stole the butter.

What costs nothing is worth nothing.

Of hasty counsel take good heed, for haste is very rarely speed.

Take counsel before it goes ill, lest it go worse.

Covetousness is always filling a bottomless vessel.

Wicked cows have short horns.

Milk the cow, but don't pull off the udder.

The cow does not know the value of her tail till she has lost it.

Men that crawl, never fall.

A flying crow always catches something.

A crown is no cure for the headache.

Darkness and night are mothers of thought.

A brilliant daughter makes a brittle wife.

Daughters may be seen but not heard.

Every day is not a holiday.

Who is tired of happy days, let him take a wife.

He waits long that waits for another man's death.

He that is embarked with the devil must sail with him.

Talk of the devil and you hear his bones rattle.

The devil has his martyrs among men.

Where the dike is lowest the water first runs out.

To do nothing teaches evil.

A dog with a bone knows no friend.

Barking dogs don't bite.

Better have a dog for your friend than your enemy.

Stroke your dog, and he'll spoil your clothes.

When the dog is down, everyone is ready to bite him.

Dogs have teeth in all countries.

Many open a door to shut a window.

Sweep in front of your own door before you look after your neighbor's.

The open door invites the thief.

Good drink drives out bad thoughts.

After great droughts come great rains.

Economy is a great revenue.

To get eggs there must be some cackling.

Unlaid eggs are uncertain chickens.

Where there is nothing, the emperor loses his right.

Everything has an end with the exception of God.

For great evils strong remedies.

Set your expense according to your trade.

What the eye sees not, the heart craves not.

The eyes are bigger than the belly.

The eye of the master makes the horse fat, and the eye of the mistress makes the chambers neat.

Who has only one eye must take good care of it.

Beware of the person with two faces.

Who doesn't keep faith with God won't keep it with men.

Falling teaches us to walk safely.

Common fame seldom lies.

Long fasting doesn't save bread.

Who goes fasting to bed will sleep but lightly.

Bear patiently that which you suffer by your own fault.

A good fire makes a quick cook.

It is good to warm oneself by another's fire.

Who wants fire, let him look for it in the ashes.

Big fish jump out of the kettle.

Little fish are sweet.

After high floods come low ebbs.

Holland

Every flood has its ebb.

More flies are caught with a spoonful of syrup than with a barrel full of vinegar.

The fly flutters around the candle till it gets burnt.

It needs a cunning hand to shave a fool's head.

To every fool his cap.

Were fools silent, they would pass for wise.

There is a fool at every feast.

A fool by chance may say a wise thing.

Fools are free all the world over.

If fools ate no bread, corn would be cheap.

Fortune and glass break easily.

Better a slap from your friend than a kiss from your enemy.

With a friend behind you, you have a safe bridge.

All are not friends who smile at you.

Before you make a friend, eat a pack of salt with him.

Learn who are your friends when you are in need.

Your friend lends and your enemy asks for payment.

In the division of inheritance, friendship stands still.

Never wear a brown hat in Friesland.

Froth is not beer.

Who gives to me, teaches me to give.

God does not pay weekly, but pays at the end.

God sells knowledge for labor, honor for risk.

Help yourself and God will help you.

One God, one wife, but many friends.

Where there's no good within, no good comes out.

In the company of the good we become good.

Men can bear all things except good days.

Common goods, no goods.

The best goods are the cheapest.

The goose hisses, but does not bite.

Geese are plucked as long as they have feathers.

Whoever gossips about his relatives has no luck and no blessing.

Soon grass, soon hay.

A daily guest is a great thief in the kitchen.

There is no point in combing where there is no hair.

Hares are not caught with drums.

In small woods may be caught large hares.

When we least expect it, the hare darts out of the ditch.

Nothing in haste but catching fleas.

Hastiness is the beginning of wrath, and its end repentance.

When the head is sick the whole body is sick.

A scabby head fears the comb.

Hearsay is half lies.

A stout heart tempers adversity.

The heart does not lie.

Better once in heaven than ten times at the gate.

Where the hedge is lowest everyone goes over.

Hens like to lay where they see an egg.

The cost is high of the honey that must be licked from thorns.

After honor and state follow envy and hate.

Better poor with honor than rich with shame.

What has horns will gore.

A good horse is worth his fodder.

A horse may stumble, though he has four feet.

Better a blind horse than an empty halter.

Better ride a good horse for a year than an ass all your life.

Ill-matched horses draw badly.

One can't shoe a running horse.

Holland

A merry host makes merry guests.

It is hard to steal where the host is a thief.

Many hounds mean the death of the hare.

When the husband earns well, the wife spends well.

An idle man is the devil's pillow.

Idleness is hunger's mother; of theft it is full brother.

An inch too short is as bad as a yard.

Give him an inch and he'll take a yard.

He that would jest must take a jest, or else to let it alone were best.

He who is outside the door has already a good part of his journey behind him.

It is easier to make a lady of a peasant girl than a peasant girl of a lady.

Let me get over the lake, and I will have no fear of the brook.

Better a ruined than a lost land.

Better poor on land than rich at sea.

Who knows the language is at home everywhere.

The most learned are not the wisest.

He who is afraid of the leaves must not go into the wood.

Better a leg broken than the neck.

Who ventures to lend, loses money and friend.

Like will to like, be they poor or rich.

A louse in the cabbage is better than no meat at all.

Love makes labor light.

Who writes love letters grows thin; who carries them, fat.

He that has the luck leads the bride to church.

A man without money is like a ship without sails.

A man overboard, a mouth less to feed.

Where a man feels pain he lays his hand.

He must shoot well who always hits the mark.

To marry once is a duty, twice a folly, and three times—madness.

Holland

Marry in haste and repent at leisure.

One should not think about it too much when marrying or taking pills.

He must indeed be a good master who never does wrong.

No better masters than poverty and want.

After meat comes mustard.

Might is not right.

The end of mirth is the beginning of sorrow.

A miser's money takes the place of wisdom.

Fair money can cover much that's foul.

Sow not money on the sea lest it sink.

Behind every mountain lies a valley.

The higher the mountain the lower the valley, the taller the tree the harder the fall.

In time a mouse will gnaw through a cable.

It is better to blow than burn your mouth.

It is hard to blow with a full mouth.

Out of the abundance of the heart the mouth speaks.

One nail drives in another.

He who slanders his neighbor makes a rod for his own back.

Many seek good nights and waste good days.

Nobility of soul is more honorable than nobility of birth.

Every one must row with the oars he has.

All offices are greasy.

No office so humble but it is better than nothing.

What the old ones sing, the young ones whistle.

Opportunity makes desire.

An ox and an ass don't yoke well to the same plow.

Pastors come for your wine and officers for your daughters.

A handful of patience is worth more than a bushel of brains.

Patience surpasses learning.

No one can have peace longer than his neighbor pleases.

Better keep peace than make peace.

An ennobled peasant does not know his own father.

A penny saved is better than a florin earned.

One penny in the pot makes more noise than when it is full.

The third person makes good company.

If you pull one pig by the tail all the rest squeak.

Roast pigeons don't fly through the air.

The best pilots are ashore.

If you touch pitch you will get dirty.

Pleasures steal away the mind.

Poverty is the reward of idleness.

All are not princes who ride with the emperor.

In the land of promise a man may die of hunger.

Promises make debts, and debts make promises.

No greater promisers than they who have nothing to give.

When prosperity smiles, beware of its guiles.

Who serves the public serves a fickle master.

You cannot make a silk purse from a sow's ear.

When two quarrel both are in the wrong.

Hasty questions require slow answers.

Quickly done; long repented.

It's good to watch the rain from a dry standpoint.

An old rat won't go into the trap.

The young ravens are beaked like the old.

Better reap two days too soon than one too late.

Take nothing in hand that may bring repentance.

Rest makes rusty.

Better return half way than lose yourself.

Reward sweetens labor.

The rich have many friends.

The richest man, whate'er his lot, is the one content with what he's got.

Good right needs good help.

Soon ripe, soon rotten; soon wise, soon foolish.

He who would catch a rogue must watch behind the door.

The farther from Rome the nearer to God.

He who would gather roses must not fear thorns.

Roses fall, but the thorns remain.

Cast no roses before swine.

It is good rowing with the sail set.

When the sack is full it pricks up its ears.

It is safest to sail within reach of the shore.

He that saves something today will have something tomorrow.

Self-love is blind.

Who has many servants has many thieves.

Shame lasts longer than poverty.

Who fears no shame comes to no honor.

Coupled sheep drown one another.

No sheep runs into the mouth of a sleeping wolf.

The scabbier the sheep the harder it bleats.

When one sheep is over the dam, the rest follow.

When the shepherd strays, the sheep stray.

My shirt is closer to me than my cloak.

There is more to dancing than a pair of dancing shoes.

Skill and assurance make an invincible combination.

Were the sky to fall, not an earthen pot would be left whole.

Sloth is the beginning of vice.

He that despises the small is not worthy of the great.

What the sober man thinks, the drunkard tells.

It is hasty speed that doesn't succeed.

Better to be squinting than blind.

It is too late to lock the stable door when the horses have already been stolen.

When the stomach is full the heart is glad.

One sprinkles the most sugar where the tart is burnt.

It is hard to swim against the current.

Teachers die, but books live on.

Tender surgeons make foul wounds.

Much talk, little work.

Everyone is a thief in his own craft.

Little thieves have iron chains; big thieves have gold ones.

There are more thieves than are hanged.

When thieves fall out, honest men get their goods back.

Good things require time.

He would be wise who knew all things beforehand.

When things go well it is easy to advise.

Who undertakes many things at once seldom does anything well.

He who has no thirst has no business at the fountain.

Thistles and thorns prick sore, but evil tongues prick even more.

Time and place make the thief.

Time destroys all things.

Our time runs on like a stream; first fall the leaves and then the tree.

Tall trees catch much wind.

The nobler the tree, the more bends the twig.

When the tree falls everyone runs to cut the branches.

Trees often transplanted seldom prosper.

From trivial things great arguments often arise.

Sooner or later the truth comes to light.

Truth is lost with too much debating.

Nobody's sweetheart is ugly.

Who undertakes too much, succeeds but little.

A usurer, a miller, a banker, and a publican are the four evangelists of Lucifer.

Virtue consists of action.

Wasting is a bad habit, saving is a sure income.

Who watches not catches not.

Great wealth, great care.

They who fight with golden weapons are pretty sure to prove they are right.

It is a bad well that you have to fill with water.

Stay a while, and lose a mile.

A young wife, new bread, and green wood devastate a house.

Neither reprove nor flatter your wife where people hear or see it.

Who has a bad wife, his hell begins on earth.

When it is God's will to plague a man, a mouse can bite him to death.

Good wine praises itself.

Poor folk's wisdom counts very little.

That is good wisdom which is wisdom in the end.

Wisdom in the man, patience in the wife, brings peace to the house and a happy life.

He would be wise who knew all things beforehand.

He is so wise that he goes upon the ice three days before it freezes.

A wolf hankers after sheep even at his last gasp.

All women are good Lutherans—they would rather preach than hear mass.

Women who are often at the looking-glass seldom spin.

Woods have ears and fields have eyes.

An honest man's word is his bond.

When hard work goes out of the door, poverty comes in at the window.

With hard work, you can get fire out of a stone.

The world likes to be cheated.

He who wants a new world must first buy the old.

A wreck on shore is a beacon at sea.

What is wrong today won't be right tomorrow.

It is good spinning from another's yarn.

Young folk, silly folk; old folk, cold folk.

The young may die, the old must.

Hungary

Adam ate the apple, and our teeth still ache.

A bashful beggar has an empty wallet.

I can chew for you, my child, but you must swallow by yourself.

It is a fine thing to die for one's fatherland, but a still finer thing to live for it.

A flatterer is a secret enemy.

He who is struck by the lightning doesn't hear the thunder.

A loan, though old, is not a gift.

An ox remains an ox, even if driven to Vienna.

A prudent man does not make the goat his gardener.

One road leads to heaven but many lead to hell.

An old spinster is not worth more than an unposted letter.

There is no coat big enough to hide both poverty and drunkenness.

Blushing is the paint of good habits.

Where there is no bridge the smallest plank is of great value.

In the long run even a dog will compromise with the cat.

Come a little closer when your sword is too short.

He who accepts the gift loses his liberty.

If it's God's will the broom will lose its handle.

He who trusts is happy; the doubter is wise.

Try to be in good company, even when you are alone.

The crowd is not led by the head but by the heart.

No one was ever hung for what he was thinking.

In the dark all cats and all girls are beautiful.

Beloved children have many names.

Look at the mother, marry the daughter.

Nobody can rest in his own shadow.

He who wants to go fishing must not be afraid of the water.

Better dry bread in peacetime than meat in wartime.

He who is feared by many must be afraid of many.

The woman of a man without sorrows is almost a widow.

If women were not vain, men could teach them how to be.

Even the white lily casts a shadow.

He who slowly gets angry will stay angry for a long time.

Peccadillos at home, deadly sins abroad.

Iceland

A sitting crow starves.

Mediocrity is climbing molehills without sweating.

The revenge that is postponed is not forgotten.

All old sayings have something in them.

Two make an army against one.

Hunger, work, and sweat are the best herbs.

A greasy kitchen; a will with not much in it.

Better to drink the milk than to eat the cow.

It would be good to have two mouths and speak to yourself with
    both.

Need is not governed by the law.

Need is a bad negotiator.

It is difficult to steal when the boss is a thief.

On the ladder to success there is always somebody on the rung above you and who uses your head to steady himself.

Few are like father, no one is like mother.

A story is only half told if there is only one side presented.

Every story has two sides and every song has twelve versions.

Much always longs for more.

A man yearns for his paradise but it could become his hell.

Better wise language than well combed hair.

Bad birds seldom bring good weather.

Useless wisdom is double foolishness.

You can't complain about the sea if you suffer shipwreck for the second time.

India
(Bengal, Bihar, Hindustan, Kashmir, Madras)

What does the blind man know of the beauty of the tulip?

Brains are not to be found in the beard.

A buffalo does not feel the weight of his own horns.

Be like a camel—carrying sweets but dining on thorns.

When a camel is at the foot of a mountain only then judge his height.

The crab instructs its young: "Walk straight ahead—like me."

The deceitful have no friends.

Dependence on another is perpetual disappointment.

Always be well dressed, even when begging.

Eating while seated makes one of large size; eating while standing makes one strong.

When an elephant is in trouble, even a frog will kick him.

There is enmity between to dig and to let dig.

Faith keeps the world going.

Many families are built on laughter.

He who has come through the fire will fade in the sun.

To sing to the deaf, to talk with the dumb, and to dance for the blind are three foolish things.

The grown-up pays attention to what you are doing; the child sees beyond that.

The heart at rest sees a feast in everything.

Every man is the guardian of his own honor.

If you call a lady a slave, she laughs, but if you call a slave a slave, he cries.

A lie has no author, nor a liar a conscience.

Since love departs at dawn, create, O God, a night that has no morn.

A man laughs at others and weeps for himself.

Use medicine as well as prayers.

One of the two partners always bites the best part of the apple.

Be peaceful yet vigilant—a sheep will bite someone without a stick.

Pearls are of no value in a desert.

The poor looks for food and the rich man for appetite.

We are both queens, so who will hang out the laundry?

Regularity is the best medicine.

A lot of people become saints because of their stomach.

When the sculptor is dead his statues ask him for a soul.

Why save when your son is a good son? Why save when your son is a bad son?

If you can't give any sugar then speak sweetly.

The hot sun melts away the snow; when anger comes, does wisdom go.

The tree casts its shadow on everything, even upon the woodcutter.

The truth is half a quarrel.

India

You cannot separate water by beating it with a fork.

Weeping washes the face.

It is little use to dig a well after the house has caught fire.

Never strike your wife, not even with a flower.

Happy is the woman whose husband does not speak to her.

The word of a woman is a bundle of water.

The world flatters the elephant and tramples on the ant.

There is no hand to catch time.

No sin is hidden to the soul.

The tongue is safe; even among thirty teeth.

The sieve says to the needle, "You have a hole in your tail."

Whoever eats a pancake never counts the holes in it.

Truth has no branches.

A dog always bites under the knee.

Pull someone by the ears and his head will follow.

A foolish bride gets no presents.

After eating nine hundred rats, the cat is now going on a pilgrimage.

The cock goes to town for only four days and returns home a peacock.

The potter sleeps soundly, for no one would steal clay.

The dog's tail stays crooked even if he is buried for twelve years.

An adder with its poisonous fangs taken out is nothing more than a piece of rope.

We admire what we do not understand.

The ambitious one makes friends with the elephant, then tramples upon the ant.

He who answers is inferior to the one who asks the question.

When you have an ass for a friend, expect nothing but kicks.

The baby is not yet born, and yet you say that his nose is like his grandfather's.

Be bad to the bad; good to the good; be a flower to other flowers and a thorn to other thorns.

He that is baldheaded has no need of combs.

When the bed breaks, there is the ground to lie on.

A beggar himself, can he afford to have one asking for alms at his door?

A blind man sat behind a pile of stones and thought that nobody could see him.

It is better to be blind than to see things from only one point of view.

Blind men have no need to walk.

Who is blind? He who can see no other world. Who is dumb? He who can say nothing pleasant about his lot. Who is poor? He who is troubled with too many desires. Who is rich? He who is happy with his lot.

That which blossoms must also decay.

A book is a good friend when it lays bare the errors of the past.

A cat in a cage becomes a lion.

You should not call in a cat to settle the argument of two birds.

He who does not climb, will not fall either.

You may lock up the cock, but the sun will still rise.

A coconut shell full of water is a sea to an ant.

It is only in your coffin that you sleep really well.

A guilty conscience is a lively enemy.

Better cross-eyed than blind.

The crow was killed by the storm—"He died by my curse," says the owl.

There is a great uproar made about the debt of a poor man.

Deceive me about the price but not about the goods.

You must answer the devil in his own language.

Better to have a diamond with a few small flaws than a rock that is perfect.

You may never die before death arrives.

When you are in difficulty, go to the house of your friend—not your sister's.

Every dog is a tiger in his own street.

A dog will not make himself look like a horse just by cutting off his tail.

Be careful for deep water and dogs that do not bark.

The dog's tail, even if buried for twelve years, will remain as crooked as ever.

To give jewels to a donkey is as stupid as giving a eunuch to a woman.

He who dreams for too long will become like his shadow.

Drums sound loud because they are hollow.

Never use a dwarf to measure the depth of the water.

By joining the tail to the trunk one makes up the whole elephant.

The man who has mounted an elephant will not fear the bark of a dog.

The enemy's own punishment is his envy.

It is worse to excuse than to offend.

It's better to pick a fight with your in-laws than with your neighbors.

Fish and guests smell when they are three days old.

In the end, all foxes meet at the furrier's.

It is a greater gift to give than to receive.

God laughs when you steal from a thief.

First God, then the white man.

Goodness reaches further than badness.

He who is a guest in two houses, starves.

True happiness lies in giving it to others.

The hare that escaped had eight legs.

One man's house burns so that another may warm himself.

A house without children is a graveyard.

Only the hunchback himself knows how he can lie comfortably.

Hunger drives good taste away.

Hypocrisy is a homage that vice pays to virtue.

Better than the ignorant are those who read books; better still are those who retain what they read; even better are those who understand it; the best of all are those who go to work.

Never stand in front of a judge or behind a donkey.

It is easy to forget a kindness, but one remembers unkindness.

A lawyer's fee and a harlot's wages are paid in advance.

The hands of a lawyer are always in someone's pocket.

The lawyer's pouch is a mouth of Hell.

Learning is a treasure no thief can touch.

Better lie than gossip.

To loan is to buy troubles.

To long for everything: sorrow; to accept everything: joy.

Without love everything is in vain.

He who loves drives a nail into his heart.

Love from someone who is bad is worse than his hatred.

It is love that makes the impossible possible.

In love beggar and king are equal.

Luck is infatuated with the efficient.

Man is like a bubble of water on the ocean.

Man loves his own mistakes.

A man without a woman is only half a man.

Without men in the neighborhood all the women are chaste.

Money is the best servant.

When money is not a servant it is a master.

The money you dream about will not pay your bills.

Money hides in the tiger's ear.

A man without money is like a bow without arrows.

Where the needle goes, the thread follows.

Only the nightingale understands the rose.

The pain is sometimes preferable to the treatment.

Patience is the most beautiful prayer.

A pearl is worthless as long as it is still in its shell.

Good people, like clouds, receive only to give away.

A person who misses a chance and the monkey who misses its branch—both cannot be saved.

If you are up to your knees in pleasure, then you are up to your waist in grief.

Don't poison someone whom you can kill with sweets.

The voice of the poor has no echo.

Poverty destroys all virtues.

Poverty makes thieves, like love makes poets.

The worst kind of poverty is to have many debts.

Worldly prosperity is like writing on water.

Follow the river and you will get to the sea.

If you live on the river, befriend the crocodile.

The sandal tree perfumes the axe that fells it.

There are many people who can sing, but don't know the words.

Rather be a slave to a rich man than the spouse of a poor man.

Smiles that you broadcast, will always come back to you.

Though the snake be small, it is still wise to hit it with a big stick.

The soldier's wife is always a widow.

A spoiled son becomes a gambler, while a spoiled daughter becomes a harlot.

For the first five years of your son's life treat him as a prince, for the next ten years as a slave, then as a friend for the rest of his life.

What is sport to the boy is the death of the bird.

The spouse of a woman is a man, the spouse of a man is his livelihood.

I gave him a staff for his support and he uses it to break my head.

Stolen sugar is the sweetest.

If you throw a handful of stones, one at least will hit.

You do not stumble over a mountain, but you do over a stone.

Theologians, dogs, and singers always disagree.

A thief is a thief, whether he steals a diamond or a cucumber.

The thief that is not caught is a king.

In a tree that you can't climb, there are always a thousand fruits.

Turkeys, parrots, and hares don't know what gratitude is.

There are only two things from which to choose: profit or loss.

Only two things matter in this world: a son and a daughter.

There are three uncertainties: woman, wind, and wealth.

In a deserted village the jackass is king.

War is to a man what bed is to a woman.

All the water in the sea doesn't even reach the knees of the man who fears not death.

When a woman laughs an experienced man will know how much it will cost him.

A beautiful woman belongs to everyone; an ugly one is yours alone.

A house without a woman is the devil's own lodging.

Where there is a glut of words, there is a dearth of intelligence.

Friendly words are convincing.

He who works as a slave, eats as a king.

One man's beard is burning, and another warms his hands by it.

Not all the buds on a bush will blossom.

If not today—when?

Have faith—God calls forth life even from eggs.

A harvest of peace grows from seeds of contentment.

What good is giving sugar to the dead?

It is hard for an ex-king to become a night watchman.

Life is like the flame of a lamp; it needs a little oil now and then.

Do what the mullah says, but don't do what he does.

One and one sometimes make eleven.

It's easy to throw something into the river but hard to get it out again.

No strength within, no respect without.

Where the sun shines, there is also shade.

One person can burn water, while another can't even burn oil.

A doctor is only a doctor when he has killed one or two patients.

Your own wealth is flowers and wine; the other man's is but weeds.

Justice is better than admiration

If you are going to kill, then kill an elephant; if you are going to steal make sure it's a treasure.

He who wants fruit should not pick flowers.

A rap on the ringed finger does not hurt.

A fight in your neighbor's house is refreshing.

To the world wisdom is folly; to the wise the world is foolish.

Abstinence is the best medicine.

When you drink milk under the palm tree, people will say that it is palm wine.

Garlic is as good as ten mothers.

If a man from humble beginnings gets rich, he will carry his umbrella at midnight.

Undeserved punishment is better than that which is deserved.

He who has a true friend, has no need of a mirror.

Indonesia

Different fields, different grasshoppers; different seas, different fish.

Nothing is difficult if you're used to it.

The name of Love's fiancée is Divorce.

Beware, the enemy lies under your blanket.

People seek out big shots as flies seek out the elephant's tail.

Once the rice is pudding, it's too late to reclaim the rice.

If you go into a goat stable, bleat; if you go into a water buffalo stable, bellow.

The sea becomes the shore, the shore becomes the sea.

The shadow should be the same length as the body.

The firm tree does not fear the storm.

Death is the bride of life.

When you begin to understand the situation, you know you must have been ill-informed.

A moth will eat the finest linen.

Calm water does not mean there are no crocodiles.

A fire will sear and the sun burn yet more, but neither can match the ardor of a man's heart.

Don't stay on the dew until the sun reaches its highest.

There are not many who would announce their faults with a gong.

A man finds what he takes to be small; it will only be big again when he loses it.

The laughter of someone pining for his beloved is like that of someone who is always crying.

Before you let your voice be heard, first lick your lips.

If an eel is with fish, he shows his tail; if he is with snakes, he shows his head.

They are flies that are born of a wasp.

Goodness shouts. Evil whispers.

Iran

Acquaintance without patience is like a candle with no light.

I gave so much advice that hair grew on my tongue.

Listening to good advice is the way to wealth.

Giving advice to the ignorant is like the rain falling on muddy ground.

He is still alive because he cannot afford a funeral.

To the ant, a few drops of dew is a flood.

For an ant to have wings would be his undoing.

You cannot applaud with one hand.

Arabic is a language, Persian is a delicacy and Turkish is an art.

The arrow that has left the bow never returns.

An arrow can be pulled out of a wound, but a hurtful word stays forever in your heart.

Who sows barley cannot reap wheat.

A beggar will always be a beggar even if they give him the whole world as a gift.

Beware a rickety wall, a savage dog, and a quarrelsome person.

A blind man who sees is better than a sighted man who is blind.

If you enter the city of the blind, cover your eyes.

Thick body, weak soul.

Sometimes the body becomes healthy by being very sick.

The branch that bears the most fruit bends itself thankfully towards the ground.

Bravery without foresight is like a blind horse.

Make bread while the oven is hot.

Bribery makes both parties happy.

The bride who wears four petticoats has a lot to hide.

Where the camel is sold for a cent, the ass is worthless.

A camel does not drink with a spoon.

When the cat and the mouse agree, the grocer is ruined.

"That smells bad," said the cat about meat that it cannot reach.

Do not let the cat watch over the bacon.

Whoever has no children has no light in his eyes.

A child is a bridge to heaven.

As long as the clouds don't weep, the pasture cannot laugh.

If there are two cooks in one house, the soup is either too salty or too cold.

Credit is better than wealth.

The cripple will always find a stone to kick.

Iran

When I am dead the world can be an ocean or a dried up ditch.

You can't escape death and guests.

Debts are like women, once you have them you can't get rid of them.

In the hotel of decisions the guests sleep well.

There are three things that have to be done quickly: burying the dead, opening the door for a stranger, and fixing your daughter's wedding.

The dog is a lion in his own house.

For his master the dog is a lion.

A dog by your side is better than a brother miles away.

Never open a door that you can't lock again.

Doubt is the key to knowledge.

The drowning man is not troubled by rain.

The big drum only sounds well from a distance.

With one ear he hears, and with the other he dismisses.

The earth is a host who kills his guests.

He who eats alone is Satan's brother.

I eat what others have planted and I plant what others want to eat.

Whatever you eat will rot, whatever you give will blossom into a rose.

He who has only one enemy, meets him everywhere.

I have no right to rejoice at the death of my enemy when I do not have eternal life myself.

It is a real compliment that comes from an enemy.

There are three kinds of enemy: the enemy himself, the friends of your enemy, and the enemies of your friends.

Use your enemy's hand to catch a snake.

While yearning for excess we lose the necessities.

The eyes can do a thousand things that the fingers can't.

The loveliest of faces are to be seen by moonlight, when one sees half with the eye and half with the fancy.

If you fall into a pit, Providence is under no obligation to come and look for you.

When fate strikes physicians are useless.

You only appreciate your father the day you become a father yourself.

Every fault that a Sultan pleases can be a quality.

There are four things in this life of which we have more than we think: faults, debts, years and enemies.

Fear those who do not fear God.

The pleasure of finding something is worth more than what you find.

There is no need for fish in an empty pond.

It's better to fly and stay alive than to die a hero.

Flies will never leave the shop of a sweetmaker.

Flies will easily fly into the honey—their problem is how to get out.

The fool's excuse is bigger than the mistake he made.

If a fool borrows a book cut off his hand; but cut off both hands of the fool who brings it back.

Forgiveness hides a pleasure that you can't get back from revenge.

When fortune turns against you, even jelly breaks your teeth.

A friend is a poem.

I can only get better if I have good friends.

In this world generous people have no money and those with money are not generous.

A gentle hand may lead even an elephant by a single hair.

The hand that gives is also the one that receives.

God gives to us according to the measure of our hearts.

God provides, but he needs a nudge.

Gold bears more gold. The lack of gold only a headache.

Our real grave is not in the ground but in men's hearts.

A greedy man is always poor.

The guard's sleep is the lamplight of the thief.

Woe is he who claims to have found happiness.

Iran

You cannot pick the fruit of happiness from the tree of injustice.

At harvest time the gardener is deaf.

The bigger a man's head, the worse his headache.

Not every head deserves a crown.

Where the heart is, there is happiness.

Only a heart can find the way to another heart.

A broken hand works, but not a broken heart.

The hearth is winter's bed of tulips.

The fatter the hen the smaller is the hole to lay eggs.

Don't count the teeth of a horse that was given to you.

How a house is decorated will tell us about the owner.

The owner has one house; the tenant has a thousand.

"If" married "But" and their child was called "Maybe."

Ignorance is death, science is life.

As the ignorant keep on talking, the wise man arrives at a conclusion.

Inebriation enhances the truth.

Injustice all around is justice.

The frightened jackal will never eat good grapes.

The jealous eye will uncover hidden faults.

To describe your joy is half the pleasure of it.

A judge who is on your side is worth more than a hundred witnesses.

If the king says at midday that it is night, look up at the stars.

Nobody knows me better than I do myself.

The tree of laziness produces hunger.

A letter is half a visit.

Liars are forgetful.

Lies will blossom but never bear fruit.

The lie's lantern will shed no light.

Life is a dream from which death wakes us up.

Life is like perpetual drunkenness, the pleasure passes but the headache remains.

When a lion is old, he becomes the plaything of jackals.

He whose heart is aroused by love will never die.

Don't just take love, experience it.

It is not from the love of God that the cat catches mice.

The lover who gives you her body but not her heart is generous with thornless roses.

Go and wake up your luck.

Not everyone who sings a lullaby stays awake.

A man's servant can live for a hundred years; the slave of a woman dies in six months.

As soon as a man gets new trousers, he thinks about a new wife.

A man without a child is a king without sorrows.

Every man is the king of his own beard.

A man without passion is no son of Adam.

It takes two days to learn everything about a man; to know animals you will need more time.

Learn good manners from those who don't have them.

Maturity comes from wisdom not in the passing of years.

The tears of the roasting meat kindle the fire even more.

The mediator in a fight gets all the blows.

A mirror does not reflect a broken heart.

You can close the city gates but not the mouths of men.

The mud that you throw will fall on your own head.

You cannot hang everything on one nail.

Necessity changes a lion into a fox.

Great needs grow from great possessions.

The needle makes clothes but stays naked.

In your neighbors' soup there is always one fatty morsel.

He who sits waiting for his neighbor will go to bed hungry.

Night hides a world but reveals a universe.

If you want to be with Noah, don't be afraid of floods.

Taking pity on a bloodthirsty panther does a great injustice to the sheep.

Have patience, everything is difficult before it gets easy.

Persians think that hen eggs are laid by a swan.

Persian was the language of love spoken by Adam and Eve, but the angel that took them away from Paradise spoke Turkish.

One place is everywhere, everywhere is nowhere.

Why use poison if you can kill with honey?

Politeness is like a coin—giving it away makes the receiver rich.

The wisdom of the poor is as good as a palace in the desert.

The poor always pay double.

The poor man's lantern sheds no light.

The power of the stream comes from the source.

No matter how you practice you can never make a nightingale from an owl.

He who hankers after praise should move on.

Too much praise is worse than an insult.

If the prince picks fruit the slave tears up the tree.

A well made remark gets no answer.

A rich man can't afford revolutions.

Riddles already solved look easy.

The larger a man's roof, the more snow it collects.

Rose water is not for the backs of old folk, but for the breasts of young lovers.

There is no saint without a past and no sinner without a future.

The secret that you keep is your slave. But you are the slave of the secret that you let out.

Who seeks finds? No, who finds seeks.

I complained because I had no shoes, until I met a man with no feet.

The shoemaker's shoes have no heels.

One sin is too much, a hundred prayers are not enough.

To sin in secret is more pleasant than having pleasure in the open.

If you really have to sin, then choose a sin that you enjoy.

The sky is the same color wherever you go.

A snake can change its skin but not its disposition.

When the snake is old, the frog will tease him.

An ungrateful son is a wart on his father's nose—he leaves it, it's ugly, he removes it, it hurts.

He that sows shall also reap.

One spark is enough to burn a hundred worlds.

The public improves the speaker's speech.

The halfwit spoke, and the brainless believed.

Everyone thinks his own spit tastes good.

When a stone hits glass, the glass breaks. When glass hits a stone, the glass breaks.

If the Sultan demands five eggs, let his soldiers roast a thousand chickens.

Treat your superior as a father, your equal as a brother, and your inferior as a son.

A sword in the hands of a drunken slave is less dangerous than science in the hands of the unscrupulous.

Who has not had a taste longs to do so, but for whom has tasted then the longing is a hundred times more.

The strictness of the teacher is better to bear than the prejudice of the father.

Every tear has a smile behind it.

A tear at the right moment is better than a misplaced smile.

A thief is a king until he is caught.

What the thief stole has always been called expensive.

Who has ever seen tomorrow?

The tongue of men is the whip of God.

A sharp tongue will cut off its own head.

If you tell the truth too early, you are laughed at—too late and you are stoned.

The virtuous will be praised but not envied.

The walls have mice, the mice have ears.

Four walls make a man free.

He who doesn't go to war roars like a lion.

Whoever can walk on water is probably made of straw.

One sip of wine is an antidote against death, cupfuls poison life.

In winter a fire is better than a muscat blossom.

It is a wise man who can laugh at his own jokes.

The wise man who does not put his knowledge into practice is like a bee that gives no honey.

As the wise man looks for a bridge the fool crosses the river.

A wolf's repentance died a long time ago.

Expect trust from a dog but not from a woman.

Women are just like cats—they always land on their feet.

A coquettish woman is like a shadow—as you chase her she runs away, and if you run away, she chases after you.

You don't put a wooden pot on the fire twice.

Little by little the wool becomes a carpet.

Do not use words that are too big for your mouth.

Work is twice done by the man in a hurry.

The world is a rose; smell it and pass it on to your friends.

If you can give me no ointment for my wound, can you help me by not rubbing salt in?

Iraq

A beautiful bride needs no dowry.

Tell me who your friends are, and I'll tell you who you are.

One night of anarchy does more harm than a hundred years of tyranny.

Whoever writes a book, should be ready to accept criticism.

Stealing leads to poverty.

Sometimes you have to sacrifice your beard in order to save your head.

The poor are the silent of the land.

The day will wipe out all the promises of the night.

Ireland

Age is honorable and youth is noble.

This is better than the thing we never had.

The man with the boots does not mind where he places his foot.

It takes time to build castles.

What the child sees, the child does. What the child does, the child is.

The raggy colt often made a powerful horse.

The covetous person is always in want.

It is often that a cow does not take after its breed.

The day will come when the cow will have use for her tail.

If you hit my dog you hit myself.

A drink precedes a story.

Good as drink is, it ends in thirst.

It is sweet to drink but bitter to pay for.

When the drop is inside the sense is outside.

Falling is easier than rising.

The well fed does not understand the lean.

When fire is applied to a stone it cracks.

There is no fireside like your own fireside.

It is not a fish until it is on the bank.

A friend's eye is a good mirror.

Both your friend and your enemy think you will never die.

The full person does not understand the needs of the hungry.

May you have a bright future—as the chimney sweep said to his son.

When the goat goes to church, he does not stop till he gets to the altar.

Put silk on a goat, and it's still a goat.

God likes help when helping people.

God often pays debts without money.

The mills of God grind slowly but they grind finely.

God's help is nearer than the door.

Good luck comes in slender currents, misfortune in a rolling tide.

You've got to do your own growing, no matter how tall your grandfather was.

A person's heart is in his feet.

The light heart lives long.

It is a bad hen that does not scratch herself.

A hen is heavy when carried far.

The hole is more honorable than the patch.

Though honey is sweet, don't lick it off a briar.

It is the good horse that draws its own cart.

As the big hound is, so will the pup be.

A hound's food is in its legs.

Instinct is stronger than upbringing.

It is better to exist unknown to the law.

When the liquor was gone the fun was gone.

You must live with a person to know a person. If you want to know me come and live with me.

A loan long continued usually confers ownership.

A lock is better than suspicion.

There is no luck except where there is discipline.

If you want to be criticized, marry.

Money swore an oath that nobody that did not love it should ever have it.

The person who doesn't scatter the morning dew will not comb grey hairs.

Need teaches a plan.

There is no need like the lack of a friend.

Patience is poultice for all wounds.

People live in each other's shelter.

It is the quiet pigs that eat the meal.

One may live without one's friends but not without one's pipe.

A poor person is often worthy.

Quiet people are well able to look after themselves.

Lack of resource has hanged many a person.

When you are right no one remembers; when you are wrong no one forgets.

He who gets a name for early rising can stay in bed until midday.

Listen to the sound of the river and you will get a trout.

It is a long road that has no turning.

You are not a fully fledged sailor unless you have sailed under full sail, and you have not built a wall unless you have rounded a corner.

It is not a secret if it is known by three people.

Two thirds of the work is the semblance.

Three diseases without shame: love, itch, and thirst.

The wearer best knows where the shoe pinches.

A silent mouth is musical.

The smallest thing outlives the human being.

If you do not sow in the spring you will not reap in the autumn.

He who comes with a story to you brings two away from you.

There is no strength without unity.

Thirst is the end of drinking and sorrow is the end of drunkenness.

Even a small thorn causes festering.

Time is a great story teller.

A trade not properly learned is an enemy.

When a twig grows hard it is difficult to twist it. Every beginning is weak.

Two shorten the road.

It's not a matter of upper and lower class but of being up awhile and down awhile.

Walk straight, my son—as the old crab said to the young crab.

Wine divulges truth.

A barrel that contains the wine will retain the drop in its staves.

Women do not drink liquor, but it disappears when they are present.

Mere words do not feed the friars.

The work praises the man.

The world would not make a racehorse of a donkey.

Praise the young and they will blossom.

Youth sheds many a skin. The steed does not retain its speed forever.

Youth does not mind where it sets its foot.

Islamic Proverbs

If I had two loaves of bread, I would sell one and buy hyacinths, for they would feed my soul.

When God wishes a man well, He gives him insight into his faults.

Good deeds banish bad ones.

Light your lamp first at home and afterwards at the mosque.

If you hear that a mountain has moved, believe; but if you hear that a man has changed his character, believe it not.

A kind speech and forgiveness is better than alms followed by injury.

Allah does not love the aggressors.

A hand that has been chopped off cannot steal any more.

Man was created in a hurry.

Israel

Most people forget everything except being ungrateful.
Lies are accepted once, not twice.
The ink of a scholar is worth as much as the martyr's blood.
Silence is a brother of delight.
When your enemies attack, bathe in their blood.

Israel

Do not try to make yourself so big, you are not so small.
You can't force anyone to love you or to lend you money.
Love is a sweet dream, and marriage is the alarm clock.
Better an honest smack in the face than a false kiss.
Never kiss an ugly girl; she will tell everyone.
Poverty is no shame—but is no great honor either.
He who has no hand cannot clench his fist.
The worst life is better than the best death.

Italy

A small woman always seems newly married.
A donkey cannot trot for long.
The scent of every flower is short lived.
The cheat always lies at the feet of the cheated.
By asking the impossible you will get the best.
It is the small expenses that empty your purse.
As the snow melts the filth shows through.
Absence is the enemy of love.
Adam must have an Eve to blame for his faults.
Write down the advice of him who loves you, though you like it not
    at present.
The best advice one can give to the hungry is bread.

It is not enough to aim; you must hit.

One would not be alone even in Paradise.

It is a good answer which knows when to stop.

A good anvil fears no hammer.

The anvil lasts longer than the hammer.

The best armor is to keep out of range.

Under white ashes there is glowing coal.

A rakish bachelor makes a jealous husband.

He is a sorry barber who has but one comb.

What worth has beauty if it is not seen?

She who is born a beauty is born betrothed.

Bed is the poor man's opera.

He who begins many things finishes but few.

It is not for the blind to give an opinion on colors.

Half a brain is enough for him who says little.

Many are brave when the enemy flees.

A new broom is good for three days.

He who builds by the roadside has many surveyors.

A burden that one chooses is not felt.

All is not butter that comes from the cow.

The buyer needs a hundred eyes, the seller not one.

Applaud the man who cheats a cheater.

The comforter's head never aches.

Good company on the road is the shortest of short cuts.

It is better to be condemned by many doctors than by one judge.

Conscience is as good as a thousand witnesses.

Give neither counsel nor salt till you are asked for it.

Who has no courage must have legs.

One with the courage to laugh is master of the world almost as much
as the one who is ready to die.

Italy

Between two cowards, the first to detect the other has the advantage.

When the danger has passed, the saints are soon forgotten.

When I'm dead, everybody's dead—and the pig too.

Every door may be shut but death's door.

If you are determined—just do it!

He that is afraid of the devil does not grow rich.

One devil does not make hell.

Speak of the devil and he appears.

Of three things the devil makes a salad: lawyers' tongues, notaries' fingers, and a third that shall be nameless.

The dying cannot leave their wisdom or experience to their heirs.

Diseases are the visits of God.

A doctor and a clown know more than a doctor alone.

Every dog is a lion at home.

Where there are no hounds the fox is king.

Those who sleep with dogs will rise with fleas.

Drink water like an ox, wine like the king of Spain.

The eagle does not wage war against frogs.

Six feet of earth make us all equal.

Out of a white egg often comes a black chick.

Break the legs of an evil custom.

Every excuse is good, if it works.

The eye is blind if the mind is absent.

Have an open face, but conceal your thoughts.

Failures are but mileposts on the road to success.

A favor to come is better than a hundred received.

Short is the road that leads from fear to hatred.

The feast passes and the fool remains.

Feather by feather the goose is plucked.

The fish rots from the head.

Don't even take a bath with fools, because they'll throw away the soap.

Fools grow without watering.

Only a fool asks, "What do you want with my wife?"

Even the fool says a wise word sometimes.

Foolish boys, wise men.

There's no fool like a learned fool.

A fool's spark glows in all men.

Let every fox take care of his own tail.

Give your friend a pig and your enemy a peach.

To preserve friendship, one must build walls.

God keep me from my friends; from my enemies I will keep myself.

Old friends are always new.

Better one true friend than a hundred relatives.

Trust not the praise of a friend nor the contempt of an enemy.

Even a frog would bite if it had teeth.

Where there is nothing to gain, there is a lot to lose.

Once the game is over, the king and the pawn go back into the same box.

It is a bad game where nobody wins.

Gold is the devil's fishhook.

A golden cage does not feed the bird.

Good is good, but better beats it.

Everything is good for something.

One may have good eyes and see nothing.

If it rained macaroni, what a fine time for gluttons!

Happiness that lasts too long spoils the heart.

He who has, is.

He who has nothing, lacks nothing.

He who does as he likes has no headache.

He who enjoys good health is rich, though he knows it not.

The smaller the heart, the longer the tongue.

Make yourself all honey and the flies will devour you.

Since the house is on fire let us warm ourselves.

He who is not impatient is not in love.

By asking for the impossible, obtain the best possible.

The remedy for injuries is not to remember them.

He who is born with a weak intellect and a goiter can never be cured.

The joker confesses.

Everyone loves justice in the affairs of another.

A kiss without a moustache is like beef without mustard.

To know everything is to know nothing.

He who knows little quickly tells it.

He who knows nothing doubts nothing.

He who laughs too much, is hiding his grief.

No sooner is a law made than a way around it is discovered.

No good lawyer ever goes to court himself.

Beware of him who has nothing to lose.

If you want to buy love, love itself is the price you'll have to pay.

Love rules without rules.

Love kills time and time kills love.

Lovers' purses are tied with cobwebs.

When ill luck falls asleep, let none wake her.

To be lucky you need a little wit.

Men are as old as they feel, women as old as they look.

Go early to market and as late as you can to battle.

Be sure before you marry of a house wherein to tarry.

God sends us the meat, but it is the Devil who sends us cooks.

Mills and wives are ever wanting.

Never point out the mistakes of another with a dirty finger.

If you throw money away with your hands, you'll look for it later with your feet.

Who would make money must begin by spending it.

Public money is like holy water, everyone helps himself to it.

Mother-in-law and daughter-in-law, storm and hail.

Big mouthfuls often choke.

You cannot make the mule drink when he is not thirsty.

A mule that thinks he is a stag discovers his mistake when he comes to leap over the ditch.

Does your neighbor bore you? Lend him some money.

God save me from a bad neighbor and a beginner on the fiddle.

Who offends writes on sand, who is offended on marble.

Nothing improves the taste of pasta more than a good appetite.

The salt of patience seasons everything.

He who has no patience, has nothing at all.

A pear will never fall into a closed mouth.

The end of the pig is the beginning of the sausage.

It's a bad plan that cannot be changed.

What does not poison, fattens.

The poorhouse is filled with honest people.

He who has the Pope for a cousin soon becomes a Cardinal.

Three are powerful: the Pope, the king, and the man who has nothing.

The best way to get praise is to die.

Those who don't understand prayer—let them go to sea.

If pride were a disease, how many would be already dead?

The priest's friend loses his faith, the doctor's his health, and the lawyer's his fortune.

Too much prosperity makes most men fools.

He who serves the public has a sorry master.

Who serves the public, serves no one.

Never let people see the bottom of your purse or of your mind.

Who seeks a quarrel will find it near at hand.

A hundred-year-old revenge still has its baby teeth.

If you would be rich in a year, you may be hanged in six months.

I may have lost the ring, but I still have the fingers!

There is no worse robber than a bad book.

Beat the rogue and he will be your friend.

With so many roosters crowing, the sun never comes up.

Who will not be ruled by the rudder must be ruled by the rock.

All are not saints who go to church.

What shall I say when it is better to say nothing?

There is a deep sea between saying and doing.

"They say so," is half a lie.

It is better if you could say "Here he ran away" than "Here he was killed."

It's a foolish sheep that makes the wolf its confessor.

When the ship has sunk everyone knows how she might have been saved.

It is better to wear out one's shoes than one's sheets.

It is the first shower that wets.

You cannot write down a meaningful silence.

A hidden sin is half forgiven.

It may be quieter to sleep alone, but not warmer.

The smoke of my own house is better than another man's fire.

He is a friend when you sneeze—all he says is "God bless you."

One who speaks fair words feeds you with an empty spoon.

If you would succeed, you must not be too good.

Do not sell sun in July.

When the sun is highest it casts the least shadow.

Who depends on another man's table often dines late.

Nothing dries faster than tears.

He wastes his tears who weeps before the judge.

If you scatter thorns, don't go barefoot.

The second thought is always the best.

When it thunders the thief becomes honest.

Let not your tongue say what your head may pay for.

Teeth placed in front of the tongue give good advice.

Translators, traitors.

When the tree is down, everyone runs to it with a hatchet to cut wood.

A little truth helps the lie go down.

Vices are learned without a master.

Virginity is noted only in its absence.

Virtue comes not from chance but long study.

To a weaving that has begun, God sends threads.

You must marry a widow while she is still mourning.

With the first wife is matrimony, the second company, the third heresy.

One should learn to sail in all winds.

A cask of wine works more miracles than a church full of saints.

When wine comes in, modesty leaves.

A meal without wine is like a day without sunshine.

That which the wise man does first, the fool does last.

No woman ever speaks the naked truth.

He who takes a woman gives away his freedom.

No wonder lasts more than three days.

Better to lose the wool than the sheep.

Years and sins are always more than admitted.

"Yes" and "no" govern the world.

If you want the daughter, you must kiss the mother.

Who suffers from love, feels no pain.

You don't go to heaven in a carriage.

The purse of loved ones is tied with a gossamer thread.

He who goes not into battle cannot wear a crown.

Tenderness can be a bad judge.

Better a living donkey than a dead doctor.

The donkey won't drink if he can't see water.

It is easy to frighten the bull from the window.

The river does not swell with clear water.

If you have a good cellar at home don't go drinking at the tavern.

Old saints don't get incense anymore.

Love begins with song and music and ends in a sea of tears.

He who never begins will never end.

Bitter fruit will fall before the ripe.

Whoever stays awake longest must blow out the candle.

Ivory Coast

Mutual affection is when each gives his share.

Too much discussion will lead to a row.

Two flavors confuse the palate.

Everybody loves a fool, but nobody wants him for a son.

Mutual gifts cement friendship.

Ingratitude is sooner or later fatal to its author.

Their mosquito won't bite me.

A bad son gives his mother a bad name.

He who gives a monkey as a present doesn't keep hold of its tail.

A poor man's sheep will never get fat.

In the village that you don't know, the chickens have teeth.

Taking aim for too long can ruin your eyes.

In the villages where there are no oxen, the sheep's feet seem strong.

The panther and the sheep never hunt together.

He who cannot sleep can still dream.

He who talks incessantly, talks nonsense.

The twig that falls in the water will never become a fish.

If you are not going to bite, don't show your teeth.

Teeth will never quarrel with the tongue.

The stranger has big eyes but he doesn't see anything.

A friend will wipe away sweat but not blood.

Better a bad wife than an empty house.

Taking water from the same well doesn't make all the wives' gravy taste good.

Jamaica

A little axe can cut down a big tree.

Barking saves biting.

Going to bed without dinner is better than waking up in debt.

When you buy beef, you buy bones; when you buy land, you buy rocks.

You can stop a bird from flying over you, but you can't stop it building a nest.

The black man steals just half of very little, but the white man steals the whole sugar plantation.

The nearer the bone, the sweeter the meat.

Bushes have ears, walls have eyes.

If chickens were judges, cockroaches would be sentenced.

Clothes cover up character.

You will often see a high collar above an empty stomach.

A good conscience is better than a big wage.

Cows do not indulge in horseplay.

Those who can't dance blame it on the music.

An old debt is better than an old grudge.

Eat with the devil but give him a long spoon.

Pay the doctor, praise the Lord.

Every dog knows his dinnertime.

When a dog has money, he buys cheese.

Behind the dog it is "dog," in front of it, it's "mister dog."

You cannot tie up a dog with a chain of sausages.

When you go to a donkey's house, don't talk about ears.

Not everything that is good to eat is good to talk about.

You can't have two faces under one hat.

When you point your finger at someone, look where the other fingers point.

If a flea had money, it would buy its own dog.

If you follow a fool, you're a fool yourself.

Tired feet always say that the path is long.

The hungry fowl wakes early.

Make a friend when you don't need one.

If you want to know who your friends are, lie by the roadside and pretend to be drunk.

When your own funeral is approaching, you don't pick and choose your grave diggers.

You shake a man's hand, you don't shake his heart.

Not everything you hear is good for conversation.

If "How are you?" cost a cent, few would hear it.

Too much hurry, and get there tomorrow; take time, get there today.

That which you do not know is older than you.

When the affected lady is doing well she eats her peas with a pin.

A lawyer looks at you with one eye, but he looks at your pocket with two.

Marriage has teeth and it bites hard.

Keep both eyes open before you are married and afterwards close only one.

Japan

Meat that the cat brings in never gets to your plate.
You can't take the milk back from the coffee.
Save money and money will save you.
A little pepper burns a big man's mouth.
Empty pots will never boil over.
Prayer only from the mouth is no prayer.
You can say anything to a man with a full stomach.
Sleep has no master.
The soldiers' blood, the general's reputation.
The spider and the fly can't make a deal.
If you don't take it, you don't have it.
Today can't catch tomorrow.
A man with trousers that are too short should wear long suspenders.
Sleepy turtles never catch up with the sunrise.
The umbrella was made for rainy days, the white man uses it for the sun.
Virtue never goes far without the company of idleness.
Beautiful woman, beautiful trouble.
Scratch an old woman's back and she will let you taste her pepper pot.
Words die and men keep on living.

Japan

Abuse often starts with praise.
The acolyte at the gate reads scriptures he has never learned.
Advertising is the mother of trade.
An ant's nest could bring down a hill.
Apple blossoms are beautiful, but rice dumplings are better.
A single arrow is easily broken; a quiver of ten is not.
To ask is a temporary shame; not to ask, an eternal one.

"It's awful, I hate it" is hardly the other side of "That is beautiful and I loved it."

Better than a banquet somewhere else is a good cup of tea and a bowl of rice at home.

A bath refreshes the body, tea refreshes the mind.

Beginning is easy—to keep going is hard.

If the skin of your belly is tight, the skin of your eyelids can sleep.

If the bird hadn't sung, it wouldn't have been shot.

The caged bird dreams of clouds.

Though the blind man cannot see it, light remains light.

A fallen blossom never returns to the branch.

Boasting begins where wisdom stops.

If you are in a boat you are more afraid of fire than you are of water.

A boat that is not tied up will drift along with the stream.

Too many hands will row the boat up a mountain.

Never watch a bonfire wearing a straw coat.

You have to bow a few times before you can stand upright.

He who burns his mouth on the soup will blow on a cold fish dish.

Good luck in business is like the froth on an ox's face.

No one buys what he recommends himself.

He who buys useless things, later sells things that he needs.

Don't take seriously the cat who mourns for a mouse.

A borrowed cat catches no mice.

A good cat does not need a collar of gold.

A centipede, though dead, will not fall.

When the character of a man is not clear to you, look at his friends.

The character of a man lies not in his body but in his soul.

Character can be built on daily routine.

A dead cherry tree will not blossom.

It is better to be the head of a chicken than the rear of an ox.

When you have children yourself, you begin to understand what you owe your parents.

The child who died too soon was always beautiful and intelligent.

Children grow up, with or without parents.

There is no such thing as dirty clothes when it is cold.

Only when the coffin is closed will we see how long lasting is the name.

Cold tea and cold rice are bearable, but cold looks and cold words are not.

How good at combing is the bald priest.

If you have no one else, then confer with your knee.

Once conquered—always a traitor.

The consequence is the reward of the cause.

The crow that mimics a cormorant gets drowned.

Who cares if a crow is male or female?

Cupidity has no peak.

The day you decide to do it is your lucky day.

Day has its eyes, night has its ears.

Each day you can admire the moon, the snow and the flowers.

Once dead the good and the bad are covered by the same moss.

Great deeds come from times of shortage.

He who is dependant on others must make friends with the dog.

He who is desperate will squeeze oil out of a grain of sand.

The devil was good looking at eighteen, and course tea makes a bitter first cup.

You don't have to die: heaven and hell are in this world too.

It is easy to die—the difficulty lies in living.

A dying man discovers the honesty with which he was born.

After three years even a disaster can be good for something.

Victims of the same disease have a lot to talk about.

Disgrace is like the grain of a tree trunk—time makes it bigger instead of erasing it.

Don't tell others to do what you cannot do.

When you do something wholeheartedly, you are not in need of helpers.

Don't call in the doctor after the funeral.

If you turn into a dog, be sure to choose a rich family.

The dog that wags its tail won't be beaten.

The dog called "Sorrow," without eating, will be fat in every house.

First the man takes a drink; then the drink takes a drink; after that the drink takes the man.

Drink and sing: the dark night is ahead of us.

The taste of cold water after drinking, is a pleasure that the teetotaller will never know.

Dumplings are better than flowers.

The path of duty lies in what is near at hand, but men look for it in what is remote.

Pursue your duties and don't let them pursue you.

Eat before falling in love.

Eggs and promises are easily broken.

To endure what is unendurable is true endurance.

He who knows not when he has enough, is poor.

The eye that is still says more than a chattering mouth.

Consider the facts seven times before you suspect someone.

Fall seven times, stand up the eighth.

If you are going to fall it's muddy everywhere.

Every fashion goes out of style.

The goodness of the father reaches higher than a mountain; that of the mother goes deeper than the ocean.

To receive a favor is to sell one's liberty.

Fear blows wind into your sails.

More festive than the feast itself is the day before.

If you are going out for a fight leave your best hat at home.

After the fight both parties give each other a good smack.

When there are two fires in one room, only one will smoke.

A fish gets bigger when it gets away.

Where there is fish, there is water.

Flattery is the best persuader of people.

The most beautiful flowers flourish in the shade.

Many flowers, few fruits.

Yesterday's flowers are today's dreams.

There is no such thing as bad food when you are really hungry.

Even a fool knows the glow of gold.

Fools and scissors require good handling.

Forgiving the unrepentant is like drawing pictures on water.

Fortune will call at the smiling gate.

The fortune-teller never knows his own.

Absent friends get further away every day.

The frog in his pond sneers at the ocean.

You should climb Mount Fujiyama once in your life. Climb it twice
and you're a fool.

When you talk about future happenings the devil starts to laugh.

He who makes the first bad move always loses the game.

If you would shoot a general, shoot his horse first.

Under a powerful general there are no feeble soldiers.

Generals conquer, soldiers are killed.

When a girl in the teahouse smiles at you, look the other way.

God lives in an honest heart.

He who has gold is served by the devil.

What is good is not necessarily beautiful.

You will never learn enough looking for only the good things in life;
you will always be a pupil.

Good things are never cheap.

A wild goose may be worth a hundred pieces of gold, but you first have to spend three pieces of gold to buy an arrow.

When you have a good government the grass will grow over your troubles.

Grief itches but scratching it makes it worse.

Any ground is good enough to be buried in.

The guest who seeks special attention muddies the host's tea.

Happiness rarely keeps company with an empty stomach.

Happiness spring-cleans the heart.

One moment of intense happiness prolongs life by a thousand years.

If you run after two hares, you will catch neither.

If you hate a man, let him live.

A man's heart changes as often as does the autumn sky.

The human heart is neither of stone nor wood.

When the heat has passed, you forget about the shade of trees.

When you reject gifts from heaven you will be rewarded in hell.

You can see heaven through the eye of the needle.

There is no escape from heaven's web.

Even in hell you meet relations.

The hen tells the cock to crow.

A good husband is healthy and absent.

Do not stay too long when the husband is not home.

An idiot is eloquent when he stays silent.

He who admits to his ignorance shows it once only; he who tries to hide it shows it frequently.

It is better to be ignorant than mistaken.

Indifference is a generous kind of intolerance.

He who insults another, digs two graves.

Over-intelligent people can't find friends.

Invalids live the longest.

Japan

A joke is often the hole through which truth whistles.

A journey of a thousand miles starts with one step.

Into the house where joy lives, happiness will gladly come.

One joy can drive away a hundred sorrows.

Never judge things of which you only know the shadow.

A man who always wears his best kimono has no Sunday clothes.

Better to wash an old kimono than borrow a new one.

To know and to act are one and the same.

Time spent laughing is time spent with the gods.

No one was ever hurt by laughter.

Where there is laughter happiness likes to be.

The lawyer will extend the frontiers of a fight.

Lazy people have no spare time.

The lazy one stands up between one armchair and another.

There are no national frontiers to learning.

A lie has no legs but scandalous wings.

It's better to lie a little than to be unhappy.

Life is the source of all things.

Life is a long journey with a heavy bag on its back.

Life? That is a candle in the wind; frost upon a roof; the twitching of the fish in a pan.

Even when months and days are long, life is short.

Plan your life at New Year's eve, your day at dawn.

At the bottom of the lighthouse it is dark.

The sack of longing has no bottom.

When you are looking upwards you see no frontiers.

The lotus flower blooms in the mud.

A man in love mistakes a pimple for a dimple.

He who treads the path of love walks a thousand meters as if it were only one.

If you make love in the shade you get cold.

In the eyes of a lover a pock-marked face is one with pretty dimples.

Two lovers in the rain have no need of an umbrella.

If you are looking for bad luck, you will soon find it.

Man is the instrument of illness.

As soon as a man leaves his house he has seven enemies.

A man of straw is still a man.

Man longs to see that which he is afraid to see.

A powerful man has big ears.

Men and women are never placed too far apart to be near.

There is no coincidence in getting married.

The matchmaker always asks for too much money for his eight hundred lies.

Good medicine often has a bitter taste.

Every meeting is the beginning of a good-bye.

Money grows on the tree of persistence.

Making money is like digging with a needle. Spending it is like pouring water into sand.

Money has no ears but it hears; no legs but it walks.

A monkey makes fun of the red behinds of his fellow monkeys.

The head of a monkey, the headdress of a prince.

When the moon is full, it begins to wane.

The mouth of a man is a terrible opening.

Too much is worse than too little.

The nail that sticks up gets hammered down.

Serve your neighbors as you would be served yourself.

One cannot scoop up the ocean with a sea shell.

When someone offends you, you haven't given him enough love.

Old age cures us of our youth.

There are old men of three years old and children of a hundred.

Old horses don't forget the way.

A man can endure the worst pain—of others.

Japan

Even a sheet of paper has two sides.

The past is the future of the present.

Pears and women are the sweetest in the parts that are heaviest.

If I peddle salt, it rains; if I peddle flour, the wind blows.

The pensioner gets the wages of the death.

A pig used to dirt turns its nose up at rice.

The plagiarist turns the body inside-out and changes the bones.

Thirty-six plans of how to win the battle are not so good as one plan to withdraw from the fight.

Poets know all about famous places without having been there.

Poetry moves heaven and earth.

When you are polite, the others think they are wearing flowers.

Too much politeness is impertinent.

The poor have no time to spare.

Poor men sleep the best.

If one man praises you, a thousand will repeat the praise.

A single prayer moves heaven.

Where profit is, loss is hiding nearby.

Do not prophesy to the man who can see further than you can.

You can't see the whole sky through a bamboo pole.

A proposal without patience breaks its own heart.

The heaviest rains fall on the house that leaks most.

If you believe everything you read, you had better not read.

A good religion does not need miracles.

Never rely on the glory of the morning or the smiles of your mother-in-law.

Sometimes it takes only an hour to get a reputation that lasts for a thousand years.

Growing rice gives you more than poetry will.

He is rich who knows when he has enough.

Deceive the rich and powerful if you will, but don't insult them.

216

He who is always right will never get round the world.

No road is too long in the company of a friend.

The hard road turns the traveller into the same dust that he has to swallow.

Say what you have to say, tomorrow.

If you are going to sit on it for three years, the seat will certainly get warm.

Seeing is poison for the eyes.

He who is too servile ruins his back.

Even thinking about sexual pleasure has its roots in greed.

If you are eager to be in the shadow, leave your axe at home.

He who sits in the shade won't take an axe to the tree.

Don't scratch your shoe when it's your foot that itches.

The prettiest of shoes makes a sorry hat.

You won't get sick if you have plenty of work.

The other side also has another side.

Silence makes irritation grow.

He who talks to a silent listener will soon stand naked.

A silent man is the best one to listen to.

People who are asleep can't fall down.

He who smells does not know it himself.

He who wears a smile instead of worrying is always the strongest.

You can't straighten a snake by putting it in a bamboo cane.

When ten thousand soldiers lie rotting, the general's reputation is enhanced.

If you love your son, make him leave home.

If you love your son, let him travel.

Sorrow is the seed of wealth.

It is useful to first see the spark before the fire.

The sparrow flying behind the hawk thinks the hawk is fleeing.

The inarticulate speak longest.

The speaker may well be a fool but the listener is wise.

The spendthrift beats his money as if it were a carpet.

To the starving man the beauty of Fujiyama has no meaning.

Steal goods and you'll go to prison, steal lands and you are a king.

It is no use cutting a stick when the fight is over.

Even the stone you trip on is part of your destiny.

As soon as stones can swim, leaves will sink.

Stupidity begins with honesty.

If every day was a sunny day, who would not wish for rain?

Suspicion bears dark devils.

Don't take a golden sword to cut a radish.

Great talents mature late.

The fast talker makes mistakes.

Even a thief takes ten years to learn his trade.

If you think about things too long, good thoughts will disappear.

When you are thirsty, it's too late to think of digging the well.

Tigers die and leave their skins; people die and leave their names.

Time waits for no one.

Never admit that there is a tomorrow.

The tongue is more to be feared than the sword.

A three inch tongue—the iron bulwark of politics.

If you are travelling towards the East, you will inevitably move away from the West.

If you carry treasure, don't travel at night.

Large trees are envied by the wind.

If you wish to learn the highest truth, begin with the alphabet.

The turtle underestimates the value of fast feet.

It is precisely the uncertainty of this world that makes life worth living.

Unhappiness can be a bridge to happiness.

The unscrupulous succeed every time.

After three years useless things are useful too.

We learn little from victory, but a great deal from defeat.

After victory, tighten your helmet chord.

Great villainy is often called loyalty.

Virtue is not knowing but doing.

Virtue carries an empty purse.

Hidden virtues ring like a soft bell.

Nothing so visible than what you want to hide.

Vision without action is a daydream. Action without vision is a nightmare.

A gilt-edged visiting card often hides an ugly face.

If you wait long enough, it will be good weather.

Depend on your walking stick, not on other people.

He who wants what God wants of him will lead a free and happy life.

You warm up something for ten days and it goes cold in one.

Water will always take the form of the vase it fills.

Only he who knows his own weaknesses can endure those of others.

Wealth gets in the way of wisdom.

Pick your wife in the kitchen.

Wine is water adulterated by foolish talk.

Only through suffering and sorrow do we acquire the wisdom not found in books.

Wisdom is lost in a fat man's body.

Wisdom and virtue are like the two wheels of a cart.

A beautiful woman is like an axe in one's life.

Because of their figure, vain women stay cold.

Without women there is no day and no night.

A woman has many mouths.

Look for a thrifty woman—even though it may cost you a pair of shoes.

Women's quarrels cause the men's wars.

Unspoken words are the flowers of silence.

Truthful words are seldom pleasant.

The second word makes the fray.

Quiet worms will bore a hole in the wall.

You can worship a sardine's head if you believe in it.

Better to write down something one time than to read something ten times.

Your years will still remain the same whether you laugh or cry.

Kalmyk Proverbs

The swine do not know what heaven is.

Every stick has two ends.

Kanuri Proverbs
(West Africa)

At the bottom of patience there is heaven.

Kenya

Absence makes the heart forget.

Try this bracelet: if it fits you wear it; but if it hurts you, throw it away no matter how much it sparkles.

Once you have been tossed by a buffalo, a black ox looks like a buffalo.

Do not slaughter a calf before its mother's eyes.

It is the duty of children to wait on elders, and not the elders on children.

There is no cure that does not have its price.

He who is unable to dance blames it in the stony yard.

A white dog does not bite another white dog.

One finger alone cannot even kill a louse.

After a foolish deed comes remorse.

Soon found, soon lost.

You may laugh at a friend's roof; don't laugh at his sleeping accommodation.

Nobody walks with another man's gait.

If you receive a gift don't measure it.

What's too hard for a man must be worth looking into.

Affairs of the home should not be discussed in the public square.

Just because he harmed your goat, do not go out and kill his bull.

Hearts do not meet one another like roads.

When you take a knife away from a child, give him a piece of wood instead.

Who does not know one thing knows another.

No attention is paid to him who is always complaining.

At the harvest you know how good the millet is.

There is no phrase that doesn't have a double meaning.

Do not say the first thing that comes to your mind.

Seeing is different from being told.

A slave has no choice.

Sticks in a bundle are unbreakable.

Talking to one another is loving one another.

Thunder is not yet rain.

If a dead tree falls, it carries with it a live one.

Virtue is better than wealth.

A loved one has no pimples.

Never let a hyena know how well you can bite.

Each has his own way of moving.

Don't count what they get—they count what they don't get.

Only scratch where you can reach.

Old age devours your youth.

The water of the river flows on without waiting for the thirsty man.
When the figs are ripe all the birds want to eat.
A flea can trouble a lion more than the lion can harm a flea.
Only believe a woman one day later.

Kikuyu Proverbs
(East Africa)

No one puts his finger back where it was once bitten.
Death makes no appointment.
He who doesn't know the road holds back even the one that does.

Korea

A newborn baby has no fear of tigers.
Tall branches are apt to be broken.
Tap even a stone bridge before crossing.
The bull that is used to the sun shivers by the light of the moon.
Butterflies come to pretty flowers.
The bad calligrapher is choosy about his brushes.
Aim high in your career but stay humble in your heart.
Even children of the same mother look different.
When you have three daughters, you sleep with the door open.
A fish wouldn't get into trouble if it kept its mouth shut.
There is no flower that lasts ten days and no might lasts ten years.
The frog forgets that he was once a tadpole.
Better in the grave than be a slave.
Even honey can taste bitter if it's used as medicine.
A poor old horse will have a worn out tail.
If you kick a stone in anger, you'll hurt your own foot.

A kitchen knife cannot carve its own handle.

The matchmaker gets three cups of wine when he succeeds and three slaps on the cheek when he fails.

Even a monk can't shave his own head.

A sheet of paper is lighter if two of you don't try to carry it.

If a pedestrian sees a horse he will want to ride it.

Carve the peg only after studying the hole.

A physician's neighbor is never a doctor.

A day-old pigeon cannot fly over a mountain pass.

It is a bad plowman that quarrels with his ox.

Put off for one day and ten days will pass by.

No sleep, no dream.

Even the best song becomes tiresome if heard too often.

Give an extra piece of cake to a stepchild.

You cannot strike a face that is smiling.

Do not draw your sword to kill a fly.

The thief hates the moon.

Useful trees are cut down first.

A turtle can only get on it by sticking its neck out.

In the valley where there are no tigers the hare is king.

Virginity can be lost in one night.

If you want a well, only dig in one place.

There is no winter without snow, no spring without sunshine, and no happiness without companions.

Wise men philosophize as the fools live on.

The nicest woman is your own; the nicest harvest is your neighbors.

Woman was born three days earlier than the devil.

Words have no wings but they can fly a thousand miles.

Three years will eradicate even murderous thoughts.

A man's youth will never die, unless he kills himself.

Kurdistan

Search yourself, and you will find Allah.

Do not throw the arrow which will return against you.

If you talk to the blacksmith you'll get hit by sparks.

Not every cloud brings rain.

Those who do not go to war roar like lions.

A threat does not lengthen your sword.

Loneliness is a nest for the thoughts.

With a mule you have a son, with a son-in-law you only have a mule.

With fortune on your side you can sow salt and harvest grass.

Some will enjoy the honey, others will have to put up with the sting.

One sturdy house is worth a hundred in ruins.

The devil will not bother you in a house full of children.

When a bald man dies the mourners give him curly hair as a present.

After dinner a Kuru kills a man or kidnaps a woman.

It is up to the people to feed the dogs; it's up to the Cardias to feed the Turks.

A hundred men can sit together quietly but when two dogs get together there will be a fight.

Any man with two wives becomes a porter.

Better one day a man than ten days a woman.

The man is a river, the woman a lake.

When Madame drops her cup of tea it makes no noise.

A girl without a mother is like a mountain with no paths; a girl without a father is like a mountain with no streams.

He who wants pearls has to dive into the sea.

Only by falling do you learn how to mount a horse.

If God didn't like beautiful women, he wouldn't have made them.

God created women and women created the hearth.

A woman is a fortress, a man her prisoner.

If you cannot build a town, build a heart.

He who loves a woman is a nephew of the sun.

No one says, "My pasture is not sweet."

Your son can be a prince, your daughter will be a mother.

Kyrgyzstan

A dry spoon will tear the mouth.

Only God has no faults, only water is pure.

Better to be the lowest in your own land than a Sultan in a foreign land.

If you are going out to steal, go alone—otherwise there is a witness.

A dirty soul can be cleansed when one speaks.

Laos

If you like to have things easy, you'll have difficulties; if you like problems, you will succeed.

If you must be a servant, serve the rich; if you must be a dog, let it be a temple dog.

Live with vultures, and become a vulture; live with crows, and become a crow.

Listen with one ear; be suspicious with the other.

When you've heard it you must see it; when you've seen it make a judgement with your heart.

Happiness flies away from those who want it most.

The voice of a poor man does not carry very far.

One piece of wood will not make a fire.

Lapland

The memories of one's youth make for long, long thoughts.

Latvia

He who shares the meat is always left with the bone.

Everyone knows the bear, but the bear knows no one.

No one can climb a tree with no branches.

Who stands by the door of his house is not yet gone away.

The cheese betrays the milk.

Don't raise your club so high; it will only fall on your head.

Cowardice will not prolong life.

Freedom does not lengthen life.

The wise man will be cheated only once.

Latvia

Once you've cut the bread, you cannot put it together again.

If you can't use your eyes, follow your nose.

Sleep is the poor man's treasure.

A good backside will easily find a bench to sit on.

Promised berries will not fill the basket.

Even the devil himself does not know where women sharpen their knives.

Let the devil into church and he will climb into the pulpit.

On the hook of truth only small carp will bite; in the net of falsehood the big salmon are caught.

In dense woods the trees grow straight.

Your belly is not a book.

"We have rowed well," said the flea as the fishing boat arrives at its mooring.

A strange glass is emptied in one draught; your own glass not even in ten.

Lebanon

Good advice once was worth a camel; now that it is free of charge, no one takes it.

A cemetery never refuses a corpse.

A clear conscience shines not only in the eyes.

A donkey is a donkey though it may carry the Sultan's treasure.

He who took the donkey up to the roof should bring it down.

Lock your door rather than suspect your neighbor.

Better to have one thousand enemies outside the house than to have one single enemy inside it.

God hears things upside down.

Do good and throw it into the sea—if it is not appreciated by an ungrateful man, it will be appreciated by God.

He who gossips to you will gossip about you.

Two things cannot be hidden: being astride a camel and being pregnant.

He who wants to eat honey should endure the stings.

If you fall in love let her be a beauty; if you should steal, let it be a camel.

He who has money can eat ice cream in hell.

Nights of pleasure are short.

Do today what you want to postpone until tomorrow.

He who slaps himself on the face should not cry ouch.

If a rich man eats a snake people say, "This is wisdom!" If a poor man eats a snake people say, "This is folly!"

The son of an old man is an orphan, and his wife is a widow.

If summer had a mother, she would weep at summer's passing.

Whatever your uncle gives you, take.

A wretched year has twenty-four months.

He who knew you when you were young will not respect you when you grow up.

A polite devil is more agreeable than a rude saint.

You become like that which you own.

A bite from a loving mouth is worth more than a kiss from any other.

If you follow the lead of the cockerel, you'll be led to the poulterer.

A dog will always be a dog, even if he is raised by lions.

If someone puts their trust in you, don't sever it.

If you spit in the face of a coward he'll tell you that it's raining.

A dressed up lie is worth more than a badly told truth.

When you're out of luck in the coffin making business, no one dies.

No matter how fast the poplar grows, it will never reach heaven.

If you beat my drum, I will blow your whistle.

It is easier to be a happy bachelor for a year than a widower for a month.

Some men will build a wine cellar when they have found just one grape.

You cannot cook your eggs with wind.

It's normal for a sieve to have holes in it.

When you come back from a trip bring something for the family—even if it is only a stone.

If you are too sparing with the cat's food, the rats will eat your ears.

Lesotho

Sickness comes with a waning moon; a new moon cures disease.

It is best to bind up the finger before it is cut.

An itching palm is a sign of good luck.

Liberia

Do not eat your chicken and throw its feathers in the front yard.

Don't look where you fell, but where you slipped.

Libya

Though the palm tree in the jungle is big, who knows how big its
    yield will be?
A little rain each day will fill the rivers to overflowing.
When building a house, don't measure the timbers in the forest.
If the townspeople are happy, look for the cook.
Only when the tree is big and strong can you tether a cow to it.
To the patient man will come all the riches of the world.

Libya

If you get mixed with bran you'll soon be pecked by chickens.
All that is round is not a cake.
If everyone thought alike, no goods would ever be sold.
If your pocket gets empty, your faults will be many.
Every raisin contains a pip.
Stretch your legs according to the length of your bedspread.

Lithuania

The breath of others always stinks.
If it weren't for sorrow and bad times, every day would be Christmas.
Fear and love do not go together.
Who gives, has.
God gave teeth; He will give bread.
To be without learning, is to be without eyes.
Offer the lazy man an egg, and he'll want you to peel it for him.
To a starving man bread is sweeter than honey.
It is easier to give orders than to work.
The older the goat the tighter the rope.
Don't laugh when your neighbors oven is on fire.
There is an herb for every kind of sickness but not for death.

Even the smallest drop is appreciated by the drunkard.

There is no worse devil than a farmer who wants to be a gentleman.

As one devil goes out, another one comes in.

Without gold even the daylight is dark.

Not all that glitters is gold; not all that is sticky is tar.

Gold glitters even in the mud.

Dogs cannot make dreams come true—people must do that.

Good eyes don't fear smoke.

For every head a hat.

The calf isn't even born yet and there he is sharpening his carving knife.

The church is nearby, God is far away.

It is difficult to teach a cow to climb a tree.

You are learning all your life and you die stupid.

There is no need to whip docile horses.

If you go to bed hungry, you'll wake up without having slept.

Smoke in your own country is purer than fire in a foreign land.

With the intellect of another you won't get very far.

The beauty of a housewife will not put more fat into the soup.

Even the hardest of winters fears the spring.

From a big cloud comes little rain.

Words do not fill your purse.

Smoke spreads further than the fire.

Sleep on a bed of silver and dream of gold.

A man without a beard is like bread without a crust.

Luxembourg

A woman is at her strongest when she faints.

Truth is what women do not tell.

A man's eyes are for seeing, a woman's for being seen.

A woman is as old as she wishes to tell you.

In the eyes of its mother every turkey is a swan.

To the fiancé—milk; to the bride—butter; to the husband—cheese.

You will catch no birds with a club.

Your wife and your wheelbarrow—lend them to no one.

The wife cries before the wedding, the husband after.

A woman who likes to wash will find water.

When girls whistle, the Holy Virgin cries.

Keep your eye on girls that don't tell their mothers everything.

Words are but dwarfs, examples are giants.

Madagascar

Don't help a bull out of a ditch, for when he's out he'll butt you.

If you try to cleanse others—just like soap, you will waste away in the process!

Cross the river among a crowd and the crocodile won't eat you.

Don't kick a sleeping dog.

The dog's bark is not might, but fright.

The eel that got away is as fat as your thigh.

The end of an ox is beef, and the end of a lie is grief.

Indecision is like the stepchild: if he doesn't wash his hands, he is called dirty; if he does, he is wasting the water.

Life is a shadow and a mist; it passes quickly by, and is no more.

Love is like young rice: transplanted, still it grows.

Don't be so much in love that you can't tell when it's raining.

Let your love be like drizzle: it comes softly, but still swells the river.

Marriage is not a tight knot, but a slip knot.

Don't take a second mouthful before you have swallowed the first.

Sorrow is like a precious treasure, shown only to friends.

Greet everyone cordially when you don't know who your in-laws are going to be.

The barking dog gives you no power—it gives you fear.

To love the law is to lose money.

He is truly hungry who accepts defeat in a fight over meat.

When you are looking for a country with no tombstones you will find yourself in the land of cannibals.

As long as the mouse keeps still you can be sure that the cat stays on guard.

Advice is a stranger; if he's welcome he stays for the night; if not, he leaves the same day.

Ants can attack with a grain of rice.

You can't blame the axe for the noise made by the chicken you are about to slaughter.

Do not scare the birds you are going to shoot.

You may well have caught a bird, but have you a fire to roast it on?

Even the bottom of a basket finds something to hold.

A canoe does not know who is king. When it turns over, everyone gets wet.

Do not kick away the canoe which helped you to cross the river.

When you treat someone like a wild cat, he will steal your chickens.

Behave like the chameleon: look forward and observe behind.

A chicken that hatches a crocodile's eggs is looking for trouble.

You can catch a cricket in your hand but its song is all over the field.

When the crocodiles leave, the caymans come.

A starving crocodile is never pleasant.

Debts make the thief.

The dying person cannot wait for the shroud to be woven.

Nothing is so difficult that diligence cannot master it.

Distracted by what is far away, he does not see his nose.

Divorce a young woman and you make another man happy.

Madagascar

Only thin dogs become wild.

When the ducks are quacking the frogs take it as a warning.

The earth is God's bride—she feeds the living and cherishes the dead.

The earth is a giant cooking pot and men are the meat therein.

If we don't fight we remain equals, if we do fight then one of us wins.

It is not the fire in the fireplace which warms the house, but the couple who get along well.

From all the fish in the pot you can only make one soup.

Flint and gunpowder: every time they meet there is an explosion.

The food which is prepared has no master.

"If it is not a boy it will be a girl," says the fortune-teller.

Friendship reminds us of fathers, love of mothers.

May your friendship not be like a stone: if it breaks you cannot put the pieces together. May it be like iron: when it breaks, you can weld the pieces back together.

To deny God's existence is like jumping with your eyes closed.

One can't give a grasshopper to a child if one has not caught it yet.

Better to be guilty in the eyes of men than in the eyes of God.

If the hill is on fire the grasshoppers are roasted.

Idleness moves so slowly that it will be overtaken by misery.

Iron does not clang by itself.

The king inherits a country—the people only hard work.

When the king reigns it is thanks to the people; when a river sings it's thanks to the stones.

It is the softness of the lime that is fatal to the bird.

Living is not a reward and dying is no crime.

Love is just like rice—plant it elsewhere and it grows.

If love is torn apart you cannot stitch the pieces together again.

A man finds many faults in a woman when he wants to divorce, and finds many charms in one's fiancée.

Better to lose a little money than a little friendship.

Money is like a guest: it comes today, leaves tomorrow.

Be like the mouth and the hand: when the hand is hurt the mouth blows on it, when the mouth is hurt the hand rubs it.

Sadness is a valuable treasure—only discovered in people you love.

The sin for which you repent is the father of virtue; but a virtue that you talk about, is the mother of sin.

Do not waste your time looking for soft ground to drive your spade in.

Wealth is like hair in the nose: it hurts to be separated whether from a little or from a lot.

Do not measure up the wood before the tree is cut down.

Words are like the spider's web: a shelter for the clever ones and a trap for the not-so-clever.

Words are like newly hatched eggs: they already have wings.

Words go further than bullets.

Malawi

One little arrow does not kill a serpent.

Do not be like the mosquito that bites the owner of the house.

Malaysia

Anger has no eyes.

Ants die in sugar.

Don't use an axe to do embroidery.

Just as a bamboo cane forms a round jet of water, so taking counsel together makes men of one mind.

If you are going to bathe, get thoroughly wet.

The betrothed of good is evil; the betrothed of life is death; the betrothed of love is divorce.

The body pays for a slip of the foot and gold pays for a slip of the tongue.

The body is killed by the mouth.

Buffaloes are held by ropes, man by his words.

One muddy buffalo makes the whole herd dirty.

Where there's a carcass, there will be vultures.

Clapping with the right hand only will not make a noise.

Do not measure another man's coat on your body.

Go away and the conversation changes.

Crabs teach their offspring to walk straight.

The cradle is rocked but the baby is pinched.

Crime leaves a trail like a water beetle; like a snail, it leaves its silver track; like a horse-mango, it leaves its smell.

Don't think there are no crocodiles just because the water's calm.

When the curry is tasty, the rice is hard.

The day will come when cats have horns and Dutchmen will be circumcised.

A deer tethered with a golden chain can escape to the forest to eat grass.

You can measure the depth of the sea but what about a man's heart?

We all will die, but our tombs will differ.

A diplomat should be yielding and supple as a creeper that can be bent but not broken.

Don't dirty the place where you have eaten.

Blow your horn in a herd of elephants; crow in the company of cockerels; bleat in a flock of goats.

It is the fate of the coconut husk to float, for the stone to sink.

Fear to let fall a drop, will always make you spill a lot.

Anything with scales counts as a fish.

Fish don't get caught in deep water.

The most fragrant of flowers are eaten by the green-fly.

Those who are at one regarding food are at one in life.

Gold is a debt we can repay, but kindness not till our dying day.

If you have, give; if you need, seek.

A piece of incense may be as large as the knee, but unless burned emits no fragrance.

Every joy will follow in grief's footsteps.

Kick away the ladder and your feet are left dangling.

As if it were't bad enough to fall, the ladder lands on top of you.

He can see a louse as far away as China but is not aware of an elephant on his nose.

Leave her now and then if you would really love your wife.

As a child, is a man wrapped in his mother's womb; as an adult, in tradition; comes death, and he is wrapped in earth.

Every man is a prince in his own bed.

Low is the mountain, high the expectations.

The smallest pepper is hottest.

If you dip your arm into the picklepot let it be up to the elbow.

The proportion of things thrill the eye.

One day of rain far surpasses a whole year of drought.

When you are crossing over a river you might be eaten by crocodiles, but don't let yourself get bitten by the little fish.

Rocks need no protection from the rain.

Where there is sea there will always be pirates.

The more shoots, the more leaves.

Though near shore, you're still in the ocean.

When the sky falls down, the earth shall melt.

The less soup, the more spoons.

Where there is sugar, there are mice.

Don't think back on someone whose name you forgot, he is probably someone else by now.

Don't teach the tiger cub to eat meat.

The teeth sometimes bite the tongue.

When a dead tree falls, the woodpeckers profit from his death.

Though a tree grows ever so high, the falling leaves return to its roots.

The turtle lays thousands of eggs without anyone knowing, but when the hen lays an egg, the whole country is informed.

An upstart is a sparrow eager to marry a hornbill.

When it's warm the pea loses its pod.

However big the whale may be, the tiny harpoon can rob him of life.

The widow is just as fiery as the horse that threw her.

He who has learned how to steal, must learn how to hang.

Mali

One does not give a gift without a motive.

When mosquitoes work, they bite and then they sing.

A deaf man may not have heard the thunder but he surely will see the rain.

The hyena chasing two antelopes at the same time will go to bed hungry.

Life is like a ballet performance—danced only once.

A man is what he thinks.

You must decide where you are going in the evening, if you intend to leave early in the morning.

You cannot wage war without the sound of gunpowder.

If you've nothing to do, dig a spinster's grave.

A turtle is not proud of his long neck.

You will never drown where you always take a bath.

Slowly but surely the excrement of foreign poets will come to your village.

A woman who offers sex to everyone will get kicked by everyone.

Malta

You cannot serve God and the devil.

Do good and forget it; do ill and remember it.

Good health is the sister of beauty.

He who goes to bed hungry dreams of pancakes.

After taking ninety-nine years to climb a stairway, the tortoise falls and says there is a curse on haste.

The evil weed produces the largest number of weeds.

Malta would be a nice place, if every knight were a tree.

A good mule can be sold in his own territory.

If you don't eat you will die; overeating will shorten your life.

When it's raining and the sun shines—then a Turk is born.

The weather vane will not work without wind.

A woman has even cheated the devil.

Long skirts carry dust, but short skirts carry away souls.

A man and a sheaf of straw make two.

A good cow gets sold in its own country.

A kiss without a hug is like a flower without fragrance.

A lovely girl attracts attention by her good looks, an ugly girl by the help of a mirror.

Where the heart loves, there the legs walk.

When the husband is a hen and the wife is a cock, the house is topsy-turvy.

The wagtail hops and flaps its wings, but the male dove feeds and coos.

The world is nonsense: what looks beautiful in the morning looks ugly in the evening.

The world is a wheel and men are the felloes, and the devil prowling around spins.

When a miser dies, the heirs feel as happy as when they kill a pig.

With money you can build a road in the sea.

Malta

Money begets money, and fleas beget fleas.

Manchuria

You won't see a good drunk in a teahouse.
In a house where there are many beautiful daughters the soup kettle
    will never get polished.
A man will be born in his house and will die in the desert.
When three men march together, one of them must be the boss.
The crook will turn into a mule—that the honest man will ride.
A wolf will still be a wolf even if he hasn't eaten your sheep.

Maori
(New Zealand)

Hold on tight to the words of your ancestors.
Boast during the day; be humble at night.
Old canoes can be restored, but youth and beauty cannot.
When one chief falls, another rises.
A hand that is ready to hit may cause you great trouble.
The block of wood should not dictate to the carver.
Be quick to follow up an advantage.
Even food can attack.
Only the foolish visit the land of the cannibals.
The more you ask how much longer it will take, the longer the jour-
    ney will seem.
In peace be faithful; in war be valiant.
Never spend time with people who don't respect you.
Persist as resolutely as you persist in eating.
Who lives in a quiet house has plenty.
A house full of people is a house full of different points of view.
The prudent embark when the sea is calm—the rash when it's stormy.

Let someone else sing your praise.

In this world I greet my oldest survivor—the earth.

A warrior dies in battle; a mountain climber on the rocks, but a farmer dies of old age.

Don't lean on your fellow men—theirs is an ever moving support.

The land is a mother that never dies.

Turn your face to the sun and the shadows fall behind you.

Martinique

Chickens can't speak well of their own soup.

The good dog never gets a good bone.

You jump up, but you come down all the same.

When you bump into someone, begging your pardon doesn't put it right.

Not everybody who wears spurs is a jockey.

Thieves don't like to see their comrades carrying the bags.

Where there is a bone, there are dogs.

If you are born fat you will not die thin.

A dog doesn't like bananas, but he can't bear to think that chickens eat them.

The blow is taken on the nose but it's the eyes that cry.

If an ox doesn't know the size of his arse he won't eat an apricot stone.

The sheep drinks but it's the goat that gets drunk.

Breasts are never too heavy for the chest.

Masai Proverbs
(East Africa)

It is impossible to bend the arm of God.

Mauritania

He whose clothes are too fine, shall go about in rags.
He who begins a conversation, does not foresee the end.
Before one cooks, one must have the meat.
Open your mouth before you eat.
Not all the tree's blossoms will bear fruit.
Too large a morsel chokes the child.
If you watch your pot, your food will not burn.
A stone from the hand of a friend is an apple.
One must talk little, and listen a lot.
It is only the water that is spilled; the bowl is not broken!
He who has no spoon will burn his hands.

Mauritius

The mosquito is small—but when he sings, your cars are full of him.

Mexico

Agreements should be clearly expressed, and chocolate should be
    served thick.
Do not refuse the body what it asks for.
Foreign bread is good for your son.
Tell me what you want to buy and I will tell you what you are.
Nobody wants to buy a sleeping horse.
Though a cage may be made of gold, it is still a cage.
We are all made of the same clay, but not from the same mold.
Cleanliness is the luxury of the poor.
A good cock will crow on every dungheap.
The eleventh commandment: Thou shalt not contradict.

He who really wants to die will not complain if he is buried standing up.

For every dog there is an appropriate stick.

Duty before devotion.

The envious never give praise, they only take it in.

He who is accustomed to evil is offended by good.

He is not fat—it is his belt that doesn't fit.

No fate is worse than a life without a love.

Everyone makes firewood of a fallen tree.

Fortune is like a wall that falls on those who lean on it.

If you give away what you have, you will not yearn for what you see.

God is bigger than your problems.

God did not give wings to scorpions.

He who doesn't speak will get no help from God.

I never ask God to give me anything; I only ask him to put me where things are.

Never confuse gratitude with love.

The heir's tears are but a mask to disguise his joy.

Your hometown is like a small fatherland.

The house does not rest upon the ground, but upon a woman.

Hunger brings people down, but pride can help them get up.

The lion believes that everyone shares its state of mind.

Love is blind—but not the neighbors.

Love is too rare to be lost on jealousy.

A jealous lover becomes an indifferent spouse.

The lover of a student does not always become the wife of a graduate.

Marriage is the only war in which you sleep with the enemy.

One string is good enough to a good musician.

Necessity is a great teacher.

When two paupers get married it is the beginning of a generation of beggars.

The person who asks for little deserves nothing.

A person born to be a flower pot will not go beyond the porch.

Those who rescue are always crucified.

It's not enough to know how to ride—one must also know how to fall.

The road to hell is strewn with roses.

Even the saints' patience has its limits.

Only men with thick lips should smoke a cigar.

If it is not stolen, it is a legacy.

If it does not stink, it is not a foot.

Let the water you cannot drink flow by.

Where there are weapons, there will be wars.

Nobody leaves this world alive.

You cannot worship an unknown saint.

Monaco

An old chicken makes tasty soup.

Mongolia

Even foul water will quench fire.

The distance between heaven and earth is no greater than one thought.

Two bears in one cave will not end up well.

He who wants to build high must dig deep.

Once you have locked your door you are the emperor in your own domain.

If you are sick, think about your life; if you are better, think about your gold.

Of the good we have an understanding, for fools we keep a stick upstairs.

He who drinks, dies; he who does not drink, dies as well.

One idiot can ask more questions than ten wise men can answer.

A donkey that carries me is worth more than a horse that kicks me.

The donkey recognizes the tracks of a horse.

Greed keeps men forever poor, even the abundance of this world will not make them rich.

A cat likes to eat fresh fish but it will not go into the water.

If you are going to steal bells plug your ears.

The living are denied a table; the dead get a whole coffin.

The more you listen the more you give yourself room for doubt.

Men and women sleep on the same pillow, but they have different dreams.

The winner has many friends, the loser has good friends.

You can't put two saddles on the same horse.

Rich is he who has no debts, fortunate he who lives without handicap.

Don't undo your bootlaces until you have seen the river.

Times are not always the same; the grass is not always green.

A tiger wearing a bell will starve.

The fish sees the bait not the hook; a man sees not the danger—only the profit.

Who cleans up the dirt washes away happiness.

Wise men talk about ideas, intellectuals about facts, and the ordinary man talks about what he eats.

It's difficult to take a wolf cub without bringing in the whole pack.

In a good word there are three winters' warmth; in one malicious word there is pain for six frosty months.

There are men who walk through the woods and see no trees.

Don't look for bad things in the good that you do.

Montenegro

When three wise men say you are an ass, bray.

The Pope and a peasant know more than the Pope alone.

Better an apple pie than apple blossom.

It's better to drink and feel sick than not to drink and feel bad.

Common grief is lighter to bear.

Even the grave of the Lord has a paid guard.

Once a word has been uttered it belongs to those who hear it.

Moorish Proverbs

He who fears something gives it power over him.

If you have the moon, ignore the stars.

A forest would want to be burned by its own wood.

Hypocrisy is the mother of peace.

It's easy to say "May Allah roast the lion's mother," when the lion isn't there.

Men have thought about their marriage a whole year long—and it lasts but one night.

One lie can fill a sack; a second will empty it again.

He who inherits a hill must climb it.

Morocco

Strong attachment is difficult—it makes one mad or kills.

If you see him riding on a bamboo-cane, say to him, "Good health to your horse!"

Every beetle is a gazelle in the eyes of its mother.

Reading books removes sorrows from the heart.

Manage with bread and salted butter until God brings something to eat with it.

An old cat will never learn to dance.

Do not respond to a barking dog.

Perform good deeds; you will not regret them.

Friendship is honey—but don't eat it all.

A garden without a fence is like a dog without a tail.

The hen lays an egg, and the cock feels the pain in his backside.

It is better to be the object of jealousy, than of pity.

He who flatters with laughter wants to see you cry.

A fly will not get into a closed mouth.

A good name is more valuable than a velvet garment.

Evening promises are like butter: morning comes, and it's all melted.

Whoever does not respect you, insults you.

Over truth there is light.

A wise man without a book is like a workman with no tools.

Teaching in youth is like carving in stone.

Work and you will be strong; sit and you will smell.

Cold teaches a man how to steal charcoal.

It is worse to be wounded by words than a sword.

There is no queue at the gate of Patience.

When my child and I have eaten—then clear the table.

If you don't understand it with a wink, you certainly will with a blow.

If the judge is against you, you should withdraw the complaint.

In every false step there is something good.

If a rich man steals it is a mistake; if a poor man makes a mistake he
has stolen.

If there were no cold Friday evenings and boring Saturdays, no one
would get married any more.

A little nod is enough for the wise man; an ass needs a fist.

Mozambique

Once a man has been bitten by a lion, he buys a dog.
You cannot dance well on only one leg.
Witch doctors do not sell their potions to each other.
On a dead tree there are no monkeys.
He who led me in the night, will be thanked by me at daybreak.
A snake that you can see does not bite.
No tattoo is made without blood.
If you do not travel, you will marry your own sister.
Slander by the stream will be heard by the frogs.
Never marry a woman who has bigger feet than you.

Myanmar

The anger of the prudent never shows.
They call their aunt only when her cucumbers are ripe.
Do not bathe if there is no water.
Beware of a man's shadow and a bee's sting.
The blind person is not afraid of ghosts.
If you don't have a brain, join the army; if you don't have rice, use
    beans instead.
Often a branch is broken off the tree by the one who has rested in its
    shadow.
When the cat gets too old, the mice are not afraid any more.
Once the cattle have been split up, then the tiger strikes.
If a centipede loses a leg, it can still walk.
A child without a mother is like a fish in shallow water.
Bad children? Guilty parents!
There is no cure for an unknown illness.
Day will not break thanks to the cackling of the chicken.

The dead know the price of wood.

Doctors must be old and lawyers must be young.

Too many doctors caused the boy's death.

When the healthy dog fights with a mad dog, it is the ears of the healthy one that are bitten off.

Dust does not rise because a dog-flea hops.

With fowls, the pedigree; with men, breeding.

Only when a new government comes to power do you learn to appreciate the values of the old one.

The life of a guest is seven days.

The strings of the harp must be not too tight, and not too slack.

He who comes from hell is not afraid of hot ashes.

The hero appears only when the tiger is dead.

You can only be honest if you are well fed.

An inflated idea can burst the bubble of your happiness.

Karma is the mother and karma is the father.

The more you know, the luckier you get.

A man with little learning is like the frog who thinks its pond is an ocean.

It is as difficult to win love as it is to pack salt in pine needles.

Where there is love, there is peace.

What is now top of the mast, will be firewood soon.

It is never later than midnight.

The monkey never complains that he has no comb.

He who carries the word "no" with him will never be poor even when he is old.

The strongest ox is only as strong as the old ox with a broken leg.

Old oxen like soft grass.

If you take big paces you leave big spaces.

Worthless people blame their karma.

Spread the word of a Psalm and it becomes a popular song.

You can't get rice by pounding bran.

One sesame seed won't make oil.

Only the sufferers know how their bellies ache.

Sugarcane is always sweet—people only sometimes so.

The talkers aren't strong; the strong don't talk.

Only tall things cast shadows.

He who carries too much tenderness will become a slave.

The tree is felled... let's plant a new one.

A good tree can lodge ten thousand birds. ✓

Namibia

A braggart is recognized by his headgear.

He who has bad breath cannot smell it.

The ears do not lose their interest.

A glutton is never satisfied.

An heir also inherits quarrels.

Even a weak lion is not bitten by a dog.

A parasite cannot live alone.

It's easy to weed your neighbor's field.

Where there are birds, there is water.

If your mouth turns into a knife, it will cut off your lips.

The bone given to you by the king is meat.

Those who live together cannot hide their behinds from each other.

A fool laughs at himself.

God speaks a foreign tongue.

That which leaks cannot stay full.

Native American Proverbs

Every animal knows more than you do.

We do not inherit the land from our ancestors; we borrow it from our children.

When the last tree has been cut down, the last river has been polluted and the last fish has been caught—only then do you realize that money can't buy everything.

Don't judge a man until you have walked two moons in his moccasins.

A man can't get rich if he takes proper care of his family.

When the white man wins, it is a battle. When the Indian wins, it is a massacre.

Do not let grass grow on the path of friendship.

Nobody gets out of the bed to sleep on the floor.

If it does not kill you, it will bring you happiness.

Live and learn, die and forget it all.

A pearl is worthless as long as it is in its shell.

The river is my brother for it carries my canoe.

Do not change horses in the middle of the river.

The lazy ox drinks dirty water.

Haste is the mother of inaccuracy.

There is nothing so eloquent as the rattlesnake's tail.

One shower doesn't make a flood.

Lovely women, lovely quarrels.

Worms don't like the robin's song.

When the earth is hot, the worm stays in the ground.

The devil goes away and heaven comes to stay.

After dark all cats are leopards.

Do not wrong or hate your neighbor for it is not he that you wrong but yourself.

If you see no reason for giving thanks, the fault lies in yourself.

What the people believe is true.

Tell me and I'll forget. Show me, and I may not remember. Involve me, and I'll understand.

Man has responsibility, not power.

Life is not separate from death. It only looks that way.

Listen or your tongue will keep you deaf.

You can't wake a person who is pretending to be asleep.

Nepal

The farmer grows the corn, but the bear eats it.

Depend on others and you'll go hungry.

Even the devil slaves for the fortunate.

You have a lot of friends if you have money; otherwise there are only strangers.

The god who made the mouth will provide the food.

Hold short services for minor gods.

It is the mind that wins or loses.

Opportunities come but do not linger.

A speaker needs no tools.

Too much sugar is bitter.

Vanity blossoms but bears no fruit.

Wealth is both an enemy and a friend.

New Zealand

Let us hurry and finish up the food; when visitors arrive, the meal will be over.

Nicaragua

You make a road by walking on it.

Have patience, fleas, the night is long!

Niger

Ashes fly back into the face of him who throws them.

He who does not mend his clothes will soon have none.

Familiarity breeds contempt; distance breeds respect.

He who marries a beauty marries trouble.

The rat cannot call the cat to account.

He who boasts much can do little.

However hard a thing is thrown into the air, it always falls to the ground.

People in trouble remember Allah.

Allah preserve us from "If only I'd known!"

Birth is the only remedy against death.

If a blind man says lets throw stones, be assured that he has stepped on one.

By crawling, a child learns to stand.

If you can't dance well, you'd better not get up.

However poor the elephant, it will be worth more than ten frogs.

The elephant's track treads out the camel's.

From the well of envy, only a fool drinks the water.

Proportion your expenses to what you have, not what you expect.

The only insurance against fire is to have two houses.

Fishing without a net is just bathing.

A person is a guest for one or two days, but becomes an intruder on the third.

Being happy is better than being king.

Don't look for speed in a cheap horse; be content if it neighs.

Hurrying and worrying are not the same as strength.

The teeth that laugh are also those that bite.

Man is like pepper—you only know him when you've ground him.

Even in Mecca people make money.

Mud houses don't burn.

When the music changes, so does the dance.

Choose your neighbors before you buy your house.

One pebble doesn't make a floor.

The quarrel that doesn't concern you is pleasant to hear about.

Your own rags are better than another's gown.

A smiling face dispels unhappiness.

The stars shine brightest when the moon is gone.

Midday sun is the remedy for a cold.

One cry of "Thief!" and the whole marketplace is on the lookout.

Choose your fellow traveller before you start on your journey.

Ugliness with a good character is better than beauty.

He who does not lose his way by night will not lose his way by day.

The well gives, but the bucket refuses.

Nigeria

All is never said.

The king's ambassador is without sin.

He who runs from the white ant may stumble upon the stinging ant.

He who lives in the attic knows where the roof leaks.

He who wishes to barter, does not like his belongings.

If you find "Miss This Year" beautiful, then you'll find "Miss Next Year" even more so.

Some birds avoid the water, ducks look for it.

The bird flies high, but always returns to earth.

The blind say that eyes have no sense of smell.

If the bull would throw you, lie down.

The one being carried does not realize how far away the town is.

If there is character, ugliness becomes beauty; if there is none, beauty becomes ugliness.

Children of the same mother do not always agree.

What the child says, he has heard at home.

When you cook a guinea fowl, the partridge gets a headache.

If crocodiles eat their own eggs what would they do to the flesh of a frog.

The dying man is not saved by medicine.

Earth is the queen of beds.

Evil knows where evil sleeps.

It is more fun doing evil than putting it right.

Fire has no brother.

The fire that burns a royal palace only enhances its splendor.

Before firing, you must take aim.

Hold on to a true friend with both hands.

A friendly person is never a good-for-nothing.

The frog does not jump in the daytime without reason.

One goat cannot carry another goat's tail.

Grass does not grow on the nose of a thief.

As long as you stay in a group, the lion will stay hungry.

Guilt is like the footprint of a hippopotamus.

If you have run out of gunpowder, use your gun as a club.

Horns do not grow before the head.

The hunter does not rub himself in oil and lie by the fire to sleep.

Hyenas are caught with stinking bait.

The body of Joy is not so big.

You can't jump from one tree to another but you can from one man to another.

Not to know is bad; not to want to know is worse.

The day you are leaving is not the time to start your preparations.

Someone else's legs are no good to you when you're travelling.

Lending is the firstborn of poverty.

The lion's power lies in our fear of him.

Until the lions have their historians, tales of the hunt shall always glorify the hunter.

"Now the marriage begins," says the woman who has been beaten with thorns.

Meat does not eat meat.

If you want to give a sick man medicine, let him first be really ill—so that he can see how well the medicine works.

That which brings misfortune is not big.

Money kills more than do weapons.

Only a mother would carry the child that bites.

A mother is gold, a father is a mirror.

More than one mother can make tasty soup.

When the mouse laughs at the cat, there is a hole nearby.

The head of your neighbor is a kingdom and his heart a wood.

The one-eyed man thanks God only when he sees a man blind in both eyes.

Overabundance is not far from want.

A pig that is used to wallowing in the mud looks for a clean person to rub against.

What a prostitute earns she calls presents from her husband's friends.

If you put a razor in your mouth, you will spit blood.

If you rise too early, the dew will wet you.

The river may dry up but she keeps her name.

The house roof fights the rain, but he who is sheltered ignores it.

Seeing is better than hearing.

He who is sick will not refuse medicine.

When you are sick you promise a goat, but when you are well again make do with a chicken.

If the stomachache were in the foot, one would go lame.

The stone in the water does not know how hot the hill is, parched by the sun.

A tiger does not have to proclaim its tigritude.

Time destroys all things.

When one is in trouble, one remembers God.

Warm water never forgets that it was once cold.

A wealthy man will always have followers.

The whip hits at the legs, not the guilt.

It is the woman whose child has been eaten by a witch who best knows the evils of witchcraft.

The advice of a woman ends with "Oh, if I had only known!"

The woman is cold water that kills you; deep water that you drown in.

A woman who has not been twice married cannot know what a perfect marriage is.

Words are sweet but they can never replace food.

Fine words do not produce food.

Voluntary work is better than slavery.

A person always breaking off from work never finishes anything.

Although the snake does not fly it has caught the bird whose home is in the sky.

If all seeds that fall were to grow, then no one could follow the path under the trees.

The crocodile does not die under the water so that we can call the monkey to celebrate its funeral.

The family is like the forest. If you are outside, it is dense; if you are inside, you see that each tree has its own position.

Norway

One should never rub bottoms with a porcupine.

Fowls will not spare a cockroach that falls in their mist.

You do not need a big stick to break a cock's head.

Marriage is like a groundnut, you have to crack it to see what is inside.

The rain wets the leopard's spots but does not wash them off.

Norway

Ask for advice, then use your head.

Bad is called good when worse happens.

Black soil produces white bread.

Better an iron dictatorship than a golden anarchy.

He who has a dog need not bark himself.

He who does no evil does a lot of good.

Every family has its hanger-on.

Fish bite best on a golden hook.

There is never a fish without a bone, and no man without faults.

Good fortune is loaned, not owned.

It is better to be a free man in a small house than a slave in a big one.

Better a free bird than a king in captivity.

Go often to the house of a friend; for weeds soon choke up the unused path.

In the game no one is brother to others.

To be a hero hang on for a minute longer.

The taller the house, the heavier the storm.

The less you know, the less you forget.

What three men know then the whole world knows.

Latecomers see the least.

It is the law that judges, not the judge.

A blushing lie is better than the pale truth.

257

Men look more like their uncles on the mother's side.

He who leaves a good name does not die poor.

The pardon may be more severe than the penalty.

The stomach is not content with nice words.

The thief thinks everybody steals.

Time has strong teeth.

Tomorrow is the day that idlers get busy.

The coat of truth is often lined with lies.

There is no wind that blows right for the sailor who doesn't know where the harbor is.

It is the great north wind that made the Vikings.

Wise men learn at another's expense.

Not all the words that were ever uttered are worth weighing on golden scales.

Oji
(West Africa)

If you want heaven to know, tell it to the wind.

When the mouth stumbles, it is worse than when the foot does.

A forest that has sheltered you, you should not call a patch of scrub.

Pakistan

A fat wife is like a blanket in winter.

Palestine

The empty gives way to the full.

Do good and throw it in the sea.

Palestine

Those who dig an evil hole will fall into it.

The house is our father's and the strangers came to kick us out.

There will be a day for the oppressor when he will be crushed like garlic.

One hand can't clap.

The ignorant is his own enemy.

The one who loves does not hate.

Every eye has its look.

The eye does not get over the eyebrow.

Whatever is written on the forehead is always seen.

You will not dare mistreat the face you see in the morning.

The eye is the one that eats.

If you feed the mouth, the eye becomes shy.

Once deep pools, now a crossing place.

If you sit at a crossroads, you will get sick.

Don't just cross a river—cross it bearing fire!

Far from grave, no praying.

The heart is a tree; it grows where it wants.

"Long ago" did not live long ago.

If only I were a bird! Ah, but eating caterpillars?

Too far for jackals? No worthwhile tree here!

One thumb alone does not kill a louse.

Only the soil knows when a young mouse is ill.

Care now, be cared for later.

You only hear three voices in this world: the babbling of the stream, Jewish law, and money.

Pride is the mask of our sins.

Go with the powerful and people will kneel before you.

Sell what you have bought while the dust is still on your shoes.

Peru

The continuous drip polishes the stone.

You go out for wool but come back shorn.

Little by little one walks far.

In life the son is scornful of the father, in business the father is of the son.

You won't catch trout without wetting your feet.

The sleeping lobster is carried away in the stream.

Never kill a brooding bird.

Philippines

Postpone today's anger until tomorrow.

If you sow arrows, you will reap sorrows.

The hardest person to wake up is the person who is already awake.

If a bamboo tube makes a loud sound, it is empty.

Not all that is black is charcoal.

Borrowed clothes are either too tight or too loose.

If the bow is sinking, the stern follows.

A young branch can be straightened, a mature one breaks.

A brave man will face a situation no matter how dreadful.

Caution minimizes loss.

No child was ever born without having been conceived.

Coincidence defeats a well-laid plan.

The noisiest drum has nothing but air inside.

Tell me who your father is, and I'll tell you who you are.

The fly on the back of a water buffalo thinks that it's taller than the buffalo.

There is no bad food in a famine.

There's no glory without sacrifice.

Poland

Wherever you go, habit follows.

The real hero doesn't say that he is one.

Lazy people will eventually lose even their trousers.

The rattan basket criticizes the palm-leafed bag, yet both are full of holes.

People who do not break things first will never learn to create anything.

If you buy things you don't need, you'll soon be selling things you do.

A clear conscience is more valuable than wealth.

There's a crocodile in every big river.

Don't put your trust in Fortune until you are in heaven.

A country without freedom is like a prisoner with shackled hands.

It is easier to dam a river than to stop gossip.

Trying to get everything, you often get nothing.

Wherever the head goes, the tail will follow.

The bitterness of studying is preferable to the bitterness of ignorance.

If you are going a long way, go slowly.

A year's care, a minute's ruin.

The higher the bamboo, the more it can be bent.

It is easy to be born, it is difficult to be a human being.

To a dog a bone has more value than a pearl.

Marriage is not just a porridge that you spit out if it's too hot.

Children who get everything they ask for seldom succeed in life.

Tell a lie and the truth will come to light.

If the horse is already dead more hay will not help it.

Poland

Nowadays you have to go to heaven to meet an angel.

A bachelor and a dog can do anything.

Better to be paying the baker than the chemist.

Poland

Beauty does not season soup.

To believe in certainty, we must begin by doubting.

What I believe in is all that is mine.

The bell is loud because it is empty.

Where the body wants to rest, there the legs must carry it.

With a bottle and a girl one does not count the hours.

Watch the faces of those who bow low.

Every bubble bursts.

Where there is butter there are flies.

Capitalism is the exploitation of man by man. Communism is the complete opposite.

From someone else's cart you have to get off halfway.

If it were not for the hands, the clock would be useless.

Even a clock that does not work is right twice a day.

Even if a chef cooks just a fly, he would keep the breast for himself.

Corn will look better in your neighbor's field.

Both the cross and the gallows are made of wood.

The devil can swallow a woman but he can't digest her.

The worst devil is the one who prays.

A doctor will take care of the rich man; the poor man is cured with work.

It is easier to take a couple of drinks than to refuse them.

One ducat before the trial is worth three afterwards.

In church, in the taverns, and in coffins all men are equal.

The farmer is a born philosopher, the aristocrat has to learn how.

If the farmer is poor then so is the whole country.

Tasty fish have to swim three times: once in the water, then in butter, and finally in wine.

It is easier to watch over one hundred fleas than one young girl.

A fool stands always in the rain.

Friends sleep when misfortune knocks on the door.

Poland

In a game it's difficult to know when to stop.

When a girl is born it is like having six thieves invade the house.

The giver should forget, but the receiver should remember forever.

God promised me a fur coat and I'm already sweating.

Great things can best be said in silence.

That which everybody guards will soon disappear.

A guest sees more in an hour than the host in a year.

A guest hammers a nail in the wall even if he stays only one night.

Get married and you will be happy for a week; slaughter a pig and you will be happy for a month; become a priest and you will be happy for the rest of your life.

Stroke the horse until it is saddled.

In every little house there is a little louse.

Ink, if not used, will dry up.

The Italian invents it; the Frenchman makes it; the Germans sell it; the Pole buys it and the Tartar plunders it.

The liar will travel the world over, but chooses not to go back home.

The locksmith is the guilty one, but the blacksmith hangs.

Where there is love, there is happiness.

"Love one another" said Christ, but he didn't mention anything about preferences.

Love without jealousy is like a Pole with no moustache.

Love is like the moon: now full, now dark.

When the master has a cold the servants sneeze.

When I had money everyone called me brother.

The greatest love is a mother's; then a dog's; then a sweetheart's.

What reaches the mother's heart will only reach the father's knees.

A person who is always nice is not always nice.

The doorstep of the palace is very slippery.

It is a poor parish where the priest has to ring his own bells.

An iron peace is better than a golden war.

Eat in Poland, drink in Hungary, sleep in Germany, and make love in
    Italy.

If you are going to fight, pray once; if you are going to sail, pray
    twice; if you are getting married, then pray thrice.

Wherever you go, you can't get rid of yourself.

There are a thousand roads to every wrong.

In Russia as you must, in Poland as you like.

God grant me a good sword and no use for it.

He who tickles himself can laugh whenever he wants.

Truth will not make you fat but you won't choke on a lie.

Truth will take you everywhere—even to jail.

Old truths, old laws, old friends, old books, and old wine are best.

The real unlucky one will sprain his thumb when he blows his nose.

A dead man's will is the mirror of his life.

When a woman knows no more how to answer, she must be dried up.

The world is a big place but there is so little room in it.

He who climbs a ladder, must have his brains in his feet.

Time has no respect for beauty.

Water teaches us to weep, wine teaches us to sing.

Portugal

The accomplice is as bad as the thief.

If you want good advice, consult an old man.

A contented ass enjoys a long life.

It is better to receive awards that you don't deserve rather than de-
    serve them and not receive them.

What was hard to bear is sweet to remember.

The queen bee has no sting.

Pretend to be dead and the bull will leave you alone.

What is bought is cheaper than a gift.

The gentle calf sucks all the cows.

Too many candles will burn down the church.

Meowing cats catch fewer mice.

Change yourself, and your luck will change.

The chicken that stays in the farmyard, will peck the crumbs.

Death makes us equal in the grave but not in eternity.

If you have a friend who is a doctor, then send him to your enemy's house.

The dog wags his tail, not for you, but for your bread.

Beware of the door with too many keys.

If you would make an enemy, lend a man money, and ask for it back again.

Better a red face than a black heart.

Faith has no eyes; he who asks to see has no faith.

Better to have friends in the marketplace than money in your coffers.

A girl, a vineyard and a beanfield are difficult to guard.

Thinking of where you are going, you forget from whence you came.

Do good and care not to whom.

Give a grateful man more than he asks for.

Better just repair the gutter than the whole house.

To change one's habits has a smell of death.

Hell's roof is made from lost causes.

"It is nothing—they are only thrashing my husband."

No one is a good judge of his own case.

A loss not missed by your neighbor is not a real loss.

Love has no law.

"What is marriage, mother?"
　"Child, it is spinning, having children, making money, and weeping."

He who serves two masters has to lie to one.

Where there is no might, right gets lost.

Portugal

The mistress is queen, the wife is the slave.

Give me money, not advice.

Don't put money in your purse without checking it for holes.

Mouth from honey, heart of gall.

Having need of makes the ugly beautiful.

A bad neighbor will give you a needle with no thread.

He who has nothing is afraid of nothing.

An old man in love is like a flower in winter.

If you give orders and leave, the work won't get done.

Not much is achieved where everyone gives the orders.

Peace with a cudgel in hand is war.

Every peddlar speaks highly about his own needles.

No one is poor but he who thinks himself so.

If a poor man gives to you, he expects more in return.

Better to be queen for an hour than a countess for life.

Be sure not to owe anything to the rich, and don't lend anything to the poor.

Don't leave the main road for a shortcut.

Even the most beautiful sheets have small flaws.

Keep your sickness until Friday and don't fast.

You have to suffer a lot or die young.

Sweet are the tears that are dried by your loved one.

Do not tell all that you know, don't believe all you hear, and don't do all that you can.

Think of many things—do one.

Time, not medicine, cures the sick.

There's no catching trout with dry breeches.

Truth and oil come to the surface.

Truth should not be dressed up.

Visits always give pleasure—if not at the arrival, then at the departure.

A rich widow weeps in one eye and laughs with the other.

Every wine would like to be port wine.

Women are always better the following year.

Women and glasses are always in danger.

A woman with two husbands cheats both.

Better to lose the wool than the sheep.

One good word puts out the flames better than a bucket of water.

There are many ways to leave this world but only one way to come into it.

Puerto Rico

The best thing God did was to make one day follow another.

Quebecois Proverbs

He who was born for a small loaf, will never own a big one.

You can't kill a dog just to save a cat's tail.

Silk is cut best with old scissors.

When you talk about the sun, you will see her beams.

Romania

Long absent, soon forgotten.

Abundance, like want, ruins many.

Acorns were good till bread was found.

Adversity makes a man wise, not rich.

If you wish good advice, consult an old man.

When a thing is done, advice comes too late.

The anvil fears no blows.

A bean in liberty is better than a comfit in prison.

Call the bear uncle till you are safe across the bridge.

Romania

Beauty without wisdom is like a flower in the mud.

A good bee will not go to a drooping flower.

Don't throw your blanket in the fire just because it has one flea in it.

A blind man will not thank you for a looking glass.

My chicken is good, but my neighbor's looks better.

In a house where two daughters live, the cat dies of thirst.

He who is afraid of death, loses his life.

Out of a devil's egg there can only come a devil.

Make a pact with the devil until you have crossed the bridge.

The devil gives even rich men presents.

He who wants to talk with the dogs must learn to bark.

What does a donkey know about the life of a nightingale?

Better a healthy donkey than a consumptive philosopher.

Better an ugly duckling from your own village than a beauty from foreign parts.

Eating and scratching want but a beginning.

The eyes have one language everywhere.

A foreigner scratches you where you do not itch.

Gloves hide the ugliest hands.

Before you find God, you will be eaten by saints.

Where God has sown it shall flourish.

Only what you have in your hand is not a lie.

When the head does not work, the legs suffer.

What the heart thinks, the tongue speaks.

The hen that cackles in the evening lays no eggs in the morning.

Many heroes appear after the war.

Complain about the house where the husband is the wife.

Hunger goes in a straight line, desire turns in circles.

It is idle to swallow the cow and choke on the tail.

Kiss the hand that you cannot bite.

268

Romania

The lamp is not burning for those asleep.

The man who takes legal action often loses an ox to win a cat.

When a liar speaks the truth, he is sick.

The looking glass is the enemy of ugly women.

Love understands all languages.

Short love, long sighs.

The luck of idle men sits next to them.

When men take wives they stop fearing hell.

A second marriage is like a warmed-up meal.

Look first at the mother and then the daughter.

Mice always return to their own little holes.

Better a mouse in the pot than no meat at all.

The needle is small, but it sews expensive garments.

Take an ox by its horns, a man by his heart.

Even in paradise it is no fun to be alone.

The best parents are both purses for money and sacks for the corn.

There's no physician like a true friend.

The rich man makes mistakes and the poor men get the blame.

He that never rode never fell.

Self-praise is no recommendation.

Don't try to sell pumpkins to a gardener.

Even silence is an answer.

A clear sky fears not the thunder.

So long as you don't step on a snail's tail, he won't get up and bite you.

The snake bites the tamer first.

When sorrow is asleep, wake it not.

When you spit against the wind you get a dirty beard.

Do not put your spoon into the pot which does not boil for you.

One short step lengthens life.

If you want to sweep the steps clean, start at the top.

You don't go into a tavern to say your prayers.

A tent without a woman is like a violin with no strings.

The thief who isn't caught is an honest salesman.

The tongue is not steel, yet it cuts.

The man of many trades begs his bread on Sunday.

If you are travelling in the blind man's country close one eye.

The tree makes shafts for axes.

Small tree trunks can make the cart turn over.

Your wife's eyes are in your purse.

Winter will ask you what you did during the summer.

A fair day in winter is the mother of a storm.

Under a ragged coat lies wisdom.

Women have long skirts and short minds.

Nothing is more changeable than time and a woman.

A woman's tongue is a double edged knife.

From the same wood you can make a cross or a club.

If you lie upon roses when you're young, you'll lie upon thorns when
    you're old.

Better an egg today, than an ox tomorrow.

The lion won't turn on a barking puppy.

If you are already wet, you won't care about the rain.

Russia

Advertising is the driving force of business.

If age and experience came at birth,
    We would have neither youth nor mirth.

It is unpleasant to go alone, even to be drowned.

When Anger and Revenge get married, their daughter is called Cru-
    elty.

270

No apple tree is immune from worms.

Even in the ashes there will be a few sparks.

To ask is no sin, and to be refused is no calamity.

Ask a lot, but take what is offered.

You need sharp axes for knotty trees.

The newborn baby yells; you die in silence.

A bachelor is never sent as a go-between.

He who offers his back should not complain if it is beaten.

Who owns the bank owns the fish.

The bear dances but the tamer collects the money.

Only chained bears dance.

Beauty is the sister of idleness and the mother of luxury.

Better a bed of wood than a bier of gold.

The belly is like a judge that is silent yet still asks questions.

It is easier to fill twenty bellies than one pair of eyes.

On an empty belly every burden is heavy.

You know a bird from the way he flies.

Everything tastes bitter to him with gall in his mouth.

The blind cannot see—the proud will not.

Don't boast when you start out, but when you get there.

A boat stands firmer with two anchors.

Your body belongs to the Tsar, your soul to God, and your back to
   the squire.

Two boots make a pair.

Don't worry if you borrow—worry if you lend.

The boss is always right.

They bow to you when borrowing, you bow to them when collecting.

Seek the brave in prison and the stupid among the clergy.

Bread and salt never quarrel.

With a piece of bread in your hand you'll find paradise under a pine
   tree.

Around bread there will always be crumbs.

It is bread that keeps one warm, not fur.

You cannot build a wall with one stone.

You don't learn anything from buying, but you do from selling.

One can get sick of cake, but never of bread.

To know that candles are expensive is of no value to the blind man.

Thanks to one small candle the whole of Moscow burns.

As soon as your cart is turned over, everyone rushes to give you advice.

The castle gates will always open for gold-laden donkeys.

The cat with cream on her whiskers should have a good excuse ready.

When you live next to the cemetery you cannot weep for everyone.

It is easier to bear a child once a year than to shave every day.

As long as a child does not cry, it does not matter what pleases it.

Hold your children with your heart but teach them with your hands.

Small children give you headache; big children heartache.

You cannot write in the chimney with charcoal.

There are two kinds of Chinese: those who give wine and those who drink it.

Clemency is the support of justice.

Don't be so clever; cleverer ones than you are in jail.

The coat is quite new, only the holes are old.

Conversation shortens the distance, singing lightens the load.

They come into the courtroom in a suit and leave with no trousers.

You don't milk a cow with your hands in your pockets.

It's a crime if you get caught.

It's better to be a cripple than always sitting down.

Custom is stronger than law.

A bad dancer always has trouble with his balls.

One good daughter is worth seven sons.

After your daughter is married, there comes a number of potential sons-in-law.

A day is long, but a lifetime is short.

One day before you is better than ten years behind you.

Every day is a messenger of God.

In a deal there are two fools: the one who asks too much and the one who asks too little.

Death does not take the old but the ripe.

When death is there, dying is over.

Death answers before it is asked.

Death carries on its shoulders a heavy Tsar just as easily as a light beggar.

Death is a giant against whom even the Tsars must draw weapons.

Death is not found behind mountains but right behind our shoulders.

Death does not come free of charge, for it costs us our life.

He who is destined for the gallows will not be drowned.

First do it, then say it.

Only a fool will make a doctor his heir.

The dog learns to swim when the water reaches his ears.

Even good dogs have fleas.

Your dog wishes you a long life.

An old dog can't get used to chains.

For a drunkard the sea only reaches his knees.

Even an eagle will not fly higher than the sun.

You can best shoot an eagle with an arrow made from its own feathers.

Ears do not grow higher than the head.

Eat until you are half full; drink until you are half drunk.

Eggs don't teach the hens anything.

An enemy will agree, but a friend will argue.

Envy sees the sea but not the rocks.

Envy can breed swans from bad duck eggs.

Eternity makes room for a salty cucumber.

Who lives in exile finds that spring has no charm.

Our eyes are our enemies.

If the family is together, the soul is in the right place.

There are many fathers, but only one mother.

Fear the goat from the front, the horse from the rear, and a man from all sides.

A field in common is always ravaged by bears.

In a fight the rich man tries to save his face, the poor man his coat.

Fighting for your country glorifies death.

As long as the fish swims in the water, don't light up the grill.

Fishermen recognize each other from far away.

If the fool has a hunchback no one remarks about it; if a wise man has a boil everybody talks about it.

A fool is not afraid to lose his mind.

Forgiveness is a pillar of justice.

Men will not be fortunate without a helping hand from misfortune.

Men who watch their fortune grow find their houses too small.

Fortune and misfortune live in the same courtyard.

Good fortune wears a pretty dress but its underclothes do not bear investigation.

A sleeping fox counts chicken in his dreams.

One who seeks no friends is his own enemy.

A thousand friends are few; one enemy is too many.

Tell me who's your friend and I'll tell you who you are.

If you don't have a hundred rubles, make sure you have a hundred friends.

He who is frightened of a sparrow will never sow barley.

One cannot make a fur coat from a "Thank you."

Don't praise your furnace when the house is cold.

If men could foresee the future, they would still behave as they do now.

The future is for those who know how to wait.

If everyone were a gentleman, who would make the mills work?

Hang a German, even if he is a good man.

Small gifts go to places where men expect bigger ones.

Giving gifts to the rich is like pouring water into the sea.

When a girl is born all four walls weep.

A girl never grows into a lady.

Pray to God, but keep on rowing to the shore.

God is always where we don't look for him.

If God listened to every shepherd's curse, our sheep would all be dead.

God doesn't give more beards than soap.

If God sends you meal, the devil takes the sack.

Honor goes to God; the priests get the bacon.

Tell God the truth, but give money to the judge.

Trust in God, but mind your own business.

Many who have gold in the house are looking for copper outside.

Golden hands, but a wicked mouth.

When gold speaks, everything else is silent.

Gossip needs no carriage.

Habit is a shirt that we wear till death.

The hammer shatters glass but hardens steel.

If one hand were the other they would both want to be clean.

No one is hanged who has money in his pocket.

Happiness is not a horse; you cannot harness it.

What makes you happy, makes you rich.

Haste is good only for catching flies.

After the head is off, one does not cry over the hair.

You don't get a headache from what other people have drunk.

What the heart doesn't see, the eye will not see either.

If your heart is a rose, then your mouth will speak perfumed words.

The hearth in our house is warmer than our neighbor's.

Who wants heat, must endure the smoke.

No one is dragged to heaven by the hair.

You get used to everything—even hell.

Whoever wants honey must breed bees.

There is no honor when there is nothing to eat.

The horses of hope gallop, but the asses of experience go slowly.

The horse may run quickly, but it can't escape its own tail.

When he mounts his horse he forgets God; when he dismounts, he forgets his horse.

If you are a host to your guest, be a host to his dog also.

When you are in a pack of hounds, you either bark or wag your tail.

If you want to be a hundred you must start young.

Hypocrites kick with their hind feet while licking with their tongues.

Ice in spring is treacherous; new friendships are seldom sure.

An indispensable thing never has much value.

If Jesus Christ comes to help me, I laugh at the angels.

Jesus Christ was crucified by public opinion.

Do not make jokes that cost more than a ruble.

Judges and physicians kill with impunity.

When you meet a man, you judge him by his clothes; when you leave, you judge him by his heart.

A golden handshake convinces even the most skeptical judge.

A jug that has been mended lasts two hundred years.

A word of kindness is better than a fat pie.

The more you know the less will you sleep.

Law is a flag and gold is the wind that makes it wave.

Fear the law not the judge.

God wanted to punish mankind, so he created lawyers.

Lie, but don't overdo it.

In the lake of lies there are many dead fish.

There is more light than can be seen through the window.

Live and scratch—when you're dead the itching will stop.

A lizard on a cushion will still seek leaves.

An old loan repaid is like finding something new.

A lonely person is at home everywhere.

Not all who make love make marriages.

Love and eggs are best when they are fresh.

Love has its own language, but marriage falls back on the local dialect.

Love is like a glass that breaks if handled clumsily.

Those who love you will make you weep; those who hate you will make you laugh.

The person afraid of bad luck will never know good.

Bad luck is fertile.

A man without a wife is like a man in winter without a fur cap.

Take a man at his word, an ox by the horns.

A good-looking man is pleasant to look at, but it is easier to live with an amusing one.

So the man, so his shadow.

After all, every man is the son of a woman.

The man is the flame, the woman the glow.

Why marry, when your neighbor's wife is ready to go to bed with you?

Meanness looks through one eye only, ambition is blind.

An empty mill will turn without the wind.

When misers die, children open up their coffers.

Misfortune does not visit the weak-hearted.

Mistrust is an axe in the tree of love.

When money speaks truth is silent.

Money is like down—one puff and it's gone.

Money is only good for a weekday, a holiday, and a rainy day.

Other people's money has sharp teeth.

The moon gives us light but no heat.

The morning is wiser than the evening.

If you flatter the mother, you will embrace the daughter.

What comes out of one mouth goes into a hundred others.

Give a naked man a piece of cloth and he will say it is too thick.

The naked don't fear robbery.

Where necessity speaks it demands.

When a needle sees a dagger, she cries "O sister!"

If you throw nettles into your neighbors garden you will find them growing in your own.

You can't sew buttons on your neighbor's mouth.

The night walks the same road as the dream.

The nights are short for him who married late in life.

A nightingale doesn't feed on songs.

The noblemen's quarrels can be read on the backs of the peasants.

With seven nurses the child loses its eye.

The offender never forgives.

If you talk to an official you must talk rubles.

An old man telling lies is like a rich man stealing.

Never kiss an opportunity with a dirty mouth.

The first pancake is always a failure.

Partnership is an invention of the devil.

Regretting the past is like chasing after the wind.

The past is for God, the future for the Tsars.

It is good to pay with other people's money.

A bad peace is better than a good quarrel.

Eternal peace lasts until the next war.

Make peace with people; wage war with your sins.

The peasant sweats and the nobleman is always right.

If the peasant doesn't hear the thunder he won't make the sign of the cross.

Invite a peasant to your table and he'll put his feet on it.

A pessimist is a well-informed optimist.

The poorer, the more generous.

If a poor man finds a penny, it is probably a false one.

Poverty is not a sin, it's worse than that.

Poverty is a sin that the rich never forgive.

It's better to be known as a rascal than a fool.

There is no repentance after death.

Pray for revenge, and God will turn a deaf ear.

He who doesn't risk never gets to drink champagne.

The river is flat but the banks are steep.

The river's reputation ends where the sea begins.

One road for the fugitive and a hundred for the pursuer.

If rubles fell from heaven the poor would have no bag.

In Russia every day is of thirty hours.

Don't look for a sea when you can drown in a puddle.

Make yourself a sheep and the wolf is ready.

If you don't crack the shell, you can't eat the nut.

The shovel insults the poker.

A sin of gold is followed by a punishment of lead.

When we sing everybody hears us, when we sigh nobody hears us.

No one can take two skins from one ox.

The slower you go, the farther you will be.

Warm a frozen snake and it will be the first to bite you.

Soap is grey but it used to be white.

The sober man's secret is the drunkard's speech.

One son is no son, two sons is no son, but three sons is a son.

Don't blame your wife's side if your son is crosseyed.

Sorrow doesn't kill, but it blights.

There is plenty of sound in an empty barrel.

Spending is quick, earning is slow.

In a rickety stable the cow produces no milk.

First the stable, then the cow.

The stargazer's toe is often stubbed.

You cannot drive straight on a twisting lane.

A stranger's soul is like a dark forest.

Rotten straw can harm a healthy horse.

You have summer and you have winter—why, then, be in a hurry?

No year has two summers.

We all see the same sun, but we don't eat the same meal.

As long as the sun shines one does not ask for the moon.

A tale is soon told; a deed is not soon done.

Who talks little hears better.

The tears of strangers are only water.

The thief has a chicken's heart—he sleeps in fear.

The thief makes perhaps one mistake; those he stole from made a
hundred.

It will last out our time; if after us no grass grows, what does it matter
to us?

In the garden of time grows the flower of consolation.

A toad too would like to crack nuts, but he has no teeth.

You must chop down the tree that gives too much or too little shade.

Bury truth in a golden coffin, it will break it open.

Truth does not need many words.

Rather a bitter truth than a sweet lie.

The Tsar has three hands but only one ear.

He who serves the Tsar cannot serve his people.

Close to the Tsar, close to death.

A cross-eyed Tsar, one-eyed ministers, blind subjects.

When the Tsar sins the Empire must do penance.

A drop of water in the eyes of the Tsar costs the country many hand-kerchiefs.

A virgin's heart is a dark forest.

Vodka is the aunt of wine.

The vulture embraced the chicken until its last breath.

Water never loses its way.

Once you have fallen into the water, you're not scared of water any more.

Who falls in the water will hold on to the foam to save himself.

Better to turn back than to lose your way.

Badly oiled wheels will squeak.

Long whiskers cannot take the place of brains.

There are more whores in hiding than there are public ones.

The wife is twice precious only; when led into the house, and when taken out.

A wife should be as humble as a lamb, busy as a bee, as beautiful as a bird of paradise and faithful as a turtle dove.

A good wife and a wholesome cabbage soup, what more could you want?

There is nothing better than a rich wife and a generous mother-in-law.

Wine bears no blame—only the drunkard.

It is never winter in the land of hope.

A wise man sees only water in the tears of a woman.

You cannot buy wisdom abroad if there is none at home.

Wisdom is born; stupidity is learned.

Be wise, but pretend to be ignorant.

The wise man says "I am looking for truth"; and the fool, "I have found truth."

No matter how much you feed a wolf, he will always return to the forest.

Rwanda

The wolf will hire himself out very cheaply as a shepherd.

Make a friend of the wolf, but keep your axe ready.

The wolf is not afraid of the sheepdog, but he is of his chain.

When night falls the face of the wolf lights up.

A woman's tongue is longer than her hair.

You would do better to sit on a powder keg than on the knee of a woman.

One stupid woman recognizes another one from a distance.

Where you saw wood, there the sawdust will fall.

You can't keep a word of thanks in your pocket.

A friendly word is like a spring day.

A spoken word is like a sparrow that once has flown away, cannot be caught again.

Work makes you into a hunchback and then rich.

One never tires working for oneself.

Rwanda

In a court of fowls, the cockroach never wins his case.

If you are building a house and a nail breaks, do you stop building, or do you change the nail?

When the leopard is away, his cubs are eaten.

You set the trap when the rat has gone.

Pregnancy and fire cannot be kept secret.

Help from abroad always comes when the rain has stopped.

The most extensive land is the human belly.

What itches in the daughter's skirt, itches also in her mother's.

When the child falls the mother weeps; when the mother falls the child laughs.

Every cackling hen was an egg at first.

Hens keep quiet when the cock is around.

A girl only gets pregnant once.

He who has travelled alone can tell what he likes.

The rich man never dances badly.

Samoa

You shake in vain the branch that bears no fruit.

Gather the breadfruit from the farthest branches first.

The person with burned fingers asks for tongs.

A decision made at night may be changed in the morning.

Like a fish, one should look for a hole in the net.

Blessed is the moon; it goes but it comes back again.

Sin is carried in the mouth.

Sit and wait for the good chestnuts.

Stones decay; words last.

May it end with threats and not come to blows.

Sanskrit Proverbs

There are none so deaf as those who will not hear advice.

They know not their own defects who search for the defects of others.

By slitting the ears and cutting the tail, a dog is still a dog, not a horse, not an ass.

The eyes do not see what the mind does not want.

The tip of a finger cannot be touched by itself.

If a man's heart be impure, all things will appear hostile to him.

To quarrel with a man of good speech is better than to converse with a man who does not speak well.

As the spokes of a wheel are attached to the hub, so all things are attached to life.

The wise must be respected, even when the advice they give is not suitable.

Something done at the wrong time should be regarded as not done.

Take a close look at today, because yesterday is but a dream and to-morrow is barely a vision. A good well-lived today makes every yesterday a dream of a good future, and every morning is a vision of hope. Take a close look then at today.

Fear is the fever of life.

The beggar is not afraid of the drawbacks of being rich.

The diamond in your belly sparkles on your face.

Love is a crocodile in the river of desire.

What nectar can be drunk with the ears? Good advice.

You cannot cook one half of the chicken and leave the other lay eggs.

As day breaks, the glowworms say "We've lit up the world!"

A fool who knows he is a fool has a little intelligence, but a fool that thinks he is intelligent is really a fool.

Who is the happiest person in the world? An unfaithful husband.

The greatest hero is one who has control over his desires.

Truth has but one color, a lie has many.

The wind sweeps the road clean.

Where there is no honey, we have to make do with treacle.

A house without a child is like a tomb.

Snakes turn milk into poison.

You sometimes forget the harm that was done to you, but never the harm you have done to others.

An elephant never tires of carrying his own trunk.

There are three things that refresh the heart and reduce your grief: water, flowers, and a beautiful woman.

The water from the river becomes salty when it reaches the ocean.

A woman talks to one man, looks at another, and thinks about a third.

A sin that is confessed is less heavy to bear.

He who allows his day to pass by without practicing generosity and
enjoying life's pleasures is like a blacksmith's bellows: he breathes
but does not live.

Sardinia

Better pain in your purse than in your heart.

Who steals for others is hanged for himself.

Scotland

A blind man needs no looking glass.

If you don't see the bottom, don't wade.

You will never know a man till you do business with him.

It ill becomes a carpenter to be heavy-handed, a smith to be shake-
handed, or a physician to be tenderhearted.

Good company on a journey is worth a coach.

The hand that rocks the cradle rules the world.

Better to be a cuckold and not know it than to not be one and everybody say so.

What cannot be cured must be endured.

A day to come seems longer than a year that's gone.

If the Devil were dead, folk would do little for God's sake.

The Devil's a busy bishop in his own diocese.

Diet cures more than doctors.

Never draw your dirk when a blow will do it.

What may be done at any time will be done at no time.

If I had a dog as daft, I would shoot him.

Egotism is an alphabet of one letter.

Enough's as good as a feast.

Confessed faults are half mended.

There's no medicine for fear.

Be slow in choosing a friend, but slower in changing him.

Hours are Time's shafts, and one comes winged with death.

A house without a dog, a cat, or a little child is a house without joy or laughter.

A hungry man smells meat far.

He that peeks through a keyhole may see what will vex him.

All that's said in the kitchen should not be told in the hall.

He that loves law will soon get his fill of it.

Laws catch flies, but let hornets go free.

It's an ill cause that a lawyer thinks shame of.

Law's costly—take a pint and agree.

A wise lawyer never goes to law himself.

Be happy while you're living, for you're a long time dead.

Better to be off with the old love before we be on with the new.

A man cannot wive and thrive the same year.

Better half hanged than ill married.

Married folk are like rats in a trap—fain to get others in, but fain to be out themselves.

He that marries a widow will have a dead man's head often thrown in his dish.

The medicine that hurts the most is generally the best healer.

Many a mickle makes a muckle.

Money is flat and meant to be piled up.

Money is better than my lord's letter.

If ye had as little money as ye have manners, ye would be the poorest man of all your kin.

There never was a five-pound note but there was a ten-pound road for it.

A nod's as good as a wink to a blind horse.

I would as soon see your nose be cheese, and the cat get the first bite of it.

Penny wise and pound foolish.

He who will not prosper in his sleep will not prosper when awake.

Get what you can and keep what you have; that's the way to get rich.

A rich man's wooing need seldom be a long one.

Ye may not sit in Rome and strive with the Pope.

Slippery is the flagstone at the mansion-house door.

A slothful man is a beggar's brother.

From saving comes having.

Better be ill spoken of by one before all than by all before one.

Every man to his taste, as the man said when he kissed his cow.

War makes thieves, and peace hangs them.

One whisky is all right; two is too much; three is too few.

Never take a wife till you know what to do with her.

Choose your wife with her nightcap on.

A bad wound may heal, but a bad name will kill.

Senegal

Ambition begets troubles.

All birds will flock to a fruitful tree.

Even Buddhist priests of the same temple quarrel occasionally.

Eat coconuts while you have teeth.

The cow steps on the calf, but she does not hate it.

Even the fall of a dancer is a somersault.

A healthy ear can stand hearing sick words.

An intelligent enemy is better than a stupid friend.

Don't try to make someone hate the person he loves, for he will still go on loving, but he will hate you.

The heart is not a knee that can be bent.

What's the use of consulting a dead man's horoscope?

Nobody tells all he knows.

It is better to be loved than feared.

He may say that he loves you, wait and see what he does for you.

To spend the night in anger is better than to spend it repenting.

The opportunity that God sends does not wake up him who is asleep.

Three kinds of people die poor: those who divorce, those who incur debts, and those who move around too much.

The strong don't need clubs.

If you had teeth of steel, you could eat iron coconuts.

The truth is like gold: keep it locked up and you will find it exactly as you first put it away.

Spilled water is better than a broken jar.

What you give to others bears fruit for yourself.

A tree that grows in the shade of another one will die small.

The night is the king of the shadows.

A rotten fish pollutes the whole kitchen.

What a cow eats a calf drinks.

A lobster loves water, but not when he's being cooked in it.

Trusting in wealth is like looking for feathers on turtles.

The wolf dies where the pack is.

An intelligent foe is better than a stupid friend.

Poverty is an older daughter of laziness.

Kings have no friends.

The jungle is stronger than the elephant.

Serbia

It is easy to advise the wise.

The glory of ancestors should not prevent a man from winning glory for himself.

Warm bed, cold food.

To believe is easier than investigation.

Quick to believe is quickly deceived.

When big bells ring, little ones are not heard.

Better to blush once than pale a hundred times.

You don't need a candle to look for a fool.

It does no harm now and then to burn a candle for the devil.

To set fire to a church is not so bad as to speak ill of a virgin.

When coins rattle, philosophers are silent.

A dead man pays no debts.

A good deed is the best form of prayer.

Even the devil knows what is right, but he will not do it.

One devil does not scratch out another devil's eyes.

Where there are no dogs the wolves will howl.

He who drinks on credit, gets drunk twice.

Mother earth promised to tell her secrets to heaven.

A greedy father has thieves for children.

A foolish fox is caught by one leg, but a wise one by all four.

It is easy to tempt a frog to the river.

What is it to be a gentleman? Firstly it is to be thankful and secondly to complain.

You never get a headache from winning.

If you can't hold on to the horse's mane then don't try to hang on to its tail.

Jealousy and fear have big eyes.

You can judge what you make by what others make.

An empty knapsack is heavier to carry than a full one.

A man without enemies is worthless.

It is difficult to find a man but it's easy to recognize him.

The first marriage is a plate of honey, the second a glass of wine, and the third is a cup of poison.

Money and the devil know no rest.

It is better to make money in the straw market than to lose it in the money market.

Everyone is worth more than his neighbor and less than his son.

Peace pays what war wins.

A clean pig makes lean bacon.

It is not at the table but in prison that you learn who your true friends are.

There's nothing worse than a person looking for a quarrel.

A good reputation is better than a golden girdle.

Better retreat in honor than advance in disgrace.

To serve our elders is a duty, our equals it is polite, but serving the young is humiliating.

Solitude is full of God.

When a stepmother moves in, the father becomes a stepfather.

It is better to be threatened by the sword of a Turk than by the pen of a German.

Time builds castles, and time destroys them.

What makes you tired makes you stronger.

A tree near the road is easily cut down.

After a trial one party is naked and the other without a shirt.

We won the war, but lost peace.

Let war be waged in the house of him who wants it.

A wife is frightened of her first husband and a husband is frightened of his second wife.

When your wine is finished, conversation ends; when your money has been spent, you lose your friends.

Do not measure the wolf's tail till he is dead.

What is the use of a big wide world when your shoes are too small?

The wound heals, the scar remains.

Sicily

The less things change, the more they remain the same.

Who is blind, dumb and deaf will live a peaceful life of a hundred years.

Only your real friends will tell you when your face is dirty.

Freedom is a plateful of hard crusts.

Unspoken words cannot be noted.

Sierra Leone

A paddle here, a paddle there—the canoe stays still.

Do not tell the man who is carrying you that he stinks.

A cow must graze where she is tied.

It is the wandering dog that finds the old bone.

An elephant's head is no load for a child.

A big fish is caught with big bait.

He who refuses a gift will not fill his barn.

When a single hair has fallen from your head, you are not yet bald.

However full the house, the hen finds a corner to lay in.

Invite people into your parlor, and they will come into your bedroom.

Only a monkey understands a monkey.

An orange never bears a lime.

Quarrels end, but words once spoken never die.

Sweet rice is eaten quickly.

If you climb up a tree, you must climb down the same tree.

He who upsets something should know how to put it back again.

Death is the key that will open a miser's coffers.

Even though chickens don't wash, their eggs are still white.

A black cow also gives white milk.

A hundred aunts is not the same as one mother.

To try and fail is not laziness.

Slovakia

Better to eat bread in peace, then cake amid turmoil.
Who buys cheap pays twice.
Cabbage is best after it is reheated seven times.
Custom and law are sisters.
The flour tastes bitter to the mouse who has had enough.
Gold without wisdom is but clay.
There is no wise response to a foolish remark.
He who accepts favors, pawns his freedom.
In the darkness all cows are black.
Man is the head and woman is the crown upon it.
The gates of hell are always open, even at midnight.
The one who first shuts up in an argument is from a good family.
He who blows into the wind gets smoke in his eyes.

Slovenia

It is easier to believe than to go and ask.
Who is forced to go to church will not pray.
Never whisper to the deaf or wink at the blind.
Pray to God for a good harvest, but keep on hoeing!
Man's life is like a drop of dew on a leaf.
Every road does not lead to Rome.
A doorstep is the highest of all mountains.
In small churches, small saints are big.
You can do nothing about governments and winter.
God knows why he has made the wings of some birds shorter.

Solomon Islands

Foam will always find its way to the shore.

A fruit tree that grows in a dung heap will certainly blossom.

The bigger the pot the more rice will stick to it.

Somalia

A brother is like one's shoulder.

A coward is full of precaution.

Where I make a living, there is my home.

In the ocean, one does not need to sow water.

Poverty is slavery.

One cannot count on riches.

He who does not shave you does not cut you.

Do not walk into a snake pit with your eyes open.

A thief is always under suspicion.

Water and milk do not mix.

Wisdom does not come overnight.

A brave man is scared of a lion three times: first when he sees the tracks; second when he hears the first roar; and third when they are face to face.

The fowl digs out the blade that kills it.

To be without a friend is to be poor indeed.

South Africa

You are not great just because you say you are.

If he keeps on imitating everybody the monkey will one day cut his own throat.

The fool who owns an ox is seldom recognized as a fool.

South America

The heart is like a goat that has to be tied up.

Even the maid has a family.

No hill without gravestones, no valley without shadows.

When you have a lot to do, start with a meal.

A fool is a wise man's ladder.

Before you milk a cow tie it up.

He who has no intelligence is happy with it.

If you are looking for a fly in your food it means that you are full.

As great birds die the eggs rot.

When you shoot a zebra in the black stripe, the white dies too; shoot it in the white and the black dies too.

South America

The baby who doesn't cry isn't nursed.

I don't want the cheese, I just want to get out of the trap.

Become famous, then go to sleep.

The lazybones must work twice.

He who prays a lot is afraid of something.

Better a devil you know than a hundred strangers.

For our sins God has created three enemies for us: mice in the house, the fox in the mountains, and a priest in our village.

He who lives on illusions, dies of disillusion.

Two cats will not live together in one sack.

Hens perched on top will shit on those below.

Old love and wood will burn as soon as they get the chance.

Such is the fate of the sheep: either shorn or roasted.

Light in the streets, shadows in the house.

A good guitarist will play on one string.

God writes on crooked lines.

The daughter-in-law wipes away what the mother-in-law has seen.

Spain

Old debts are never paid, and the new ones get old easily.

If you are going to die you will die in the dark even if you have been in the candle business.

Laughing wife, crying purse.

Widows weep but they look for another husband.

None of us knows who we are.

You cannot hide the sun with one hand.

Spain

As the abbot sings the sacristan responds.

He who was first an acolyte, and afterwards an abbot or curate, knows what the boys do behind the altar.

Advise no one to go to war or to marry.

Never let a poor man advise you on investments.

A man who prides himself on his ancestry is like the potato plant, the best part of which is underground.

April and May make meal for the whole year.

There's no argument like that of the stick.

Never ask of him who has, but of him who wishes you well.

If three people say you are an ass, put on a bridle.

The bachelor is a peacock, the fiancé is a lion and the married man a mule.

A hundred years hence we shall all be bald.

Beads about the neck, and the devil in the heart.

Beauty and chastity are always quarreling.

If you have nothing better to do, go to bed with your own wife.

Of what you see, believe very little, of what you are told, nothing.

There are no birds in last year's nest.

He who deals with a blockhead will need a lot of brains.

An ounce of blood is worth more than a pound of friendship.

Spain

Blood boils without fire.

One cannot blow and swallow at the same time.

See to it that you have many books and many friends—but be sure
  they are good ones.

I cried when I was born and as each day passes I know why.

He who sows brambles must not go barefoot.

Who gives the bread lays down the authority.

A day without bread lasts long.

The pearls of a bride on her wedding day are the tears that will be
  shed later.

Between brothers, two witnesses and a notary.

Talking about bulls is altogether different from being in the arena.

The art of doing business lies more in paying than in buying.

Every cask smells of the wine it contains.

The cat always leaves her mark upon her friend.

If you cannot be chaste, be cautious.

Cheap things cost a lot of money.

Cheat me with the price, but not with the goods I buy.

Don't refuse a wing to the one who gave you the chicken.

What children hear their parents say by the fireside, they repeat in
  the highway.

Late children are early orphans.

Conscience is what tells you not to do what you have just done.

Cow of many—well milked and badly fed.

I thought I had made the sign of the cross—and I hurt my eye.

I dance to the tune that is played.

However early you get up you cannot hasten the dawn.

If you want to be dead, wash your head and go to bed.

The dead open the eyes of the living.

There is no remedy for death, but death itself is a remedy.

Death is the reaper who doesn't take a midday nap.

Spain

Better a quiet death than a public misfortune.

Debts are like children, the smaller they are the louder they scream.

Pay me back what you owe me; we'll talk later about what I owe you.

That's a wise delay which makes the road safe.

To deny everything is to confess everything.

There is nothing like deprivation to generate thanks for small mercies.

Limit your desires and you will improve your health.

What is much desired is not believed when it comes.

Buy from desperate people, and sell to newlyweds.

Desperation is the mistress of the impossible.

The devil climbs the bell tower in a priest's cassock.

The devil hides behind the cross.

"If the devil is going to take me," said the courtesan, "let it be in a coach."

If the devil is going to disguise himself, it will be as a monk or a lawyer.

If I die, I forgive you; if I recover, we shall see.

Dine with arrogance, sleep with shame.

Discretion is a way of hiding what you cannot help.

He who divides gets the worst share.

If two doctors visit a sick man, the sexton rings the bells.

It is better to skip one meal than to consult a hundred doctors.

Watch out for the dog that doesn't bark and the man who says nothing.

When there is real danger, the dogs don't bark.

A dog won't bite you if you are carrying a stick.

It's the grinding of his teeth that awakes the blacksmith's dog, not the noise of the hammer.

I would rather have a donkey that can carry me than a horse that throws me.

A donkey decked in gold is better than an over-laden horse.

If there is still doubt do not accuse.

Only God helps the badly dressed.

Drink nothing without seeing it; sign nothing without reading it.

The first drink with water, the second without water, the third like water.

Under a tattered cloak you will generally find a good drinker.

The earth produces all things and receives all again.

The first one to eat, the last one to work.

If your enemy is up to his waist in water, give him your hand; if the water reaches his shoulders, stand on his head.

He who never has enough, never has anything.

Experience is not always the kindest of teachers, but it is surely the best.

He who lost his faith, has nothing more to lose.

Two cannot fall out if one does not choose.

There was already twenty in the family, so my grandmother had a baby.

A day of fasting is the eve of a feast.

Fate sends almonds to toothless people.

The father a saint, the son a sinner.

Her father's fortune will make the ugliest girl attractive.

He who asks the fewest favors is the best received.

Fear and love never eat from the same plate.

To live in fear is a life half-lived.

When there is a war between fire and water, fire loses.

A hidden fire is discovered by its smoke.

The one who rings the fire bell is safe.

Painted flowers have no scent.

If fools went not to market, bad wares would not be sold.

Let fools and wind pass.

A fool is someone who trusts another fool.

Spain

The fox knows a lot, but a woman in love knows even more.

Nothing falls into the mouth of a sleeping fox.

Avoid a friend who covers you with his wings and destroys you with his beak.

A friend to everybody and to nobody is the same thing.

When a friend asks, there is no tomorrow.

Beware of a reconciled friend as of the devil.

Tell your friend a lie—and if he keeps it a secret, tell him the truth.

To offer friendship to one who is looking for love, is like giving bread to someone dying of thirst.

When two friends dip into their purse, one laughs, the other cries.

It is good to have friends, even in hell.

Young gamblers, old beggars.

Many things grow in the garden that were never sown there.

To give too much when little is asked is a form of refusal.

Say nothing when you give—only when you receive.

God comes to see without ringing the bell.

He who leaves his people will be left by God.

Good men must die, but death cannot kill their names.

If you are not good for yourself, how can you be good for others?

If it is good then the deed is more important than the intention; if it's bad then the intention is worse than the deed.

Look for the good and let the bad things come on their own.

Who gossips with you will gossip about you.

To the grateful man give more than he asks.

Compare your griefs with other men's and they will seem less.

Do not rejoice at my grief, for when mine is told, yours will be new.

Guests always have nice backs.

Habits are first gossamer then cables.

Halfway is twelve miles when you have fourteen miles to go.

Happiness itself does not stay—only moments of happiness do.

Spain

If you would live in health, grow old early.

A man too busy to take care of his health is like a mechanic too busy to take care of his tools.

The heart is like the astrologer who guesses at the truth.

Better visit hell in your lifetime than after you're dead.

Hell is full of the ungrateful.

He who helps everybody, helps nobody.

Tie up the hen that eats at your place and lays eggs elsewhere.

What have you to hide from someone who shows you his arse?

In the absence of honest men, they made my father mayor.

I know they are all honest men, but my cloak is nowhere to be found.

Honor and money cannot go in the same sack.

A man without honor smells worse than a corpse.

Better a good hope than a bad possession.

The horse may wish to do one thing, but he who saddles him another.

One takes care of the horse, another rides it.

Idiots can sometimes give good advice.

Insults should be well avenged or well endured.

Italians talk to women, Frenchmen to the learned, and the Spaniard talks to God.

On a long journey, even a straw weighs heavy.

Hidden joy is an extinguished candle.

The judge's son goes into the courtroom without fear.

Wet kisses are the messengers of the heart.

He who knows nothing doubts nothing.

He who knows nothing is as blind as him who cannot see.

Laws, like the spider's web, catch the fly and let the hawk go free.

From the leather of others you can cut long strips.

Liberty has no price.

Tell a lie and find the truth.

To lie and eat fish demand a lot of skill.

Spain

A good life, they say, keeps wrinkles at bay.

A good life is the best sermon.

Life is a gift for which we pay dearly.

Never praise life in front of death, nor the beautiful day in front of
night.

Life without a friend is death without a witness.

What cures the liver harms the spleen.

In a choice between bad company and loneliness—the second is preferable.

Where you lose nothing, you always win something.

Losers are always in the wrong.

Love kills with golden arrows.

Love is like a mousetrap: you go in when you want, but you don't get
out when you like.

Love is like war: you begin when you like and leave off when you can.

When two are in love, only one needs to eat.

When love is not madness, it is not love.

Love, pain, and money cannot be kept secret; they soon betray themselves.

Love can do much, money can do everything.

In the face of love and death, courage is useless.

Where there is love, there is pain.

Lovers always think that other people have had their eyes put out.

At twenty a man will be a peacock, at thirty a lion, at forty a camel,
at fifty a serpent, at sixty a dog, at seventy a monkey, and at eighty
nothing.

A malicious man is like a coal sack—black on the outside and even
blacker inside.

The man deliberates, the woman decides.

Men are just as God made them—and a little worse.

A man in love schemes more than a hundred lawyers.

Of the malady a man fears, he dies.

Spain

She who loves an ugly man thinks him handsome.

Man, woman, and love created fire.

When you are talking about marriage, think about your mother.

Marriage is a sack full of ninety-nine snakes and one eel.

Marriage is a little bit like buying melons, you need a little luck.

Well-married is when you have no mother-in-law and no sister-in-law.

If you want to marry wisely, marry your equal.

Memory is life's clock.

Memory is everyone's friend—it leaves you when you need it most.

Mirrors were not made for the blind.

No mirror ever reflected an ugly woman.

The most faithful mirror is an old friend.

The miser will stubbornly live poorly in order to die rich.

If you want to know the value of money, go and borrow some.

An ounce of mother is worth a ton of priest.

Even a sugar mother-in-law tastes bitter.

To drunken mothers-in-law give full jugs.

It is better to be a mouse in a cat's mouth than a man in a lawyer's hands.

The mice will never play with the kittens.

Too much bursts the bag.

There are three "too much" and three "too little" that can bring a fool down: too much spending and too little money; too much talking and too little knowledge; and too much boasting and too little earnings.

Ask for too much in order to get enough.

He who talks to a mule is one himself.

If your roof is made of glass, don't throw stones at your neighbor's house.

Wipe the nose of your neighbor's son and let him marry your daughter.

Spain

In the presence of your neighbor don't praise your wife or his.

For a bad night, a mattress of wine.

How beautiful it is to do nothing, and then rest afterward.

The oaths of one who loves a woman are not to be believed.

Old age is cruel for whores and magicians.

Don't call me a little olive until you've picked me.

Don't worry if people call you ordinary—only if you are ordinary.

A solitary ox shits more than a hundred swallows.

An old ox makes a straight furrow.

The patient who names a doctor his heir makes a big mistake.

Patience begins with tears and ends with a smile.

Always be patient with the rich and powerful.

If the peacock were to look at its feet, it would stop him strutting.

He who peeps through a hole may see what will vex him.

People are the architects of their own fortune.

A good man's pedigree is little hunted up.

A pig bought on credit grunts all the year.

The pig's tail will never make a good arrow.

He who plants the lettuce doesn't always eat the salad.

If you would be pope, you must think of nothing else.

The body of the pope takes up no more room than the sexton's.

Poverty is even worse if you have to sleep on the edge of a crowded
     bed.

Punishment is a cripple, but it arrives.

The empty purse says she is made of leather.

Indiscreet questions must be answered with a lie.

Feed the raven and he'll peck out your eyes.

If you want to be respected, you must respect yourself.

Retreating is not the same as fleeing.

He who would be rich should not collect money, but reduce his
     needs.

Spain

He who wants to bring home the riches of India, he must have them within himself.

He is always right who suspects that he is always wrong.

Nothing is gained without taking risks.

Where the river is deepest it makes the least noise.

In large rivers one finds big fish but one may also be drowned.

A rose too often smelled loses its fragrance.

An absent saint gets no candles.

Let the salad-maker be a spendthrift for oil, a miser for vinegar, a statesman for salt, and a madman for tossing.

Between two Saturdays happen many marvels.

To whom you tell your secrets you resign your liberty.

The secret of two no further will go; the secret of three a hundred will know.

If you want good service, serve yourself.

Shyness is the prison of the heart.

If the sky falls, hold up your hands.

If you want to sleep well, buy the bed of a bankrupt.

Treat the small in the way you would want to be treated by the big.

In a soap maker's house, a person who doesn't fall, slips.

He to whom God gives no sons, the devil gives nephews.

A son-in-law and a pig will show you the way only once.

It rains sorrow on him who is already wet.

Soup must be hot—insults cold.

Three Spaniards, four opinions.

Spanish is the language of lovers, Italian is for the singer, French for diplomats, and German for horses.

The snake that seduced Eve spoke Spanish.

Not everyone who wears spurs owns a horse.

An empty stomach will not listen to anything.

Stubborn men make lawyers.

Spain

Who stumbles without falling makes a bigger step.

However bright the sun may shine, leave not your cloak at home.

Suppers have killed more than doctors have ever cured.

There is no better surgeon than one with many scars.

One cannot learn to swim in a field.

A person who talks a lot is sometimes right.

Talking is easy, action is difficult.

Frivolous talk is like shooting without aiming.

Don't talk too much, because your ignorance is greater than your
knowledge.

Two great talkers never go far together.

It takes taste to account for taste.

Learn from your tears and you will win laughing.

He who forgives a thief is a thief himself.

The open house makes a good man of the thief.

Time and I against any two.

Tomorrow is often the busiest day of the week.

trouble will rain on those who are already wet.

Patched trousers, healthy testicles.

Never show the truth naked—just in its shirt.

The turd is proud that the river will carry it.

Everything in its season, and turnips in Advent.

The greatest victory is a bloodless victory.

One should eat sand rather than fall to villainy.

Walk till the blood appears on the cheek, but not the sweat on the
brow.

Let him who does not know what war is go to war.

When war begins the devil makes hell bigger.

In wartime no sweets are given out.

He who has a good looking wife, a castle on the river, or a vineyard
on the roadside is never without war.

If your wife tells you to throw yourself off a cliff, pray to God that it is a low one.

To friend and foe alike I tell them how bad she is, so that I don't have to share her with anyone.

A beautiful wife without money is like a fine house without furniture.

He that would have a beautiful wife should choose her on a Sunday.

The wind changes every day, a woman every second.

There is a great art in selling the wind.

It is better to have bread left over than to run short of wine.

Spilled wine is a sign of happiness, but break the bed and all will have long faces.

It is better to weep with wise men than to laugh with fools.

A wise man changes his mind, a fool never will.

Wit without discretion is a sword in the hand of a fool.

The wolf loses his teeth, but not his inclinations.

If you live with wolves learn to howl.

A wolf's mourning is the fox's feast.

A woman's advice is of little value, but he who does not take it is a fool.

To tell a woman what she cannot do is to tell her what she can.

The fear of women is the basis of good health.

The only chaste woman is the one who has not been asked.

Women and calendars are good only for a year.

The nightingale will run out of songs before a woman runs out of conversation.

The woman who dresses well attracts the husband from another woman's door.

Keeping a woman to her word is like trying to hold an eel by its tail.

A woman's tears are worth a lot, but cost little.

Women and wine rid a man of his common sense.

For a chaste woman God is enough.

Women, melons, and cheese are bought by the weight.

Confide in a woman and a magpie if you want something to be broadcast.

A woman's belly is a garden with many fruits.

Sickly women live longer.

Between the "yes" and "no" of a woman you can't place a pin.

Watch out for a bad woman and never trust a good one.

There is no woman who sleeps so deeply that the sound of a guitar won't bring her to the window.

Women and melons are at their best when they are really ripe.

I've fried my sausage in better pans than these.

A word and a stone let go cannot be recalled.

Friendly words gain much and cost nothing.

The spoken word sometimes loses what silence has won.

The best word still has to be spoken.

Working and painting are better from a distance.

Work improves the harvest better than the field itself.

Paid workmen have no arms.

The world is a round gulf, and he who cannot swim must go to the bottom.

Wrinkles are the gravestones of love.

Even the best writer has to erase.

Since I wronged you, I have never liked you.

You must tolerate that which you cannot change.

Early flowers give no seed.

He who shelters under a tree gets twice as wet.

A fool who knows Latin is never a real fool.

He who eats a partridge in his youth will only be left with feathers in his old age.

Love can do much, money can do more.

The more you flatter a fool, the more seriously he plays his game.

Out of love for the ox, the wolf licks the yoke.
Never beg from one who was a beggar.
A lot of weeds will grow in a stagnant pond.
The advice of foxes is dangerous for chickens.
It is no fun to guard a house with two doors.
Don't be afraid of a spot that can be removed with water.
A young woman is to an old man the horse that he rides to hell.
He who is proud of his sins, sins twice as much.
Words must be weighed not counted.
When the Spaniard sings he is either stupid or without money.
Who preaches in the desert loses his sermon.
Sorrows are valuable treasures that you only show to your friends.
Never by-pass a town where a friend lives.
The best or the worst for a man is his wife.
If the doctor is fasting it is bad for the priest.
The road of "about," leads only to the house of "never."
Near the spring nobody dies of thirst.

Sri Lanka

You would do better to be someone's victim rather than someone's certainty.
If the devil is your godfather you will be welcome in hell.
For he who has the time even the jungle is a paradise.
It's the rain that fills the rivers not the dew.

Sudan

When the monkey can't reach the ripe banana with his hand, he says it is not sweet.
Let rats shoot arrows at each other.

A little shrub may grow into a tree.

A termite can do nothing to a stone save lick it.

The poor are excused from washing with soap.

Ebb does not follow ebb—flood is in between.

The hand suffers at work, but the mouth still must eat.

Eggs and iron must not be in the same bag.

A dog cannot carry its puppies on its back.

If a dog bites you and you don't bite him back, it will say that you have no teeth.

When a hen is brooding, another hen cannot sit on her eggs.

A young crocodile does not cry when he falls in the water.

Even the sharpest ear cannot hear an ant singing.

It is sad when the elephant dies, but the whole tribe can feed on it.

If you are wearing shoes, you don't fear the thorns.

Don't cough in a hiding place.

A big chair does not make a king.

A naked man will often laugh at someone with torn clothes.

The soup would be none the worse for more meat.

Sufi Proverbs

Faith is confirmed by the heart, confessed by the tongue, and acted upon by the body.

A phantasm can be a bridge that men cross toward reality.

There wouldn't be such a thing as counterfeit gold if there were no real gold somewhere.

Sumerian Proverbs

If you lie and then tell the truth, the truth will be considered a lie.

That which is mine makes other people's things seem strange.

Whoever has walked with truth generates life.

Suriname

A dog with many masters, dies of starvation.
You don't need to open your mouth at noon to cough in the evening.
You have two ears, but you never hear words twice.

Swahili Proverbs

Aiming isn't hitting.
Haste has no blessing.
Bribery is the enemy of justice.
If you destroy a bridge, be sure you can swim.
Two crocodiles cannot agree.
Death is blind.
A distant fire does not burn.
A fly does not mind dying in coconut cream.
A letter from the heart can be read on the face.
The path of a liar is short.
Don't plant a seed in the sea.
To a physician a sick man is a garden.

Sweden

Advice should be viewed from behind.
The afternoon knows what the morning never suspected.
It is seldom the fault of one when two argue.
Choose your bedfellows by day.
When a blind man carries a lame man, both go forward.

Sweden

A piece of bread in your pocket is better than a feather in your hat.

Eaten bread is soon forgotten.

What breaks in a moment may take years to mend.

Don't throw away the old bucket until you know whether the new one is watertight.

He who builds and he who marries are never safe.

Butterflies forget that they were once caterpillars.

If you buy what you don't need, you steal from yourself.

Who is chasing after another must himself rest.

A child is a certain sorrow and uncertain joy.

The day we fear hastens toward us, the day we long for creeps.

Death is the last doctor.

Death is God's broom.

The devil visits the rich too—but he visits the poor twice.

Devils have more than twelve apostles.

The strongest among the disabled is the one who never forgets his disability.

Fear less, hope more; eat less, chew more; whine less, breathe more; talk less, say more; hate less, love more; and all good things will be yours.

Lovely flowers fade fast. Weeds last the season.

All fools are brothers.

In a small house God has His corner, in a big house He has to stand in the hall.

Happiness does not give, it only lends.

Lend to God and the earth—they both pay good interest.

A life without love is like a year without summer.

He who has long fingers should also have long legs.

Love has produced some heroes but even more idiots.

Love is like dew that falls on both nettles and lilies.

A man without money is like a boat without sails.

Sweden

As the master sleeps, the servant dreams.

The master has long arms, but they don't reach heaven.

Midsummer night is not long but it sets many cradles rocking.

The miser is his own mother-in-law.

If you marry money the devil lays an egg in your storeroom.

You cannot ask more of an ox than a steak.

A peacock has too little in its head and too much in its tail.

An upstanding peasant is bigger than a nobleman on his knees.

Don't think about the pig until it's in the poke.

After the rain the grass will grow; after wine, conversation.

If you are among the roses, your friends will look for you among the thorns.

When the sea is calm, every ship has a good captain.

Give a servant a proper meal and the cow will give more milk and the cat will drink less.

Shared joy is a double joy; shared sorrow is half a sorrow.

Who sits on your shoulders will try to climb on your head.

They who want to sing will always find a song.

Don't let your sorrow come higher than your knees.

Don't cross the stream to find water.

What matter if I suffer, if only my neighbor suffers too.

A hundred tailors, a hundred millers, and a hundred weavers make three hundred thieves.

A lazy thief is better than a lazy servant.

Better to be a poor woman than the slave of the rich.

A woman is the last judgement of the man.

Work is half of health.

Worry often gives a small thing a big shadow.

Being young is a fault which improves daily.

The young should be taught, the old should be honored.

Nobody is too young to die tomorrow.

Switzerland

It is easier to criticize than to do better.

If you close one eye, you will not hear everything.

God lets things go—but only to a point.

A greedy person and a pauper are practically one and the same.

Marriage is a covered dish.

When a merchant talks about sheep he means the hide.

Better to sell it with regret than to keep it.

A good spectator also creates.

The poor lack much, but the greedy more.

Great consolation may grow out of the smallest saying.

When in doubt who will win, be neutral.

When a neighbor gets divorced everyone thinks of his own wife.

At the bottom of the sack you will find the bill.

What good is a golden gallows if they are going to hang you.

As the stone leaves your hand it belongs to the devil.

To be a fool at the right time is also an art.

In a house of gold the clocks are of lead.

It is easier to beat two devils into a child, than one devil out.

He who mocks the cripple should be straight himself.

The night rinses what the day has soaped.

He that sleeps sound feels not the toothache.

The tongue is the worst piece of meat in the world.

Avoid those who don't like bread and children.

Where it is customary the cow is brought to bed.

One simple maxim is often worth more than two good friends.

Who cares about every little feather should not make the bed.

Words are dwarfs, deeds are giants.

It is always the fat ones who lead the dance.

Syria

It is cruelty to the innocent not to punish the guilty.

Be not water, taking the tint of all colors.

Even a soft speech has its own poison.

A borrowed mule soon gets a bad back.

In every village there is a path that leads to the mill.

A strong chicken starts to crow the moment that it comes out of the shell.

When the wolf invites you in, you had better take your dog.

Where many cocks are crowing it's dawn.

Tadzhikistan

If the mule doesn't go to the burden, then the burden will come to the mule.

Do not confide in your friend if he has other friends.

For a greedy man even his tomb is too small.

A chicken you eat only once—eggs a hundred times.

If you are an elephant don't offend the cat.

The rich eat kebab, the poor inhale smoke.

A man without a fatherland is like a nightingale without a garden.

The fox's enemy is its tail.

A woman's work is worth more than the talk of a thousand men.

Tamil Proverbs

Even an elephant can slip.

Our faults provide opportunities for others.

Learn about the future by looking at the past.

As people go their own way, destiny goes with them.

Tanzania

Kind words conquer.

Our shadow will follow us.

The one who teaches is the giver of eyes.

Why would a man without a bow look for arrows?

The beggar who asks for crumbs gets more than the one who asks for bread.

If you have planted a tree you must water it too.

Even the devil needs a friend.

You must answer the devil in his own language.

Only the cure you believe in cures.

Before you build a house you have to dig a pit.

If you are buying a cow, make sure that the price of the tail is included.

When the mother dies the father becomes an uncle.

You can buy everything, except a father and a mother.

When I drown, the whole world drowns.

He who loves the truth has many enemies.

Tanzania

Do not make the dress before the child is born.

Everything has an end.

Even flies have ears.

Events follow one another like the days of the week.

We start as fools and become wise through experience.

Do not mend your neighbor's fence before seeing to your own.

Even the night has ears.

A sheep cannot bleat in two different places at the same time.

In the world all things are two and two.

Thailand

Wait until the tree has fallen before you jump over it.

Don't help the elephant to carry his tusks.

Don't spoil a cool place under the hospitable tree.

The heart of a woman is as capricious as a drop of water on a lotus leaf.

A centipede will not stop for a cripple.

Don't spill blood until the raven has flown over.

Bald people can always find a comb.

Talk to a priest and die a thousand deaths.

Slow fires will smolder for a long time.

You should always prefer wind to water.

The bird leaves no trail.

Don't borrow another's nose to breathe with.

Little is spent with difficulty, much with ease.

On the way out, the road is rough; returning, it is smooth.

A virtuous person sleeps well.

At high tide fish eat ants; at low tide ants eat fish.

Who is timid in the woods boasts at home.

Work is the source of all good.

If you are going into the wood—don't leave your axe at home.

The dead will go to the village where the cock doesn't crow.

Gold that falls to earth never dims.

When a dog bites you, do not bite back.

The store of rice in your attic is your enemy—it makes them who have none very jealous.

With one stump you can't make a good fire.

Ten tongues that spread the word are worth less than two eyes that have seen, and two eyes that have seen are worth less than one hand that feels.

There is no other happiness but peace.

To a man wine is like water is to the boat; it can carry him or guzzle him up.

Tibet

Who can say with certainty that one will live to see the morrow?

Beat a Chinese long enough and he will talk Tibetan.

Cold hearts can find warm words.

If there is only one earring among seven daughters, there will always be a quarrel on festival days.

Eat according to the limits of your provisions; walk according to the length of your step.

My enemy's liver is the sheath of my sword.

Excellent people are honored wherever they go.

He who has had enough to eat thinks of serving God; the hungry think of stealing.

The father may well be a horse, but it's most likely that the son will be a mule.

You are only master of food that you haven't yet eaten.

Don't praise my good fortune before I'm dead and buried.

Goodness speaks in a whisper, evil shouts.

The person who gets stuck on petty happiness will not attain great happiness.

Any fool can say "Ah"—you need intelligence to say "Yes."

Only a certain amount of flowers and jewels are beautiful.

No matter if you eat a little or a lot of garlic, the smell is just as strong.

When a king is about to lose his power his orders burn more intensely than fire.

He who knows a great deal has a hundred eyes.

A lie is like a jump from a high roof.

Luck that lasts is always suspect.

The young magpie that pulls feathers out of his mother thinks that
he is showing gratitude in that way.

Men will always lose the battle against cholera and bureaucracy.

If the master gets drunk it is an honorable drunkenness; if the servant
does it is evidence of his mean disposition.

Master and servant—both have the same body odor.

The moon grows darker as it gets nearer to the sun.

It is hard work to be the mother of many pigs.

With a stout heart, a mouse can lift an elephant.

To spread the news is to multiply it.

If peace reigns in the land, a nun can govern it.

By pride one causes virtue to decline.

One good punch on your enemy's nose, gives more pleasure than
hearing well-meaning advice from your elders.

A nibbling rabbit can also die of overfeeding.

The rubbish we speak is like froth on the water, actions are drops of
gold.

Thieves never steal bells.

The unfortunate would be bitten by toothless dogs.

Water in the mouth before eating; water in the eyes when the bill
comes.

The wise understand; fools follow the reports of others.

To set fire to the wood, you need the help of the wind.

Words are mere bubbles of water; deeds are drops of gold.

Togo

If you see a frog squatting on his house, don't ask him for a chair.

A piece of wood that has been burned easily catches fire.

Dirty water cannot be washed.

Better a stupid wife than a mess at home.
The water carrier does not drink mud.
You flirt with a widow, but do you know how her husband died?
You can't look into a bottle with both eyes at the same time.

Tonga Islands

Friendship is a furrow in the sand.

Trinidad

The drum makes a great fuss because it's empty.
Fair words can buy a horse on credit.
Bathe other people's children, but don't wash behind their ears.
It's only the shoes that know if the stockings have holes.
Conversation is the food of the ears.

Tuareg Proverbs

The palm of your hand will not obscure the sun.
The eye cannot see what blows into it.
Keep your tents apart and your hearts together.

Tunisia

One hundred alcoholics are better than one gambler.
The bald woman boasts of her sister's hair.
Hit him with a bean, he will break.
If my belly is of glass, I will fill it with bread and chicken; if it is a
  closed cellar, I will fill it with cockroaches.
There is no blindness but the blindness of the heart.

We praised the bride, and she was found pregnant.

They asked the female cat why her kittens were of different colors; she said she is embarrassed to say no.

A bull went to impregnate a cow, and he came back a fetus.

He who spends a night with a chicken will cackle in the morning.

He who is covered with other people's clothes is naked.

Pretend that you are crazy, you will live.

The only difference between the cucumber and water is the moving of the teeth.

If the tail of the dog can save me, I don't care about its stench.

He who wants to be famous will have many a sleepless night.

No one will say, "My father is incontinent." Everyone will say, "He is a man of advice and wisdom."

He ate one fig and he thought the autumn had come.

They ate our food, and forgot our names.

If your friend is honey, don't lick him thoroughly.

Who came back from the grave and told the story?

Don't trust the horses if they run away, or the whores if they repent.

If the full moon loves you, why worry about the stars?

After I saw what my mother did, I will never trust a widow.

They asked the mule who his father was. He said, "My uncle is the horse."

The multitude is stronger than the king.

If there is any profit in partnership, two will share a woman.

If he gives you a rope, tie him with it.

If someone hits you with a stone, hit him with bread; your bread will return to you and his stone will return to him.

How lovely is the sun after rain, and how lovely is laughter after sorrow.

Because he has so many trades, he is unemployed.

If you are ugly, be winsome.

You should have done it on the wedding night, you fool!
The anger of a woman is mighty and the devil's trickery weak.

Turkey

Abundance doesn't know contentment, but contentment is abundance.
Allah gave hunger to one and hunger to another.
He who asks for alms blushes once; he who refuses, twice.
Don't say amen to an unacceptable prayer.
I know nothing about it, I haven't seen it; that is the best answer.
One armpit cannot hold two watermelons.
One arrow does not bring down two birds.
If the bald man knew a remedy he would rub it on his own head.
The bear knows seven songs and they are all about honey.
Sometimes you have to sacrifice your beard in order to save your head.
If your beard's on fire, others will light their pipes on it.
In the company of the blind, close your eyes.
You don't wash blood away with blood but with water.
Where you were born is less important than how you live.
The bride who brings a golden throne will sit on it herself.
A building without foundation is soon demolished.
Who burned himself with hot milk blows on ice cream.
Do not leave to the morning the business of the evening.
A ship with two captains sinks.
If a cat wants to eat her kittens, she'll say that they look like mice.
Everyone admires his own character.
He who has no children has one sorrow, he who has children has a thousand sorrows.
Cocks that crow too early will quickly find themselves in the pot.

Turkey

Coffee should be black as Hell, strong as death, and sweet as love.

Where conceit and ignorance sit, grass will not grow again.

Cotton cannot play with fire.

Cruelty is stupidity.

Death is the black camel that kneels before every door.

Idle men tempt the devil; the devil tempts all others.

He who wants to kill a dog says that he has urinated against the mosque.

The dog that is going to bite does not show its teeth.

A hungry dog will bring a lion down.

The first drink makes you a frisky gazelle, the second an impetuous zebra, the third a roaring lion, and with the fourth you become a silly donkey.

The eagle does not feed on flies.

The earth has ears, the wind has a voice.

One eats, another watches; that's how revolutions are born.

Be thine enemy an ant, see in him an elephant.

Better your enemy who you recognize than a dark friend.

One bad experience is worth more than a thousand threats.

Everything is worn out with usage—except for experience.

He that falls by himself never cries.

If you fall in a river hang on to a snake.

Don't sell the fish that is still swimming in the ocean.

No flock without dog and shepherd.

The fool castrates himself in order that he could accuse his pregnant wife of adultery.

The fool sings a love song to his wife, the wise man will talk about his dog.

The foot of a lamp is always the least lit.

A friend is one soul in two bodies.

A stupid friend is a greater plague than a wise enemy.

Turkey

None is so rich as that he can throw away a friend.

Who seeks a faultless friend remains friendless.

God made low branches for birds that cannot fly so well.

When God wants to please a poor man, He lets him lose his donkey and then helps him find it again.

Gold takes no rust.

Gold that is lent goes away laughing and comes back in tears.

The governor must fill your jars.

If your guest becomes a cook, your larder will soon be empty.

He who has to be hanged, will not drown.

Happiness is like crystal—when it shines the most, it soon cracks.

A heart in love with beauty never grows old.

Heaven was inspired by the first judge to take a bribe.

The highway is always shorter than the unknown side roads.

Honey is one thing, the price is another.

He who steals honey, licks his fingers.

He who lives on hope, dies of starvation.

Care for your horse as a friend; ride it as if it were an enemy.

The horse can die from too much barley.

A horse knows his rider by his spurs.

"If" and "when" were planted, and "nothing" grew.

He became an infidel hesitating between two mosques.

Don't ask an innkeeper the way.

Others are always interested in us, just as we are interested in them.

When two jars collide, one breaks.

Judge the linen by the hem, the girl by the mother.

One hour of justice is worth seventy hours of prayer.

He who knows much makes many mistakes.

You don't have to know much to read, but you do to cook.

If the lady of the house breaks something it is an unfortunate accident; if the servant does, then it is a terrible disaster.

323

A liar's house is on fire and no one believes him.

You may lie, but not too much.

To quote lies is also lying.

To listen to a lie is harder than to tell it.

Tell a lie on Saturday and you will be ashamed on Sunday.

Listen with both ears, but speak with only one tongue.

Before you love, learn to run through snow without leaving footprints.

For those in love, Baghdad is near Istanbul.

A person does not seek luck; luck seeks the person.

The luckiest dies in his cradle.

A man without grief is not a man.

Out of ten men there are nine wives.

A man will sacrifice his head to conquer a heart.

Man is his own mirror.

Men make the earth black from green leaves.

The real capital of a man is a mirror worth two cents.

The most difficult master is the servant who became master.

Measure a thousand times, cut once.

Even the thinnest piece of meat will happily marry a piece of bread.

Oh, misfortune, I forgive you when you come alone.

When it sees money, the flute will play itself.

Who kisses the feet of his mother, kisses the step of Paradise.

No fat mouse in a widow's house.

The mouth is not sweetened by saying "Honey, honey."

So the music, so the people.

In our eyes the neighbor's chicken is a goose.

One must ask about the delight of opium from one who smokes it.

You cannot get into Paradise without a guide.

Patience is the key to paradise.

To live in peace one must be blind, deaf, and mute.

The physician prescribes the medicine, the vulture waits for the body.

Learn politeness from the impolite.

Who has power in his hands has no need to lie; he uses violence.

Profit is the brother of loss.

A prudent man will read the letter from back to front.

Too much prudishness makes the lover sick.

He ran away from the rain and was caught in a hailstorm.

When a rich man falls they say it was an accident; when a poor man falls they say that he was drunk.

To a good rider, right or left makes no difference.

He who is only right hasn't really anything.

No matter how far down a wrong road you are, turn back.

The rose comes from the thorns that were born of roses.

The gardener who loves roses is slave to a thousand thorns.

Satan's friendship reaches the prison door.

The sea never buys fish.

Where there are no sheep, they call the goat princess.

The sheik's miracles are those of his own telling.

Sighs never fall on the ground.

Silence is music to a wise man.

Your five year old son is your instructor; at ten your slave; at fifteen your equal and after that either friend or foe.

Sorrow is to the soul what the worm is to wood.

You don't steal a bitter eggplant.

If a stone falls on an egg, it is bad for the egg; if an egg falls onto a stone, it is still bad for the egg.

There isn't a sword that would cut off a golden hand.

You cannot forge a good sword from bad iron.

Too much sympathy with the unfortunate makes you unhappy.

Never become a teacher where you yourself were a pupil.

Turkey

The thief can lie, those he has stolen from cannot.

A tongue has no bones but it can break.

He who controls his tongue, saves his head.

If everything that came from your tongue were to come into your hands, then every beggar would be a pasha.

You can proclaim the truth also in a friendly way.

Don't be fooled by how clean the turban is, the soap was probably bought on credit.

Vinegar that costs nothing is sweeter than honey.

Vinegar that is too sour even taints the glass it's kept in.

When violence comes into the house, law and justice leave through the chimney.

Things that are weak will break—as men do who think they are strong.

A weapon is an enemy even to its owner.

If you weep for all the sorrows in this world, in the end you will have no eyes.

Wine that isn't paid for is drunk twice.

The wise man says what he knows; the fool doesn't know what he is saying.

If you look for a faultless woman, you will remain a bachelor.

One night with an ugly woman and one day in the mountains both are like an eternity.

A woman has advice only for another woman.

There are many words that are like salted jam.

Don't speak sweet words when your deeds are of stone.

The world is like that: one gives a melon, the other gets the stomach cramps.

Even if the whole world conspired against you—that would not inflict a quarter of the harm you inflict yourself.

Uganda

Only a fool tries to jump in the fire.

A roaring lion kills no game.

With wealth one wins a woman.

Empty hands only please their owner.

Familiarity is like the sea that kills the fisherman.

Men will love each other as long as one is richer than the other.

He who tells no lies will not grow up.

The hunter in pursuit of an elephant does not stop to throw stones at birds.

Even the mightiest eagle comes down to the treetops to rest.

The man with one wife is the boss of all bachelors.

An infertile woman gets a lot of visitors.

Only take away the wife of a strong man when he is out.

If a woman sees a stick for beating her rival, she will throw it away in the woods.

A strawberry blossom will not moisten dry bread.

You can burn down a house, but can you hide the smoke?

When the master is away, the frogs hop in.

He who hunts two rats, catches none.

When the moon is not full, the stars shine more brightly.

He who is bitten by a snake fears a lizard.

Sickness accompanies a waning moon; a new moon cures disease.

Ukraine

Those sitting above can easily spit on those below.

Black souls wear white shirts.

Borrowed bread lies heavy on the stomach.

No matter how hard you try the bull will never give milk.

There are no old friendships in business.

The church is near, but the way is icy. The tavern is far, but I will walk carefully.

No cook ever died of starvation.

The malicious cow disturbs the whole herd.

A crow will never be a falcon.

The fear of death takes away the joy of living.

Deficiencies come by the kilo and go by the gram.

The devil always takes back his gifts.

The devil likes to hide behind a cross.

Every disadvantage has its advantage.

Drunkards know no danger.

The earth will cover the doctor's mistakes.

The word "enough" does not exist for water, fire, and women.

Fire begins with sparks.

Keep fire away from straw.

Flies will not land on a boiling pot.

The obliging fool is worse than an enemy.

Fools love not the wise, drunkards love not the sober.

To see a friend no road is too long.

Who gives in need, gives double.

God is looking for those who come to Him.

God sits on high and he sees far.

Your head is not only for putting a hat on.

He who licks knives will soon cut his tongue.

Speak highly of the lake, but stay on the bank.

The lame man laughs at the blind.

Who laughs at you also cries for you.

Only when you have eaten a lemon do you appreciate what sugar is.

There are many lies but barely one truth.

The lion is not scared of the barking of a dog.

The lion never catches mice.

To live longer is not necessarily to live more.

Love tells us many things that are not so.

Good luck is like the sun—don't look at it with your eyes open.

Good luck comes on crutches, bad luck on wings.

A man is as good as he makes others better.

Men can learn from travel and playing games.

The desire of the master is stronger than the right of the peasant.

If you love milk you have to feed the cow.

The morning is wiser than the evening before.

Mothers-in-law have eyes in their behinds.

To a satisfied mouse, even the finest grain tastes bitter.

Negligence punishes itself.

Old goats have strong horns.

Where there is a pond there are frogs.

The poor will only find false rubles.

Precaution is not cowardice—even fleas have weapons.

If everybody were rich, no one would row the boat.

Every road has two directions.

Salt will not make fat, complaining won't make your problems disappear.

Selling and cheating go hand in hand.

Silence does not harm your tongue.

If you haven't known sorrow, you can't know what joy is.

One summer's day is worth a whole week in winter.

Truth will drown when gold floats.

Vodka burns the mouth, but it's still healthy.

From too much vodka you can have a headache for a day; from two
wives, for the rest of your life.

Don't wade in muddy waters.

No wind is too cold for lovers.

Drink a glass of wine after your soup and you will be stealing a ruble from the doctor.

Wisdom is in the head, not in the beard.

A hungry wolf is stronger than a satisfied dog.

A woman is not a harmonica that you put aside when you have used it.

If you marry a young woman, make sure your friends stay outside.

If the devil is powerless, send him a woman.

A woman's beauty cannot warm a winter's night.

With a friendly word you get farther than with a club.

A friendly word is better than a heavy cake.

You don't really see the world if you only look through your own window.

Uruguay

Cunning is better than force.

It is better to lose a minute in your life, than to lose your life in a minute.

United States

There's no advice like father's—even if you don't take it.

A bad man in Zion City is a good man in Chicago.

They who drink beer think beer.

Borrowed wives, like borrowed books, are seldom returned.

Bragging saves advertising.

There are many witty men whose brains can't fill their bellies.

If you sing before breakfast, you'll cry before night.

New churches and new bars are seldom empty.

Every cloud has a silver lining.

An ignorant consent is no consent.

Buying on credit is robbing next year's crop.

The customer's always right.

Drink and frankfurters for a dime; kill a man before his time.

Eggs cannot be unscrambled.

Some families are like potatoes—all that's good of them is underground.

When a father praises his son, he flatters himself.

Good fences make good neighbors.

Fish or cut bait.

One foot is better than two crutches.

A forest is the poor man's overcoat.

There are three faithful friends: an old wife, an old dog, and ready money.

The bad gardener quarrels with his rake.

Gentlemen prefer blonds—but marry brunettes.

Hell and the courtroom are always open.

Honesty is like an icicle—if once it melts, that's the end of it.

Ignorance is bliss.

The good lawyer knows the law, the clever one knows the judge.

It takes a heap of licks to strike a nail in the dark.

If you can't lick 'em, join 'em.

Loose lips sink ships.

Love laughs at locksmiths.

It's as difficult to win love as to wrap salt in pine needles.

Lust never sleeps.

A man chases a woman until she catches him.

Don't marry without love, but don't love without reason.

Many a good hanging prevents a bad marriage.

Money talks—everything else walks.

Don't take any wooden nickels.

If you don't have a plan for yourself, you'll be part of someone else's.

The rich get richer, and the poor get babies.

No rogue like the godly rogue.

Scratch my back and I'll scratch yours.

Success has many parents, but failure is an orphan.

A tree never hits an automobile except in self-defense.

One of the greatest labor-saving inventions of today is tomorrow.

If you cut down the trees you will find the wolf.

Never trouble trouble till trouble troubles you.

Use it up, make do, or do without.

The world is a ladder for some to go up and others down.

Living in worry invites death in a hurry.

The first hundred years are the hardest.

Years know more than books.

If you eat a live toad first thing in the morning, nothing worse will happen all day long.

When you see gossamer flying, be sure the air is drying.

Never squat with your spurs on.

When you throw dirt, you lose ground.

Venezuela

There is nothing hidden between Heaven and Earth.

Vietnam

Enter alcohol, exit words.

Don't set the attic on fire just because you didn't catch any mice.

Young bamboo trees are easy to bend.

Never forget benefits done you, regardless how small.

The bird that escapes from its cage never wants to come back.

The boat follows the helm, the woman follows her husband.

Brothers and sisters are as close as hands and feet.

The mouth prays to Buddha, but the heart is full of evil.

The buffalo that arrive late will have to drink muddy water and eat dried grass.

The fat buffalo will attract the lean buffalo.

The chained buffalo doesn't enjoy grazing.

What is good for the buffalo is good for the cow.

When the cat's away the mouse sits on its throne.

The higher you climb, the heavier you fall.

The crane was killed by the fishhook.

He wanted to cure a healthy pig and ended up with a sick one.

Better to die than to live on with a bad reputation.

The dog will always attack the one with torn trousers.

Elephants are killed for their ivory, birds for their feathers.

Venture all; see what fate brings.

There is one fish in the pond, and ten anglers on the bank.

When eating the fruit, think of the person who planted the tree.

Giving just a crumb to the hungry is worth more than giving lunch to the satisfied.

Happy hours are very short.

If you want to eat pickled herring, think about the thirst you will have.

When husband and wife live in harmony, they can dry up the ocean without a bucket.

Tell me where it itches if you want me to scratch you.

If you want to gather a lot of knowledge, act as if you are ignorant.

Life is a temporary stop, death is the journey home.

Where life is exhausted, death comes.

Man is the flower of the earth.

Men made money; money never made men.

A good name is better than good habits.

If you go out a lot at night, you will probably meet ghosts.

When the pain has passed one forgets the medicine.

People live with their own idiosyncrasies and die of their own illnesses.

Receive a plum, return a peach.

A day in prison is longer than a thousand years at large.

No rain without clouds.

The rich become deaf and the mighty blind.

It's better to sleep on the floor in an incense shop than in a bed in a fishmarket.

Sun is for cucumbers, rain for rice.

People say that time goes by; time says that the people go by.

The human tongue is more poisonous than a bee's sting.

If you want to travel fast use the old roads.

A day of travelling will bring a basketful of learning.

Victory makes you into an emperor, defeat into a rebel.

If you hold high office, the whole village will share your fame.

Better a wise man's servant than an idiot's master.

Women are like raindrops: some fall on palaces, others on ricefields.

Strong wood is worth more than painted wood.

Nice words are free, so choose ones that please another's ears.

The army is the poison and the people are the water in which the poison is mixed.

There is no ivory in the mouth of a dog.

You cannot breathe through another man's nose.

It is no disgrace to move out of the way of the elephant.

When the father has eaten too much salt in his lifetime, then his son thereafter will have a great thirst.

Virgin Islands

If you think your bundle of dirty clothes is too heavy, try picking up your neighbor's.

The bucket goes down the well every day—some day it won't come up again.

A new broom sweeps clean, but an old broom knows the corners.

No matter how fast moonlight runs, daylight catches up.

You can lock your door from a thief, but not from a damned liar.

Never pick up what you didn't put down.

"Come see me" and "come live with me" are two different things.

An empty sack can't stand up; a full sack cannot bend.

Time is longer than a rope.

Willing is a good man, but Able is a better one.

Wales

Anger is the mother of treachery.

Three things it is best to avoid: a strange dog, a flood, and a man who thinks he is wise.

Birds of a color fly to the same place.

If you would get ahead, be a bridge.

The best candle is understanding.

Conscience is the nest where all good is hatched.

If every fool wore a crown, we should all be kings.

Be a friend to yourself, and others will.

Better a friend at court than gold on the finger.

Be slow in choosing a friend, but slower in changing him.

The coldness of a friend and the coldness of linen—they never lasted long.

Do good and then do it again.

Never trust overmuch to a new friend or an old enemy.

Your hand is never the worse for doing its own work.

Old age will not come alone.

If you would be praised, die.

Those not ruled by the rudder will be ruled by the rocks.

Scatter with one hand, gather with two.

A ship and a woman are ever repairing.

A work ill done must be twice done.

Walloon Proverbs

Beauty is not so much what you see as what you dream.

A tree falls the way it leans.

The chemist doesn't smell his own medicine.

When two poor men help each other, God laughs.

He started with nothing and still he has just his begging bag.

White flowers are not to be found in a coal sack.

The more the billy goat stinks, the more the nanny goat loves him.

Three hairs are quickly combed.

You only know saints by their miracles.

The best ointment comes in small boxes.

The tail is always the most difficult part to skin.

Fat geese don't fly far.

Better warn than be warned.

In dark weather the devil is in the air.

Do what you want, but make sure you are first.

He who keeps his mouth shut, dies without confession.

Don't make use of another's mouth unless it has been leant to you.

Wolof Proverbs
(Africa)

He who can do nothing, does nothing.

Without fingers the hand would be a spoon.

Not to know is bad; not to want to know is worse.

One cannot part two fighting bulls.

There are people who place a basket on your head to see what you carry.

Yemen

Compete—don't envy.

Whoever does not help himself cannot help others.

The master of the people is their servant.

A mule driver is not aware of the stink of his animals.

If you give people nuts, you'll get shells thrown at you.

A sick person is a prisoner.

Every sickness begins in the stomach.

Do not sigh, for your enemy will hear and rejoice.

What you sow, so shall you reap.

Pity the stranger, even if he is rich.

If the time has passed, there is no point in preparing.

A hungry dog will eat his own excrement.

Yiddish Proverbs

Seek advice but use your own common sense.

An imaginary ailment is worse than a disease.

A man should stay alive if only out of curiosity.

An animal's end is slaughter. A thief's end is hanging.

To every answer you can find a new question.

Never approach a goat from the front, a horse from behind, and a fool from both sides.

One ass calls the other a pack animal.

Attractiveness is better than beauty.

If you eat your bagel, you'll have nothing in your pocket but the hole.

With time even a bear can learn to dance.

The way you prepare the bed, so shall you sleep.

Better the best of the worst than the worst of the best.

If you can't bite, better not show your teeth.

From the black earth there grows the finest grain.

The longer the blind live, the more they see.

You can wash your body but not your soul.

A boil is fine as long as it's under someone else's arm.

I can find good in my boss but he is at loggerheads with me.

Over the bottle many a friend is found.

Give me, Lord, my daily bread, I will get my own brandy.

If the bride can't dance, she blames the musicians.

The heaviest burden is an empty pocket.

Two burdens: to Moses water, to God the world.

Look for cake, and lose your bread.

If I dealt in candles, the sun would never set.

One should not send a cat to deliver cream.

A cat loves fish, but won't risk its claws.

If charity cost nothing and benevolence caused no heartache, the world would be full of philanthropists.

Charm is more than beauty.

Once it was the parents who taught their children to talk; now the children teach their parents to keep quiet.

Small children won't let you sleep, bigger children won't let you live.

He who has children will never die of starvation.

Yiddish Proverbs

Don't be scared when you have no other choice.

No choice is an option.

A clock that stands still is better than one that goes wrong.

The cold strengthens you more than hunger.

When you have left a country, you have left everyone.

What can you do with a good cow that gives a lot of milk and then kicks the bucket over?

The crow flies sky high and lands on a pig.

A big crowd, but not a human being in sight!

Better to hear curses than to be pitied.

You reproach your daughter, but you mean your daughter-in-law.

A deaf man heard how a mute told that a blind man has seen how a cripple walked.

If you start thinking of death, you are no longer sure of life.

One is certain only of death.

Interest on debts grows without rain.

Better to die upright than to live on your knees.

It's never too late to die or get married.

Every man knows that he must die, but no one believes it.

Ever since dying came into fashion, life hasn't been safe.

If all pulled in one direction, the world would keel over.

By day they're ready to divorce, by night they're ready for bed.

Doctors and gravediggers are partners.

Don't settle in a place where the doctor has gout.

The doctor has a remedy for everything but poverty.

Everyone is kneaded out of the same dough but not baked in the same oven.

You can make the dream bigger than the night.

If you want your dreams to come true, don't sleep.

If you're fated to drown, you may die in a teaspoon of water.

If two people say he is drunk, the third one should sleep.

All dumb people have a lot to say.

Eggs may be smarter than the chickens, but it doesn't take long for them to stink.

He that can't endure the bad, will not live to see the good.

Spare us what we can learn to endure.

Make sure to be in with your equals if you're going to fall out with your superiors.

Everything ends in weeping.

"For example" is not proof.

Experience costs blood.

If the eyes didn't see, the hands wouldn't take.

Don't ask questions about fairy tales.

You do not fall because you are weak, you fall because you think you are strong.

He that lies on the ground cannot fall.

A farmer should not ride the king's horse.

As the fat man gets thinner, the thin one is already dead.

When a father gives to his son, they both laugh. When a son gives to his father, they both weep.

If the father marries the aunt, he's an uncle.

You find everything when you are spring cleaning.

He who runs away from the fire, falls in the water.

A flatterer must not lose his temper.

He avenged himself on fleas, and burned up his bed.

The complete fool is half prophet.

A fool will jump into the bath and forget to wash his face.

When a fool has the cow by the horns, the wise man can milk it.

What a fool can spoil, ten wise men cannot repair.

When Dame Fortune calls, offer her a chair.

There's plenty of time to bemoan bad fortune once it arrives.

A friend you get for nothing; an enemy must be bought.

If your friend becomes your enemy, he will be your enemy for life.

If you find your friend on the sofa at home with your wife, you had better sell the sofa.

One old friend is better than two new ones.

A good friend is often better than a brother.

The gatekeepers are worse than the directors.

God created a world full of little worlds.

When God wants to punish an idiot, He teaches them a few words of Hebrew.

God sends burdens... and shoulders.

If it were God's will, you could shoot with a broom too.

God is a father, happiness is a stepfather.

One God and so many enemies.

If God were living on earth, people would break His windows.

If God wants people to suffer, he sends them too much understanding.

Don't bargain with God.

If it must always be better, it can never be good enough.

A guest for a day is welcome the whole year.

Better an ounce of happiness than a pound of gold.

Health? Very nice! But where will we get potatoes?

The heart of a man may be compared to a sausage; no one can tell exactly what's inside.

If you are bitter at heart, sugar in the mouth will not help you.

The heart is small and embraces the whole wide world.

Heaven and hell can both be found on earth.

It is heavy to carry, but you cannot throw it away.

Hell itself can be no worse than the road that leads to it.

Either it doesn't help or it isn't needed.

A hero is someone who can keep his mouth shut when he's right.

If you stay at home you won't wear out your shoes.

What good is honor when you're starving?

It's good to hope, it's the waiting that spoils it.

To fall off a good horse is at least worthwhile.

The best horse needs a whip, intelligent men need advice, and devout women need a man.

Too humble is half proud.

If I try to be like him, who will be like me?

Better ten times ill than one time dead.

Come for your inheritance and you may have to pay for the funeral.

The innkeeper loves the drunkard, but not for a son-in-law.

Never try to be more foolish than the jester.

Better a Jew without a beard than a beard without a Jew.

If a Jew cannot be a shoemaker, he will dream of being a professor.

If only one race has to be chosen, why the Jews?

Laugh and everyone sees it, cry and no one sees it.

A lie can take you far away—but with no hope of return.

Life is just like a dream—but don't wake me.

The ugliest life is better than the nicest death.

Life is the biggest bargain—we get it for nothing.

If one link has broken so has the whole chain.

One does not live on joy or die of sorrow.

When the time comes for you to live, there aren't enough years.

A lock is meant only for honest men.

Look down if you want to know how tall you are.

Many complain of their looks, but none of their brains.

If you have nothing to lose, you can try everything.

You never lose a false coin.

Love me a little but long.

They have a strong love bond; he with himself and she with herself.

Love is like butter—it's good with bread.

Yiddish Proverbs

Lovers do not need much room.

Lovers and thieves always look for darkness.

A good man, but his mad dog won't let you speak to him.

What a man thinks up for himself, his worst enemy couldn't wish for him.

Men will give away their last shirt to become millionaires.

Men don't build on strange ground.

A man too good for the world is no good for his wife.

She who wants to marry her stepfather regrets it in bed.

A lazy messenger is not short of excuses.

When a miller fights with a chimney sweep, the miller gets black and the chimney sweep gets white.

In the mirror everybody sees his best friend.

Money buys everything but good sense.

It's not as good with money as it is bad without it.

With money in your pocket, you are wise, handsome and you sing well too.

Someone who can hold on to his money is worth more than the one who earns it.

Lose an hour in the morning, chase it all day.

When a mother calls her child bastard, you can take her word for it.

Mothers-in-law are fine so long as they are deaf and blind.

Necessity can break iron.

What value is a needle without an eye?

Mix with your neighbors, and you learn what's doing in your own house.

Better a thief for a neighbor than an overzealous rabbi.

There is nothing new under the sun—and that's why there remains such a mess.

Good news always comes from far away.

Not all nice things are dear, but those that are dear are nice.

Too nice can cost a lot of money.

When the ox just stumbles, they all sharpen their knives.

If you are lucky, even your ox will calve.

Parents can give their children everything except good luck.

A bad peace is better than a good war.

Pearls around the neck, stones upon the heart.

The pen wounds deeper than an arrow.

He who stands by his point of view, must be ready to suffer hunger.

Every poor man has a dry throat and wet boots.

When a poor man eats a chicken, one or the other is sick.

Every pot will find its lid.

If you pray for another, you will be helped yourself.

If praying had helped, he could have hired someone to do it.

Pride can live in the dungheap.

An unkept promise leads to a bad life.

If the pupil is smart, the teacher gets the credit.

Go quickly but don't fall off my step.

Treat me as a rabbi, but watch over me as a thief.

The rabbi drinks the wine and asks the others to be happy.

The rich man doesn't pay, the debtor does.

To be rich is not everything, but it certainly helps.

Not only that the rich man is rich, but he has such good checks too.

The truly rich are those who enjoy what they have.

If the rich could hire others to die for them, the poor could make a nice living.

Men would not be richer for being miserly; generosity does not make a man poorer.

Protest long enough that you are right, and you will be wrong.

When both parties are right, it's a bad day for "right."

The longest road is the one that leads to your pocket.

Better ruined ten times than dead once.

Yiddish Proverbs

No blessing is bestowed on a secret.

As the sheep are shorn, the lambs shiver.

Shrouds are made without pockets.

Sins hide not in your sleep but in your dreams.

I can't sing but I am a musicologist.

Better an honest slap in the face than an insincere kiss.

Sleep faster—we need the pillows.

A snake deserves no pity.

You can't make cheesecakes out of snow.

What soap is to the body, laughter is to the soul.

If one soldier knew what the other thinks, there would be no war.

A wounded soul is difficult to heal.

The less souls, the more joy.

Hire staff but do it yourself.

Do not show a stick to a dog that has been beaten.

If someone throws stones at you, throw back bread.

Stupid solutions that succeed are still stupid solutions.

The door of success is marked "push" and "pull."

From success to failure is one step; from failure to success is a long road.

Who talks a lot, talks about himself.

The talk of the day is the dream of the night.

You can't put "thank you" in your pocket.

When a thief kisses you, count your teeth.

What's left over from the thief is spent on the fortune-teller.

If triangles had a God, He'd have three sides.

Truth is the safest lie.

Nothing tastes more bitter than the truth.

Half-truth—whole lie.

Ugliness is the only guardian angel a woman has.

Walk straight and you will not fall.

If we cannot do what we want, we must want what we can.

Who dances at the wedding, weeps at the funeral.

Who wins first, loses last.

What use is wisdom when folly reigns?

Better a slap from a wise man than a kiss from a fool.

A wise man hears one word and understands two.

The wise man, even when he holds his tongue, says more than the fool when he speaks.

It is better to be in hell with a wise man than in heaven with an idiot.

The wolf is not afraid of the dog, but he doesn't like the sound of his barking.

All women are heirs to Mother Eve.

Women can keep only one secret—their own.

Lend everyone your ears, give a hand to your friends but give your lips only to a woman.

One chops the wood, and the other shouts "Oh, my back!"

Even a ball of wool has a beginning.

Words should be weighed, not counted.

Every worm has its hole.

Yoruba Proverbs

Ashes always fly back in the face of him who throws them.

Anyone who sees beauty and does not look at it will soon be poor.

One who waits for chance may wait a year.

Covetousness is the father of unfulfilled desires.

Earth is but a marketplace; heaven is home.

Gossips always suspect that others are talking about them.

If something that was going to chop off your head only knocked off your cap, you should be grateful.

When hunger gets inside you, nothing else can.

You can't stop a pig from wallowing in the mud.

Medicine left in the bottle can't help.

When the rain falls in the valley, the hill gets angry.

You cannot shave a man's head in his absence.

The person who has been a slave from birth does not value rebellion.

Sorrow doesn't kill—reckless joy does.

There is no god like one's stomach; we must sacrifice to it every day.

Truth came to market but could not be sold; however, we buy lies
with ready cash.

When wood breaks it can be repaired, but ivory breaks forever.

Work is the medicine for poverty.

The young cannot teach tradition to the old.

Diseased genitals must keep to themselves.

What you give you get, ten times over.

Before you ask a man for clothes, look at the clothes that he is wearing.

As long as there are lice in the seams of the garment there must be
bloodstains on the fingernails.

Yugoslavia

Who asks at once for a lot, returns home with an empty bag.

When the big bells ring, the little bells are not heard.

Boast to a stranger, complain only to your friends.

What is impossible to change is best to forget.

Condemn a man within earshot; praise him at a distance.

If envy would burn, there would be no use for wood.

There is little use building a fence around the garden to keep out the
rabbits.

Nine gamblers could not feed a single rooster.

Yugoslavia

It is not easy to meet Good, but it is easy to recognize it.

The place of an uninvited guest is behind the door.

He is not honest who has burned his tongue and does not tell the company the soup is hot.

Hours once lost cannot be regained.

He who humbles himself too much gets trampled upon.

No one likes to be the first to step on the ice.

He who is late may gnaw the bones.

Where there are no laws, they can't be broken.

Grain by grain, a loaf; stone by stone, a castle.

Man is learning all his life and yet he dies in ignorance.

Man is harder than rock and more fragile than an egg.

A man shows in his youth what he will be in his age.

If you wish to know what a man is, put him in authority.

It is better to look from the mountain than from the dungeon.

Patience can break through iron doors.

I am scratching myself where I am itching.

He who does not know how to serve cannot know how to command.

Where there is no wife, there is no home.

Wine from a pot is better than water from a well.

He who works has much; he who saves, still more.

Complain to the one who can help you.

Everyone will sit on a little donkey.

On your own donkey it is quicker than on someone else's racehorse.

Life is like a game in which God shuffles the cards, the devil deals them and we have to play the trumps.

A good name reaches far but a bad one reaches farther.

The eyes see everything but themselves.

A good rest is half the job.

Tell the truth and run!

If you spit against the wind, you spit in your own face.

Zambia

Where God cooks, there is no smoke.
You learn a lot about a man by his behavior when hungry.
When you show the moon to a child, it sees only your finger.
It is inevitable that two thighs will rub against each other.
Treat the days well and they will treat you well.
Many are the eyes of the person whose spouse commits adultery.
He who has a fever is not shown to the fire.
He who paddles two canoes, sinks.
When your luck deserts you, even cold food burns.
A riddle made by God has no solution.

Zanzibar

The chicken-thief does not listen to the chicken's prayer.
The death throes of an elephant are not so annoying as a living flea.
A chicken's head cannot wear a turban.
Who chooses will always have desires.
Who speaks alone is always right.
The fish caught in the net starts to think.
Things that are useful to people go into the cooking pot.
If you praise the man who taps the palm tree, he'll put water in the palm wine.
Wealth diminishes with usage; learning increases with use.

Zimbabwe

A borrowed fiddle does not finish a tune.
A coward has no scar.

The monkey does not see his own hind backside; he sees his neighbor's.

If your mouth were a knife, it would cut off your lips.

Two experts never agree.

Whoever plows with a team of donkeys must have patience.

Every elephant has to carry its own trunk around.

The more help in the cornfield the smaller the harvest.

A bull is not known in two herds.

A woman is attractive when she is somebody else's wife.

A roaring lion kills no game.

Annoy your doctor and sickness comes in laughing.

Blood is the sweat of heroes.

A careful hyena lives a long time.

Zulu Proverbs

You can't eat "almost."

Even an ant can hurt an elephant.

Darkness conceals the hippopotamus.

Death has no modesty.

No dew ever competed with the sun.

Do not leave your host's house throwing mud in his well.

You arrive Mr. Big Shot but leave Mr. Nobody.

Blessed are those who can please themselves.

Follow the customs or flee the country.

Do not call to a dog with a whip in your hand.

A fault confessed is half redressed.

The most beautiful fig may contain a worm.

He who hates, hates himself.

A horse has four legs, yet it often falls.

Zulu Proverbs

The horse that arrives early gets good drinking water.

Without life there is nothing.

A half loaf is better than no bread.

When the man is away, the monkey eats his corn and goes into his hut.

Copying everybody else all the time, the monkey one day cut his throat.

Plenty sits still, Hunger is a wanderer.

Do not talk about a rhinoceros if there is no tree nearby.

The rich are always complaining.

You cannot cross a river without getting wet.

This world is a harsh place, this world.

BIBLIOGRAPHY

Auden, W.H., and Louis Kronenberger, *The Faber Book of Aphorisms*. London: Faber and Faber, 1964.

Ayalti, Hanan J. *Jiddische Levenswijsheid.* Delft: Elmar, 1995.

Ballesteros, Octavio A. *Mexican Sayings.* Austin, Texas: Eakin Press, 1992.

Brizeux, Auguste. *Proverbes Bretons.* N.p. 1850.

Browning, D.C. *Dictionary of Quotations and Proverbs.* London: Chancellor Press, 1988.

Buddingh', C. *Citatenomnibus.* Utrecht: Het Spectrum, 1967.

Cox, H.L. *Spreekwoordenboek in vier talen.* Utrecht and Antwerp: Van Dale Lexicografie, 1989.

Crummenerl, Rainer. *Flaschen-Post.* Rostock: Deutsche Seereederei, n.d.

Darbo, Peter. *Dutch Proverbs.* Rijswijk: Elmar, 1997.

de Baïf, Mimes, Jean Antoine. *Enseignements et Proverbes.* N.p. 1576

de Ley, Gerd. *Klassiek Citatenboek.* Antwerp: Standaard Uitgeverij, 1992.

———. *1001 Buitenlandse Spreekwoorden.* Antwerp: Darbo, 1994.

de Noyers, Gilles. *Proverbia Gallicana.* N.p. 1558

Engelman, Jan. *Adam zelf.* Amsterdam: Bigot en Van Rossum, n.d.

Gleason, Norma. *A Fool in a Hurry Drinks Tea with a Fork.* New York: Citadel Press, 1994.

Gross, David C. and Esther R. Gross, *De wereld is in handen van dwazen.* Delft: Elmar, 1995.

Heywood, John. *Proverbs in the English Tongue.* N.p. 1546

Hoefnagels, Peter, and Shonwé Hoogenbergen. *Antilliaans Spreek-woordenboek.* Amsterdam: Thomas Rap, 1991.

Houghton, Patricia. *Book of Proverbs.* London: Cassell, 1992.

Kelly, James. *Scottish Proverbs.* N.p. 1721

Kleinworth, Daniel. *Wijsheid over de natuur.* Amsterdam: Omega Boek, 1988.

—————. *Liefde voor de natuur.* Amsterdam: Omega Boek, 1990.

Kluge, Manfred. *Wijsheid uit Japan.* Amsterdam: Omega Boek, 1989.

Knappert, Jan. *Namibia, Land and Peoples, Myths and Fables.* Leiden: E.J. Brill, 1981.

Leslau, Charlotte, and Wolf Leslau. *African Proverbs.* New York: Peter Pauper Press, 1962.

Maloux, Maurice. *Dictionnaire de l'Humour et du Libertinage.* Paris: Albin Michel, 1984.

Masello, Roberto. *Proverbial Wisdom.* Chicago: Contemporary Books, 1993.

Matukama, Lusendi. *Afrikaanse Verhalen en Tradities.* Brussels: C.I.E.E.A., 1993.

Mesters, G.A.. *Spreekwoordenboek.* Utrecht and Antwerpen: Het Spectrum, 1955.

Möller, Ferdinand. *Proverbes Français.* Munich: Deutscher Taschenbuch Verlag, 1979.

N.N. Altrussische Lebensweisheiten. Salzburg: Verlag Das Bergland-Buch, 1985.

Obenhuijsen, Iet. *Spiegeltje.* Amsterdam and Antwerp: Contact, 1938.

Peltzer, Karl, and Reinhard von Normann. *Das treffende Zitat.* Thun: Ott Verlag, 1979.

Petras, Kathryn, and Ross Petras. *The Whole World Book of Quotations*. New York: Addison-Wesley Publishing Company, 1994.

Pommerand, Gabriel. *Le Petit Philosophe de Poche*. Paris: Le Livre de Poche, 1962.

Pustet, Friedrich. *Wijsheid uit het Oosten*. Amsterdam: Omega Boek, 1977.

Rattray, R.S. *Ashanti Proverbs*. Oxford: Oxford University Press, 1916.

Ridout, Ronald, and Clifford Witting. *English Proverbs Explained*. London: Pan Books, 1969.

Ronner, Markus M. *Neue treffende Pointen*. Thun: Ott Verlag, 1978.

Schipper, Mineke. *Een goede vrouw is zonder hoofd, Europese spreekwoorden en zegswijzen over vrouwen*. Baar: Ambo, 1993.

———. *Een vrouw is als de aarde, Afrikaanse spreekwoorden en zegswijzen over vrouwen*. Baarn: Ambo, 1994.

Schröder, Johann. *Alte Deutsche Sprichwörter*. N.p. 1691

Tan, Mou. *Chinese woorden van wijsheid*. Delft: Elmar, n.d.

ter Laan, K. *Andermans Wijsheid*. Amsterdam: A.J.G. Strengholt, 1961.

Tripp, Rhoda Thomas. *The International Thesaurus of Quotations*. New York: Harper & Row, 1970.

Tuet, Jean Charles François. *Matinées Sénonaises ou Proverbes Français*. N.p. 1789.

van Acker, Achille. *De duivel in spreekwoord en gezegde*. Heule: Uga, 1976.

van Roy, H. *Proverbes Congo,* Tervuren, 1963.

Vanden Berghe, G. *Oosters Citatenboek.* Utrecht and Antwerp: Het Spectrum, 1968.

————. *Oosters Citatenboek 2.* Utrecht and Antwerp: Het Spectrum, 1969.

Vanden Berghe, Gaby. *Hoofdkussenbokje voor politici.* Tielt: Lannoo, 1988.

————. *Hoofdkussenboekje voor Verliefden,* Tielt: Lannoo, 1990.

————. *Het ware geluk, gelukkig maken.* Tielt: Lannoo, 1995.

————. *Kinderen zijn een brug naar de hemel.* Tielt: Lannoo, 1995.

————. *Wie dankbaar is hoeft niet te blozen.* Tielt: Lannoo, 1995.

Walser, Ferdinand. *Luganda Proverbs.* Berlin: Reimer Verlag, 1982.

Watson, G. Llewellyn. *Jamaican Sayings.* Florida: A&M University Press, 1991.

Westerhuis, Dr. D.J.A. *Latijns Citatenboek.* Utrecht and Antwerp: Het Spectrum, 1974.

Yetiv, Isaac. *1,001 Proverbs from Tunisia.* Washington, D.C.: Three Continents Press, 1987.

Zona, Guy T. *The House of the Heart Is Never Full and Other Proverbs of Africa.* New York: Simon & Schuster, 1993.

INDEX OF KEY WORDS

A book without an index is like a house
that is bolted and barred.
Hebrew Proverb

A

INDEX OF KEY WORDS

Amen
Turkey

America
Germany

Anarchy
Iraq

Ancestor
China, Maori, Serbia, Spain

Anchor
Holland

Angel
Egypt, Germany, Poland

Anger
China, France, Germany, Greece, Holland, Hungary, Malaysia, Myanmar, Philippines, Russia, Wales

Anguish
Albania, Chile

Animal
Berber Proverbs, Hebrew Proverbs, Native American Proverbs, Yiddish Proverbs

Answer
Biblical Proverbs, Cameroon, China, Denmark, India, Italy, Turkey, Yiddish Proverbs

Ant
Africa, Armenia, Borneo, Bosnia, Japan, Madagascar, Malaysia, Nigeria, Iran, Sudan, Zulu Proverbs

Antelope
Ghana, Mali

Anvil
Germany, Italy, France, Romania

Anxiety
Africa

Ape
France

Appearance
England

Applaud
Iran

Apple
Bulgaria, England, Gypsy Proverbs, Holland, Hungary, Japan, Montenegro

Apple tree
Russia

Appointment
Kikuyu

Approach
Yiddish Proverbs

April
England, Spain

Arab
Israel

Arabic
Iran

Argue
Sweden

Argument
France, Slovakia, Spain

Armchair
France

Armor
Italy

Blood vessel
Georgia

Bloom
Fiji Islands

Blossom
French Guyana, India, Japan, India, Mauritania, Montenegro, Nepal

Blow
Czech Republic, Egypt, Ethiopia, Martinique, Morocco, Samoa, Slovakia, Spain, Tuareg Proverbs

Blush
Hungary, Serbia

Boast
China, Croatia, Ghana, Holland, Japan, Maori, Niger, Russia, Thailand, Yugoslavia

Boat
Cambodia, China, Congo, Estonia, Japan, Russia, Vietnam

Body
China, Greece, Hebrew Proverbs, Malaysia, Mexico, Iran, Poland, Russia, Yiddish Proverbs

Boil
Yiddish Proverbs

Bone
Albania, Jamaica, Martinique, Namibia, Philippines

Bonfire
Japan

Book
Africa, Arabia, China, England,

Germany, India, Iraq, Latvia, Morocco, Spain

Boor
Denmark

Boot
Ireland, Russia

Bootlace
Mongolia

Boredom
Germany

Born
Africa, Ethiopia, Hebrew Proverbs, Manchuria, Martinique, Philippines, Quebec, Spain, Turkey

Borrow(er)
Biblical Proverbs, China, Egypt, Finland, Germany, Hebrew Proverbs, Philippines, Russia, Syria, Thailand, Ukraine, United States, Zimbabwe

Bosom
Biblical Proverbs

Boss
Bambara, Iceland, Manchuria, Russia, Yiddish Proverbs

Bottle
France, Poland, Togo, Yiddish Proverbs

Bottom
Madagascar, Scotland, Switzerland

Bow
China, Holland, Japan, Philip-

pines, Poland, Russia, Tamil Proverbs

Bowl
Africa, Mauritania

Boy
Creole Proverbs

Bracelet
Kenya

Brag
United States

Braggart
Namibia

Brain
Czech Republic, India, Italy, Myanmar, Poland, United States

Bramble
Spain

Bran
Libya

Branch
Croatia, Denmark, Iran, Korea, Lapland, Myanmar, Philippines, Samoa

Brandy
Finland, Germany

Brave(ry)
Arabia, Berber Proverbs, Bosnia, China, Iran, Italy, Philippines, Russia, Somalia

Brazilian
Brazil

Bread
Arabia, Croatia, Denmark, Egypt, England, Estonia, France,

Germany, Hebrew Proverbs, Hungary, Iran, Islamic Proverbs, Latvia, Lithuania, Mexico, Morocco, Russia, Slovakia, Spain, Sweden, Switzerland, Ukraine, Yiddish Proverbs, Zulu Proverbs

Breadfruit
Samoa

Break
Philippines, Sweden

Breakfast
China, United States

Breast
Creole Proverbs, Gabon, Hebrew Proverbs

Breath
Lithuania, Namibia

Breathe
Vietnam

Breeze
Canary Islands

Bribery
Iran, Swahili Proverbs

Bride
Assyria, Creole Proverbs, Congo, Holland, India, Iran, Luxembourg, Spain, Tunisia, Turkey, Yiddish Proverbs

Bridge
Germany, Hungary, Korea, Swahili Proverbs, Wales

Brood
Peru

Brook
Colombia, France

Broom
Hungary, Italy, Virgin Islands

Brother
Africa, Albania, Arabia, Bedouin
Proverbs, Benin, Czech Republic,
Somalia, Spain, Vietnam

Bubble
Poland

Bucket
Berber Proverbs, Sweden, Virgin
Islands

Bud
India

Buddha
Vietnam

Buddhist priest
Senegal

Buffalo
India, Kenya, Malaysia, Vietnam

Build
Cameroon, Ireland, Italy, Kurdis-
tan, Liberia, Mongolia, Rwanda,
Russia, Sweden, Tamil Proverbs

Building
Turkey

Bull
Arabia, Croatia, Georgia, Italy,
Korea, Madagascar, Nigeria, Por-
tugal, Spain, Tunisia, Ukraine,
Wolof Proverbs, Zimbabwe

Bullet
Arabia

Bullfrog
Armenia

Bump
Martinique

Burden
France, Italy, Tadzhikistan, Yiddish Proverbs

Burn
Germany, Holland, India, Japan,
Samoa, Turkey

Burst
Poland

Bury
Gypsy Proverbs

Bush
France, India, Jamaica

Business
Ethiopia, Greece, Japan, Leba-
non, Peru, Scotland, Spain,
Turkey, Ukraine

Businessman
China

Butter
Denmark, Italy, Luxembourg,
Morocco, Poland

Butterfly
Armenia, Korea, Morocco, Sweden

Button
Albania

Buy(er)
China, Congo, Czech Republic,
France, Germany, Italy, Japan,
Mexico, Palestine, Philippines,
Portugal, Russia, Slovakia, Swe-
den, Tamil Proverbs

Cask
Spain

Casket
Brittany

Castle
Ireland, Russia

Cat
Antilles, Arabia, Armenia, China, Denmark, England, Ethiopia, France, Georgia, Germany, Ghana, Greece, India, Japan, Lebanon, Madagascar, Mongolia, Morocco, Myanmar, Niger, Iran, Portugal, Quebec, Russia, South America, Spain, Tadzhikistan, Tunisia, Turkey, Vietnam, Yiddish Proverbs

Catch
Denmark, Cameroon, Luxembourg

Caterpillar
Palestine

Cattle
Africa, Myanmar, Ethiopia

Cause
Germany, Holland

Caution
Holland, Philippines

Cellar
Italy

Cemetery (see Graveyard)
Lebanon, Russia

Centipede
Myanmar, Japan, Thailand

Cereal
Haiti

Certainty
Poland

Chaff
Holland

Chain
Austria, Denmark, Germany

Chair
Denmark, Ghana, Sudan

Chameleon
Arabia, Madagascar

Chance
Yoruba

Change
Germany, Hebrew Proverbs, Portugal, Yugoslavia

Chapel
Czech Republic, France

Character
Germany, Japan, Nigeria, Turkey

Charcoal
France, Morocco

Charity
China, Germany, Yiddish Proverbs

Charm
Yiddish Proverbs

Chase
Holland, Sweden

Chasm
China

Chaste
Spain

Chatter
Egypt

Cheap
Arabia, Spain

Cheat
Bosnia, China, Denmark, Italy,
Lapland, Spain

Cheek
Ghana

Cheerful
Germany

Cheese
Germany, Lapland, Luxembourg,
South America

Chemist
Walloon Proverbs

Cherry
Denmark, Gaelic, Germany

Cherry tree
Japan

Chestnut
Samoa

Chew
Hungary

Chicken
Africa, Austria, Bantu Proverbs,
China, Congo, Corsica, Creole
Proverbs, England, France, Ger-
many, Ghana, Guadeloupe, Ja-
maica, Japan, Liberia, Libya,
Madagascar, Martinique, Mon-
aco, Portugal, Romania, Sanskrit
Proverbs, Sierra Leone, Spain,

Syria, Tadzhikistan, Tunisia,
Zanzibar

Chief (see Boss)
Maori

Child
Africa, Antilles, Arabia, Argen-
tina, Bambara, Belgium, Brittany, Cameroon, China, Congo,
Cyprus, Denmark, Egypt, England, Ethiopia, France, Germany,
Gypsy Proverbs, Hebrew Proverbs, Holland, Hungary, Iran, Ireland, Japan, Kenya, Korea,
Morocco, Myanmar, Niger, Nigeria, Philippines, Rwanda, Russia,
Sanskrit Proverbs, Spain, Sweden, Switzerland, Tanzania, Trinidad, Turkey, Yiddish Proverbs,
Zambia

Chimney
Russia

Chinese
Russia, Tibet

Choice
Hebrew Proverbs, Holland, Yiddish Proverbs, Zanzibar

Choke
Mauritania

Choosy
Croatia, France

Chore
Bambara

Christ
Ethiopia

Christian
Corsica, Germany

Christmas
Lithuania

Church
Czech Republic, France, Georgia, Germany, Latvia, Lithuania, Serbia, Slovenia, Ukraine, United States, Walloon Proverbs

City
Hebrew Proverbs

Claim
Germany

Clap
Malaysia, Palestine

Clay
Germany, Mexico, Slovakia

Clean
Holland, Mexico

Cleanse
Madagascar

Clemency
Russia

Clever
Russia

Client
China

Climb
France, Gabon, Germany, India, Lapland, Lithuania, Maori, Moorish Proverbs, Vietnam

Cloak
Arabia

Clock
France, Poland, Yiddish Proverbs

Close
Hungary

Clothes
Bantu Proverbs, China, Creole Proverbs, Ethiopia, Jamaica, Japan, Mauritania, Niger, Tunisia, Virgin Islands, Yoruba

Cloud
Africa, Armenia, Burundi, Denmark, England, Iran, Kurdistan, Lithuania, United States

Clown
Holland

Club
Lapland, Luxembourg

Coachman
Holland

Coal
Estonia

Coat
Albania, Holland, Hungary, Malaysia, Russia

Cock
Arabia, Bulgaria, Corsica, France, Ghana, India, Mexico, Morocco, Syria, Rwanda, Thailand, Turkey

Cockerel
Lebanon

Cockroach
Rwanda

Coconut
Ethiopia, India, Senegal, Swahili Proverbs

Africa, Spain, Switzerland, Tamil Proverbs, Ukraine, Yiddish Proverbs

Coward
Africa, Creole Proverbs, Ethiopia, Italy, Lapland, Lebanon, Somalia, Zimbabwe

Crab
Creole Proverbs, Ghana, Haiti, India, Malaysia

Cradle
France, Malaysia, Scotland

Crane
Africa, Vietnam

Crawl
Niger, Holland

Crazy
Tunisia

Credit
France, Gypsy Proverbs, Hawaii, Iran, Trinidad, United States

Cricket
Cameroon, Madagascar

Crime
Germany, Malaysia, Russia

Criminal
China

Cripple
Austria, Germany, Iran, Russia, Thailand, Switzerland

Criticism
Burundi, Germany, Iraq, Philippines, Switzerland

Crocodile
Africa, Angola, Bantu Proverbs, Creole Proverbs, Indonesia, Madagascar, Malaysia, Nigeria, Philippines, Sudan, Swahili Proverbs

Crook
Manchuria

Cross
Brittany, Ghana, Palestine, Poland, Spain, Zulu Proverbs

Cross-eyed (see Squint)
India

Crossroad
Palestine

Crow
Bulgaria, China, Creole Proverbs, Denmark, Holland, Iceland, India, Japan, Laos, Syria, Ukraine, Yiddish Proverbs

Crowd
Hungary, Madagascar, Yiddish Proverbs

Crown
Holland, Italy, Wales

Crucify
Bulgaria

Cruelty
Syria, Turkey

Crust
Denmark, Lithuania

Cry
Africa, England, France, Morocco

Cuckold
Scotland

Deaf
Afghanistan, Denmark, France,
Greece, Mali, Sanskrit Proverbs,
Slovenia, Yiddish Proverbs

Deal
China, Russia

Death
Africa, Arabia, Armenia, Den-
mark, Estonia, France, Ghana,
Holland, Indonesia, Iran, Italy,
Kikuyu, Lithuania, Native Ameri-
can Proverbs, Portugal, Romania,
Russia, Sierra Leone, Spain, Swa-
hili Proverbs, Sweden, Turkey,
Ukraine, Yiddish Proverbs,
Zanzibar, Zulu Proverbs

Debt
Catalonia, Corsica, Croatia, Estonia, India, Iran, Jamaica, Madagascar, Mongolia, Serbia, South
America, Spain, Yiddish Proverbs

Debtor
Arabia

Deceit
France, India

Deceive
France, Germany, India

Decision
Iran, Samoa

Deed
Estonia, Greece, Guinea, Hebrew
Proverbs, Islamic Proverbs, Japan, Morocco, Serbia, Switzerland

Deer
Malaysia

Defect
Sanskrit Proverbs

Deficiency
Ukraine

Delay
Spain

Deluge
France

Denial
Germany, Spain

Dependence
India, Japan, Maori, Nepal

Deprivation
Spain

Depth
Malaysia

Desert
Spain

Deserve
England, India

Desire
China, England, Ethiopia, Sanskrit Proverbs, Spain, Zanzibar

Desperate
Japan, Spain

Destination
China

Destiny (see Fate)
France, Russia, Tamil Proverbs

Determined
Italy

Devil (see Satan)
Bulgaria, Canada, Chile, Croatia,

Dumpling
Japan

Dust
Arabia, China, Myanmar

Duty
China, Japan, Mexico

Eagle
Armenia, Gabon, Germany,
Greece, Italy, Russia, Turkey,
Uganda

Ear
Africa, Armenia, Creole Prov-
erbs, Czech Republic, Finland,
France, Guyana, India, Iran,
Laos, Namibia, Russia, Sanskrit
Proverbs, Senegal, Sudan, Suri-
name, Tanzania

Early
China, England, Belgium

Earn
China

Earring
Arabia, Tibet

Earth
Afghanistan, Africa, Austria,
Bantu Proverbs, Brazil, Bulgaria,
China, Estonia, France, Iran, It-
aly, Madagascar, Maori, Mongo-
lia, Nigeria, Serbia, Spain,
Turkey, Ukraine, Venezuela,
Yoruba

Easter
France

Easy
Gaelic, Laos

Dwarf
Armenia, China, Germany, India

Dwell
Biblical Proverbs

E

Eat
Africa, Albania, China, Creole
Proverbs, Ethiopia, France, Ger-
many, India, Iran, Jamaica, Ja-
pan, Malta, Mauritania,
Morocco, Romania, Russia,
Spain, Tibet, Turkey

Ebb
Sudan

Echo
Finland

Economy
China, France, Holland

Eel
Germany, Indonesia, Madagascar,
Thailand

Egg
Antilles, Bantu Proverbs, Bul-
garia, Canada, Croatia, Den-
mark, England, Ethiopia, Gabon,
Gaelic, Germany, Guadeloupe,
Haiti, Holland, Italy, Japan, Leba-
non, Morocco, Romania,
Rwanda, Russia, South Africa,
Sudan, Tadzhikistan, United
States, Yiddish Proverbs

Egotism
Scotland

Flesh
Biblical Proverbs, France

Flint
Madagascar

Flock
Turkey

Flood
Cameroon, Holland, Sudan

Flounder
Australia

Flour
France, Slovakia

Flower
China, Egypt, Fiji Islands, Germany, India, Italy, Japan, Korea, Malaysia, Sanskrit Proverbs, Spain, Sweden, Tibet, Walloon Proverbs

Fly
Antilles, Congo, France, Georgia, Greece, Holland, Indonesia, Iran, Morocco, Philippines, South Africa, Swahili Proverbs, Tanzania, Ukraine

Foam
Solomon Islands

Foe
Senegal

Foetus
Burundi

Fog
France

Follow
Croatia

Folly
Cameroon, France

Fondle
France

Food
Afghanistan, Africa, China, Czech Republic, Denmark, Gambia, Ghana, Haiti, Japan, Madagascar, Malaysia, Maori, Nepal, New Zealand, Philippines, South Africa, Tibet, Tunisia

Fool
Albania, Arabia, Armenia, Biblical Proverbs, Chile, China, Czech Republic, Denmark, England, Ethiopia, France, Germany, Ghana, Holland, Iran, Italy, Ivory Coast, Jamaica, Japan, Kenya, Mongolia, Namibia, Poland, Russia, Sanskrit Proverbs, South Africa, Spain, Sweden, Switzerland, Tanzania, Turkey, Uganda, Ukraine, Wales, Yiddish Proverbs

Foolish
India, Maori, Serbia, Slovakia

Foot
Arabia, Armenia, Brazil, Czech Republic, Ethiopia, Jamaica, Mozambique, Oji, Turkey, United States

Force
Uruguay

Forehead
Palestine

France, Greece, Mexico, Portugal, Spain

Grave
Arabia, England, Iran, Korea, Mali, Montenegro, Palestine, Tunisia

Gravedigger
Greece

Graveyard (see Cemetery)
France

Gravity
Armenia

Great(ness)
Africa, China, Denmark, Ethiopia, Hebrew Proverbs, Poland, South Africa

Greed(y)
Iran, Mongolia, Switzerland, Tadzhikistan

Greek
Albania, England, Greece

Greet
Madagascar

Grey
Denmark

Grief
China, Japan, Montenegro, Sanskrit Proverbs, Spain

Ground
Japan, United States

Group
Nigeria

Grow
Congo, Germany, Ireland

Grown-up
India, Uganda

Guard
Madagascar, Iran, Poland, Spain

Guardian
Guyana

Guest
Africa, China, Croatia, Holland, India, Japan, Myanmar, Niger, Poland, Spain, Turkey, Yiddish Proverbs, Yugoslavia

Guilt(y)
Ghana, Madagascar, Nigeria, Syria

Guitarist
South America

Gumbo
Haiti

Gunpowder
Mali, Nigeria

Gutter
Portugal

Gypsy
Gypsy Proverbs, Greece

H

Habit
Arabia, Egypt, Germany, Philippines, Portugal, Russia, Spain

Hair
France, Germany, Holland, Sierra Leone, Walloon Proverbs

Halfway
Spain

Headgear (see Hat)
Namibia

Heal
Gambia

Health
Arabia, France, Hebrew Proverbs, Italy, Malta, Spain, Yiddish Proverbs

Hear
Jamaica, Laos

Hearsay
Holland

Heart
Afghanistan, Africa, Arabia, Bantu Proverbs, Biblical Proverbs, Cambodia, China, Denmark, Egypt, Ethiopia, Germany, Greece, Guatemala, Guinea, Holland, India, Indonesia, Iran, Ireland, Italy, Japan, Kenya, Malta, Palestine, Romania, Russia, Sanskrit Proverbs, Sardinia, Senegal, South Africa, Spain, Swahili Proverbs, Tuareg Proverbs, Turkey, Yiddish Proverbs

Hearth
Iran, Kurdistan, Russia

Heat
Japan, Russia

Heaven
Afghanistan, Africa, Albania, Arabia, Bantu Proverbs, Cambodia, China, Czech Republic, Denmark, Finland, France, Holland, Italy, Japan, Kalmyk Proverbs, Kanuri, Mongolia, Oji, Philippines, Russia, Turkey, Venezuela, Yiddish Proverbs

Heavy
Yiddish Proverbs

Hedge
Germany, Holland

Heir
Mexico, Moorish Proverbs, Namibia

Hell
Africa, Czech Republic, England, Germany, Japan, Myanmar, Portugal, Russia, Slovakia, Spain, Sri Lanka, United States, Yiddish Proverbs

Help
Kenya, Rwanda, Spain, Walloon Proverbs, Yemen, Yiddish Proverbs

Hen
Antilles, Germany, Holland, Iran, Ireland, Japan, Morocco, Romania, Rwanda, South America, Spain, Sudan

Herb
France, Lithuania

Hero
Bulgaria, Myanmar, Norway, Philippines, Romania, Sanskrit Proverbs, Yiddish Proverbs, Zimbabwe,

Herring
France, Vietnam

Hesitate
Albania, England

J

Jewel
Tibet

Job
China

Jockey
Martinique

Joke
Japan, Russia

Joker
Italy

Journey
China, Holland, Japan, Spain

Joy
China, Czech Republic, Germany, Hebrew Proverbs, Iran, Japan, Malaysia, Nigeria, Spain

Judge
Arabia, Finland, Hebrew Prov-

Karma
Myanmar

Kebab
Tadzhikistan

Keep
France

Kernel
Germany

Kettle
Estonia

Key
Africa

Keyhole
Scotland

erbs, India, Iran, Italy, Japan, Laos, Morocco, Native American Proverbs, Portugal, Russia, Serbia, Spain, Turkey

Jug
Germany, Russia

Jump
Czech Republic, Denmark, Germany, Martinique, Nigeria, Thailand

Jungle
Czech Republic, Senegal, Sri Lanka

Just
Biblical Proverbs, Estonia

Justice (see Injustice)
China, France, India, Italy, Turkey

K

Kill
Hebrew Proverbs, India, Native American Proverbs

Kimono
Japan

Kindness
China, India, Russia, Tamil Proverbs

King
Africa, Arabia, China, Estonia, France, Ghana, India, Iran, Italy, Madagascar, Namibia, Senegal, Sudan, Tibet

Kingdom
China

Manners
China, Iran

Manure
Estonia

Maple
Greece

Mark
Holland

Market
Burkina Faso, Italy

Marriage
Africa, Arabia, Austria, Burundi, Estonia, France, Germany, Haiti, Hebrew Proverbs, Jamaica, Madagascar, Mexico, Moorish Proverbs, Nigeria, Philippines, Portugal, Romania, Serbia, Spain, Switzerland, United States

Marry
Egypt, Finland, France, Hebrew Proverbs, Holland, Hungary, Ireland, Italy, Jamaica, Japan, Morocco, Mozambique, Niger, Russia, Scotland, Spain, United States, Yiddish Proverbs

Martyr
Islamic Proverbs

Mast
Myanmar

Master
Arabia, Burundi, China, Denmark, France, Germany, Gypsy Proverbs, Holland, Poland, Portugal, Suriname, Sweden, Tibet, Turkey, Uganda, Ukraine, Yemen

Matchmaker
Japan, Korea

Mate
France

Maturity
Iran

Maxim
France, Switzerland

Meal
France, New Zealand, South Africa

Meanness
Russia

Measure
Turkey

Meat
Holland, Iran, Italy, Jamaica, Lapland, Mauritania, Namibia, Nigeria, Sudan, Turkey

Mecca
Niger

Mediator
Iran

Medicine
China, Hebrew Proverbs, India, Japan, Nigeria, Scotland, Walloon Proverbs, Yoruba

Mediocrity
Iceland

Meekness
Germany

Meeting
China, Japan

Name (see Nickname)
Biblical Proverbs, Germany, Morocco, Norway, Vietnam, Yugoslavia

Narrow minded
China

Nation
Belgium, Germany

Nature
Bulgaria, Germany, Ghana, Greece

Necessity
Africa, England, Germany, Mexico, Iran, Russia, Yiddish Proverbs

Neck
Ethiopia

Need
Albania, China, France, Iceland, Ireland, Iran, Palestine, Philippines, Portugal

Needle
Africa, Armenia, Basque Province, Belgium, China, Estonia, Ethiopia, Guinea, India, Romania, Russia, Yiddish Proverbs

Negligence
Ukraine

Neighbor
Albania, Arabia, Bulgaria, China, Croatia, Czech Republic, Denmark, Egypt, France, French Guyana, Germany, Hebrew Proverbs, Holland, India, Iran, Italy, Japan, Lithuania, Namibia, Native American Proverbs, Niger, Nigeria, Portugal, Russia, Serbia,
Spain, Switzerland, Tanzania, Turkey, Virgin Islands, Walloon Proverbs, Yiddish Proverbs

Neighborhood
China

Nest
Egypt

Net
Samoa

Neutral
Switzerland

New
Biblical Proverbs, Cuba, Yiddish Proverbs

News
Africa, France, Tibet, Yiddish Proverbs

Nice
Poland, Yiddish Proverbs

Nickle
United States

Nickname
France

Night (see Midnight)
Congo, Corsica, France, Hebrew Proverbs, Holland, Iran, Iraq, Lebanon, Mozambique, Nicaragua, Russia, Samoa, Senegal, Spain, Switzerland, Tanzania, Vietnam

Nightingale
Denmark, India, Russia

Nile
Ethiopia

Partner
India, Russia, Tunisia

Partridge
Africa, Spain

Party
France

Passage
Arabia

Past
Japan, Russia

Pasta
Italy

Pastor
Holland

Pasture
Kurdistan

Patience (see Impatient)
Albania, Arabia, Bantu Proverbs, Cameroon, China, Denmark, France, Germany, Greece, Holland, India, Iran, Ireland, Italy, Kanuri, Morocco, Nicaragua, Spain, Turkey, Yugoslavia, Zimbabwe

Patient
Afghanistan, Africa, France, India, Liberia, Spain

Pauper
Armenia, Mexico

Pay
Germany, Russia

Peace
Arabia, China, France, Ghana, Holland, Hungary, India, Maori, Moorish Proverbs, Poland, Portugal, Russia, Serbia, Thailand, Tibet, Turkey, Yiddish Proverbs

Peaceful
India

Peacock
Spain, Sweden

Pear
Germany, Italy, Japan

Pearl
Africa, India, Kurdistan, Native American Proverbs, Philippines, Yiddish Proverbs

Peasant
Catalonia, Holland, Montenegro, Russia, Spain, Sweden

Pebble
Niger

Pecadillo
Hungary

Peddle
Japan

Pedestal
China

Pedestrian
Korea

Pedlar
Portugal

Peep
Spain

Peg
Korea

Pen
Arabia, Yiddish Proverbs

Pope
Italy, Montenegro, Spain

Poplar
Lebanon

Porridge
Philippines

Portion
Congo

Portugal
Chile

Position
Germany

Postpone
Lebanon

Pot
Andes Mountains, Arabia,
Cameroon, France, Germany,
Guadeloupe, Jamaica, Maurita-
nia, Solomon Islands, Yiddish
Proverbs

Potter
Africa, India

Poulterer
Lebanon

Poverty
Africa, Brazil, China, Germany,
Hebrew Proverbs, Holland, Hun-
gary, India, Israel, Russia,
Senegal, Somalia, Spain

Power
Croatia, France, Ghana, Iran, Native American Proverbs, Turkey

Powerful
Bambara, China, Italy, Palestine

Practice
England, Iran

Praise (see Dispraise, Self-praise)
Arabia, China, Czech Republic,
Denmark, Finland, Germany,
Iran, Italy, Japan, Maori, Wales,
Zanzibar

Pray
Armenia, France, Germany, Pales-
tine, Poland, Slovenia, South
America, Yiddish Proverbs

Prayer
Berber Proverbs, Germany, Italy,
Jamaica, Japan

Preacher
Germany, Spain

Precaution
Ukraine

Prediction
China

Pregnant
Bambara, Burkina Faso, Ivory
Coast, Rwanda

Prepare
Yemen

Present
China, Denmark

Pretend
France

Prevention
England

Price
France, Hebrew Proverbs

Purse
Berber Proverbs, Germany, Holland, Italy, Lithuania, Sardinia, South America, Spain

Quality
Finland

Quarrel
Hebrew Proverbs, Holland, Italy, Namibia, Native American Proverbs, Niger, Sanskrit Proverbs, Serbia, Sierra Leone

Queen
India, Portugal

Rabbi
Yiddish Proverbs

Rabbit
Tibet

Rag
Haiti, Niger, Mauritania

Rain
Africa, Arabia, Armenia, Cameroon, China, Czech Republic, England, Finland, France, Holland, Japan, Liberia, Lithuania, Malaysia, Malta, Nigeria, Romania, Rwanda, Sweden, Sri Lanka, Turkey, Vietnam, Yoruba

Rainbow
Antilles

Raisin
Libya

Ram
Germany

Put off
England, Korea

Q

Question
Cameroon, Holland, Spain

Queue
Morocco

Quick
Denmark, Holland, Yiddish Proverbs

Quiet
Ireland, Maori

R

Rap
India

Rascal
Russia

Rat
China, Ethiopia, Holland, Lebanon, Niger, Rwanda, Sudan

Rattlesnake
Native American Proverbs

Raven
Bulgaria, Holland, Thailand, Spain

Razor
Africa, Nigeria

Read
Albania, Japan, Morocco

Reality
Sufi Proverbs

Rest
Holland, Hungary, Yugoslavia

Restaurant
China

Retreat
Serbia, Spain

Return
Holland

Revenge
Arabia, Iceland, Italy, Russia

Reward
Holland

Rhinoceros
Zulu Proverbs

Rhubarb
Germany

Rhythm
Arabia

Rice
China, Creole Proverbs, Indonesia, Japan, Myanmar, Sierra Leone, Solomon Islands, Thailand

Rich
Africa, Arabia, Armenia, Brazil, China, Denmark, Ethiopia, Finland, France, Georgia, Germany, Ghana, Greece, Gypsy Proverbs, Hebrew Proverbs, Holland, India, Iran, Italy, Japan, Lebanon, Mongolia, Morocco, Native American Proverbs, Portugal, Romania, Rwanda, Scotland, Spain, Tadzhikistan, Turkey, Uganda,

Ukraine, United States, Vietnam, Yiddish Proverbs, Zulu Proverbs

Riches
Armenia, Liberia, Somalia, Spain

Rid
Poland

Riddle
Iran, Zambia

Ride
Germany, Mexico, Morocco, Romania, Turkey

Ridicule
France

Right
China, Croatia, Hawaii, Holland, Ireland, Japan, Spain, Turkey, Yiddish Proverbs, Zanzibar

Righteous(ness)
Arabia, Biblical Proverbs

Ring
India, Italy

Ripe
Holland, Kenya

Rise
Ireland, Nigeria

Risk
Russia, Spain

Rival
Burundi

River
Arabia, Basque Province, China, Congo, Czech Republic, France, Ghana, India, Ireland, Italy, Liberia, Malaysia, Mongolia, Native

American Proverbs, Nigeria, Palestine, Philippines, Russia, Spain, Sri Lanka, Zulu Proverbs

Road
Bantu Proverbs, Cameroon, China, Hungary, Ireland, Japan, Kikuyu, Mexico, Nicaragua, Poland, Portugal, Russia, Sanskrit Proverbs, Slovenia, Spain, Thailand, Turkey, Ukraine, Yiddish Proverbs

Robber
Italy

Rock
Italy, Malaysia, Wales

Rogue
Holland, Italy, United States

Roll
England

Rome
England, France, Holland, Germany, Scotland, Slovenia

Roof
Iran, Nigeria

Rooster
Italy

Rope
Antilles, Egypt, Lithuania, Tunisia, Virgin Islands

Sack
Holland, Virgin Islands

Sacrifice
Iraq

Rose
Afghanistan, Africa, China, France, Georgia, Germany, Holland, Spain, Sweden, Turkey

Rose water
Iran

Ruble
Russia

Round
Libya

Row
Holland, Latvia

Rubbish
Tibet

Rudder
Italy, Wales

Rug
Eskimo Proverbs

Ruin
Yiddish Proverbs

Rule
Bosnia, Italy, Wales

Ruler
Biblical Proverbs

Run
Brazil, Ethiopia, France, Germany

Russia
Poland, Russia

S

Saddle
Ethiopia, Mongolia

Sadness
Madagascar

Sheepskin
Bulgaria

Sheet
Portugal

Sheik
Turkey

Shell
Russia, Yemen

Shelter
Oji

Shepherd
Germany, Holland

Ship
China, Italy, Wales

Shirt
Holland

Shoe
Afghanistan, Africa, Bahamas, Germany, Holland, Iran, Ireland, Italy, Japan, Sudan, Trinidad

Shoemaker
Iran

Shoot
Cambodia, Malaysia

Shop
China

Shore
Cambodia, Malaysia

Shoulder
Denmark, Sweden

Shovel
Russia

Show
England, Native American Proverbs

Shower
Italy, Native American Proverbs

Shroud
Yiddish Proverbs

Shrub
Sudan

Shyness
Spain

Sick
Creole Proverbs, Japan, Mongolia, Nigeria, Yemen

Sickness
Basque Province, France, Ethiopia, Lesotho, Lithuania, Portugal, Uganda, Yemen, Zimbabwe

Side
Japan

Sieve
India, Belgium, Brazil, Lebanon

Sigh
Creole Proverbs, Turkey, Yemen

Sight
England

Silence
Africa, Arabia, Berber Proverbs, Egypt, England, Estonia, France, Greece, Hebrew Proverbs, Islamic Proverbs, Italy, Japan, Romania, Turkey, Ukraine

Silent
Iraq, Ireland, Japan, Slovakia

Smell
Greece, Iceland, Japan, Morocco, Namibia

Smile
Africa, Babylonian Proverbs, China, Cuba, France, India, Japan, Niger

Smoke
Italy, Lithuania, Mexico, Slovakia, Tadzhikistan, Zambia

Snail
Africa, Romania

Snake (see Rattlesnake, Serpent)
Africa, Arabia, Bambara, China, Congo, Egypt, Ethiopia, France, India, Iran, Japan, Lebanon, Mozambique, Nigeria, Romania, Russia, Sanskrit Proverbs, Uganda, Yiddish Proverbs

Snake-pit
Somalia

Sneeze
Italy

Snore
Creole Proverbs, Denmark

Snow
Italy, China, Yiddish Proverbs

Soap
Hebrew Proverbs, Russia, Spain, Sudan, Yiddish Proverbs

Sober
Denmark, Holland, Russia

Society
Greece

Sock
China

Soil
Palestine

Soldier
China, Germany, Hebrew Proverbs, India, Jamaica, Japan, Yiddish Proverbs

Solitude (see Loneliness)
Serbia

Solution
Croatia

Son
Afghanistan, Congo, Denmark, India, Iran, Japan, Kurdistan, Lebanon, Peru, Russia, Spain, Turkey, Vietnam,

Son-in-law
China, Hebrew Proverbs, Kurdistan, Spain

Song
Bulgaria, Gypsy Proverbs, Korea

Songbird
China

Sorrow
Denmark, Finland, Germany, Japan, Lithuania, Madagascar, Romania, Russia, Spain, Sweden, Turkey, Ukraine, Yoruba

Soul
Arabia, China, France, Kyrgyzstan, Yiddish Proverbs

Sound
Russia

erbs, Turkey, Ukraine, Yiddish
Proverbs, Yoruba, Yugoslavia

Try
Cameroon, Sierra Leone

Tsar
Russia

Tumor
China

Turban
Turkey, Zanzibar

Turd
Spain

Turk
Albania, Arabia, Bulgaria, Kurdistan, Malta

Turkey
India

Turnip
Spain

Turtle
Jamaica, Japan, Korea, Malaysia, Mali

Twig
Ireland, Ivory Coast

Two
Africa, France, Germany, Iceland, India, Ireland, Tanzania, Burkina Faso

Tyranny (see Dictatorship)
Iraq

Tyrant
Egypt

U

Ugly
Burundi, China, Germany, Holland, Israel, Malta, Niger, Tunisia, Yiddish Proverbs

Umbrella
India, Jamaica

Unanimity
Denmark

Uncertainty
India, Japan

Uncle
Lebanon, Tamil Proverbs

Understand
Arabia, Indonesia, Morocco

Undertake
Holland

Undressed (see Naked)
Zambia

Unfortunate
Arabia, Tibet

Ungrateful
Islamic Proverbs

Unhappy
Germany, Japan

Uninvited
Germany

Unlucky
Poland

Unscrupulous
Japan

Upper class
Ireland

Youth
  Arabia, Egypt, France, Ireland,
  Kenya, Korea, Lapland, Morocco

Z

Zebra
  South Africa

Also of interest from Hippocrene . . .

A CLASSIFIED COLLECTION OF TAMIL PROVERBS
edited by Rev. Herman Jensen
499 pages   3,644 entries
0-7818-0592-9 $19.95pb

**COMPREHENSIVE BILINGUAL DICTIONARY
OF FRENCH PROVERBS**
400 pages   5 x 8   6,000 entries
0-7818-0594-5 $24.95pb

**COMPREHENSIVE BILINGUAL DICTIONARY
OF RUSSIAN PROVERBS**
edited by Peter Mertvago
477 pages   8 ½ x 11   5,335 entries   index
0-7818-0424-8 $35.00pb

DICTIONARY OF PROVERBS AND THEIR ORIGINS
by Linda and Roger Flavell
250 pages   5 x 8
0-7818-0591-0 $14.95pb

DICTIONARY OF 1000 FRENCH PROVERBS
edited by Peter Mertvago
131 pages   5 x 7
0-7818-0400-0 $11.95pb

DICTIONARY OF 1000 GERMAN PROVERBS
edited by Peter Mertvago
131 pages   5 ½ x 8 ½
0-7 818-0471-X $11.95pb

DICTIONARY OF 1000 ITALIAN PROVERBS
edited by Peter Mertvago
131 pages 5 ½ x 8 ½
0-7818-0458-2 $11.95pb

DICTIONARY OF 1000 JEWISH PROVERBS
edited by David Gross
131 pages 5 ½ x 8 ½
0-7818-0529--5 $11.95pb

DICTIONARY OF 1000 POLISH PROVERBS
edited by Miroslaw Lipinski
131 pages 5 ½ x 8 ½
0-7818-0482-5 $11.95pb

DICTIONARY OF 1000 RUSSIAN PROVERBS
edited by Peter Mertvago
130 pages 5 ½ x 8 ½
0-7818-0564-3 $11.95pb

DICTIONARY OF 1000 SPANISH PROVERBS
edited by Peter Mertvago
131 pages 5 ½ x 8 ½
0-7818-0412-4 $11.95pb

TREASURY OF LOVE PROVERBS FROM MANY LANDS
146 pages 6 x 9 illustrated
0-7818-0563-5 $17.50hc

TREASURY OF LOVE QUOTATIONS
FROM MANY LANDS
120 pages 6 x 9 illustrated
0-7818-0574-0 $17.50hc

**TREASURY OF AFRICAN LOVE
POEMS AND PROVERBS**
edited by Nicholas Awde
128 pages   5 x 7
0-7818-0483-3 $11.95hc

**TREASURY OF ARABIC LOVE POEMS,
QUOTATIONS AND PROVERBS**
edited by Farid Bitar
128 pages   5 x 7
0-7818-0395-0 $11.95hc

**TREASURY OF CZECH LOVE POEMS, QUOTATIONS AND
PROVERBS**
edited by Marcela Rydlová-Erlich
128 pages   5 x 7
0-7818-0571-6 $11.95hc

**TREASURY OF FINNISH LOVE POEMS, QUOTATIONS
AND PROVERBS**
edited by Börje Vähämäki
128 pages   5 x 7
0-7818-0397-7 $11.95hc

**TREASURY OF FRENCH LOVE POEMS, QUOTATIONS
AND PROVERBS**
edited by Richard A. Branyon
128 pages   5 x 7
0-7818-0307-1 $11.95hc

TREASURY OF FRENCH LOVE AUDIO CASSETTES
2 cassettes: 0-7818-0359-4 $12.95

**TREASURY OF CLASSIC FRENCH LOVE SHORT STORIES
IN FRENCH AND ENGLISH**
edited by Lisa Neal
128 pages   5 x 7
0-7818-0511-2 $11.95

**TREASURY OF GERMAN LOVE POEMS, QUOTATIONS
AND PROVERBS**
edited by Alumut Hille
128 pages   5 x 7
0-7818-0296-2 $11.95hc

**TREASURY OF GERMAN LOVE
AUDIO CASSETTES**
2 cassettes: 0-7818-0360-8 $12.95

**TREASURY OF HUNGARIAN LOVE POEMS,
QUOTATIONS AND PROVERBS**
edited by Katherine Gyékenyesi Gatto
128 pages   5 X 7
0-7818-0477-9 $11.95hc

**TREASURY OF ITALIAN LOVE POEMS, QUOTATIONS
AND PROVERBS**
edited by Richard A. Branyon
128 pages   5 x 7
0-7818-0352-7 $11.95hc

**TREASURY OF ITALIAN LOVE
AUDIO CASSETTES**
2 cassettes: 0-7818-0366-7 $12.95

TREASURY OF JEWISH LOVE POEMS,
 QUOTATIONS AND PROVERBS
edited by David Gross
128 pages   5 x 7
0-7818-0308-X $11.95hc

TREASURY OF POLISH LOVE POEMS,
QUOTATIONS AND PROVERBS
edited by Miroslaw Lipinski
128 pages   5 X 7
0-7818-0297-0 $11.95hc

TREASURY OF POLISH LOVE
AUDIO CASSETTES
2 cassettes: 0-7818-0361-6 $12.95

TREASURY OF CLASSIC POLISH LOVE SHORT STORIES
IN POLISH AND ENGLISH
edited by Miroslaw Lipinski
128 pages   5 x 7
0-7818-0513-9 $11.95pb

TREASURY OF ROMAN LOVE POEMS,
QUOTATIONS AND PROVERBS
edited by Richard A. Branyon
128 pages   5 x 7
0-7818-0309-8 $11.95hc

TREASURY OF RUSSIAN LOVE POEMS,
QUOTATIONS AND PROVERBS
edited by Victorya Andreyeva
128 pages   5 x 7   0-7818-0298-9 $11.95hc

TREASURY OF RUSSIAN LOVE POEMS
AUDIO CASSETTE
0-7818-0364-0 $12.95

TREASURY OF SPANISH LOVE POEMS,
QUOTATIONS AND PROVERBS
edited by Juan and Susan Serrano
128 pages 5 x 7 0-7818-0358-6 $11.95hc

TREASURY OF SPANISH LOVE AUDIO CASSETTES
2 cassettes: 0-7818-0365-9 $12.95

TREASURY OF UKRAINIAN LOVE POEMS,
QUOTATIONS AND PROVERBS
edited by Hélène Turkewicz-Sanko
128 pages 5 x 7
0-7818-0517-1 $11.95hc

TREASURY OF CLASSIC SPANISH LOVE SHORT STORIES
IN SPANISH AND ENGLISH
edited by Bonnie May
128 pages 5 x 7 0-7818-0512-0 $11.95hc

All prices subject to change. TO PURCHASE HIPPOCRENE
BOOKS contact your local bookstore, call (718) 454-2366, or write
to: HIPPOCRENE BOOKS, 171 Madison Avenue, New York, NY
10016. Please enclose check or money order, adding $5.00 shipping
(UPS) for the first book and $.50 for each additional book.

Enjoy these fine travel books from Hippocrene . . .

KENYA AND NORTHERN TANZANIA:
THE CLASSIC SAFARI GUIDE, 9th Edition
by Richard Cox
300 pages   4 x 7
0-7818-0519-8 $18.95pb

NAMIBIA: THE INDEPENDENT TRAVELER'S GUIDE
by Sottt and Lucinda Bradshaw
313 pages   5 ½ x 8 ¼   26 maps & 22 illustrations, photos
0-7818-0254-7 $16.95pb

AUSTRALIA COMPANION GUIDE
by Graeme and Tasmin Newman
294 pages   5 ½ x 8 ½   b/w photos, maps
0-87052-034-2 $16.95pb

THORTON COX BUDGET GUIDE TO THE CZECH
REPUBLIC
by Astrid Holtslag
310 pages   5 x 7   b/w photos, maps
0-7 818-0228-8 $16.5pb

HUNGARY INSIDER'S GUIDE
by Nicholas Parsons
366 pages   5 ½ x 8 ½   59 b/w photos & 12 maps
0-87052-976 -5 $16.95pb

COMPANION GUIDE TO IRELAND, 2nd Edition
by Henry Weisser
300 pages   5 ½ x 8 ½   b/w photos, 4 maps, charts
0-7818-0170-2 $14.95pb

PODHALE: A COMPANION GUIDE TO
THE POLISH HIGHLANDS
by Jan Gutt Mostowy
276 pages   6 x 9   36 illustrations
0-7818-0522-8 $19.95hc

THE RUSSIAN FAR EAST
by Erik and Alegra Harris Azulay
311 pages   6 ½ x 8¼   maps & photos
0-7818-0325-X $18.95pb

U.S.A. GUIDE TO THE UNDERGROUND RAILROAD
by Charles Blockson
380 pages   5 ¼ x 8 ½   b/w photos & illustrations
0-7818-0253-9 $22.95hc
0-7818-0429-9 $16.95pb

EXPLORING THE BERKSHIRES
by Herbert Whitman
168 pages   5 ½ x 8 ½   illustrations
0-87052-979-X $9.95pb

EXPLORING THE LITCHFIELD HILLS
by Herbert Whitman
112 pages   5 ½ x 8 ¼   illustrations
0-7818-0045-5 $9.95pb

U.S.A. GUIDE TO THE HISTORIC BLACK SOUTH
by James Haskins and Joann Biondi
300 pages   5 ½ x 8 ½   b/w photos
0- 7818-0140-0 $14.95pb

U.S.A. GUIDE TO HISTORIC HISPANIC AMEREICA
by Oscar and Joy Jones
168 pages   5 ½ x 8 ½   b/w photos & maps
0-7818-0141-9 $14.95pb

THE SOUTHWEST: A FAMILY ADVENTURE
by Tish Minear and Janet Limon
440 pages   5 ½ x 8 ¼   27 b/w photos & 50 line drawings
0-87052-640-5 $16.95pb

All prices subject to change. TO PURCHASE HIPPOCRENE
BOOKS contact your local bookstore, call (718) 454-2366, or write
to: HIPPOCRENE BOOKS, 171 Madison Avenue, New York, NY
10016. Please enclose check or money order, adding $5.00 shipping
(UPS) for the first book and $.50 for each additional book.